*f*P

ALSO BY SAM HARRIS

The End of Faith

Letter to a Christian Nation

Praise for THE MORAL LANDSCAPE

"Sam Harris breathes intellectual fire into an ancient debate. Reading this thrilling, audacious book, you feel the ground shifting beneath your feet. Reason has never had a more passionate advocate."

—**Ian McEwan**, author of *Atonement* and winner of the Man Booker Prize for *Amsterdam*

"A lively, provocative, and timely new look at one of the deepest problems in the world of ideas. Harris makes a powerful case for a morality that is based on human flourishing and thoroughly enmeshed with science and rationality. It is a tremendously appealing vision, and one that no thinking person can afford to ignore."

—**Steven Pinker**, Professor of Psychology at Harvard University and author of *How the Mind Works* and *The Blank Slate*

"Beautifully written as they were (the elegance of his prose is a distilled blend of honesty and clarity) there was little in Sam Harris's previous books that couldn't have been written by any of his fellow 'horsemen' of the 'new atheism.' This book is different, though every bit as readable as the other two. I was one of those who had unthinkingly bought into the hectoring myth that science can say nothing about morals. To my surprise, *The Moral Landscape* has changed all that for me. It should change it for philosophers too. Philosophers of mind have already discovered that they can't duck the study of neuroscience, and the best of them have raised their game as a result. Sam Harris shows that the same should be true of moral philosophers, and it will turn their world exhilaratingly upside down. As for religion, and the preposterous idea that we need God to be good, nobody wields a sharper bayonet than Sam Harris."

—**Richard Dawkins**, University of Oxford

"Reading Sam Harris is like drinking water from a cool stream on a hot day. He has the rare ability to frame arguments that are not only stimulating, they are downright nourishing, even if you don't always agree with him! In this new book he argues from a philosophical and a neurobiological perspective that science can and should determine morality. His discussions will provoke secular liberals and religious conservatives alike, who jointly argue from different perspectives that there always will be an unbridgeable chasm between merely knowing what is and discerning what should be. As was the case with Harris's previous books, readers are bound to come away with previously firm convictions about the world challenged, and a vital new awareness about the nature and value of science and reason in our lives."

—**Lawrence M. Krauss**, Foundation Professor and Director of the Origins Project at Arizona State University and author of *The Physics of Star Trek* and *Quantum Man: Richard Feynman's Life in Science*

THE MORAL LANDSCAPE

How Science Can Determine Human Values

SAM HARRIS

Free Press

New York London Toronto Sydney

*f*P
Free Press
A Division of Simon & Schuster, Inc.
1230 Avenue of the Americas
New York, NY 10020

This Free Press export edition October 2010

Manufactured in the United States of America

10 9 8 7 6 5 4 3 2 1

ISBN 978-1-4516-1278-3
ISBN 978-1-4391-7123-3 (ebook)

For Emma

CONTENTS

Introduction

THE MORAL LANDSCAPE

The people of Albania have a venerable tradition of vendetta called *Kanun:* if a man commits a murder, his victim's family can kill any one of his male relatives in reprisal. If a boy has the misfortune of being the son or brother of a murderer, he must spend his days and nights in hiding, forgoing a proper education, adequate health care, and the pleasures of a normal life. Untold numbers of Albanian men and boys live as prisoners of their homes even now.[1] Can we say that the Albanians are morally wrong to have structured their society in this way? Is their tradition of blood feud a form of evil? Are their values inferior to our own?

Most people imagine that science cannot pose, much less answer, questions of this sort. How could we ever say, as a matter of scientific fact, that one way of life is better, or more moral, than another? Whose definition of "better" or "moral" would we use? While many scientists now study the evolution of morality, as well as its underlying neurobiology, the purpose of their research is merely to describe how human beings think and behave. No one expects science to tell us how we *ought* to think and behave. Controversies about human values are controversies about which science officially has no opinion.[2]

I will argue, however, that questions about values—about meaning, morality, and life's larger purpose—are really questions about the well-being of conscious creatures. Values, therefore, translate into facts that can be scientifically understood: regarding positive and negative social emotions, retributive impulses, the effects of specific laws and social institutions on human relationships, the neurophysiology of happiness and suffering, etc. The most important of these facts are bound to transcend culture—just as facts about physical and mental health do. Cancer in the highlands of New Guinea is still cancer; cholera is still cholera; schizophrenia is still schizophrenia; and so, too, I will argue, compassion is still compassion, and well-being is still well-being.[3] And if there are important cultural differences in how people flourish—if, for instance, there are incompatible but equivalent ways to raise happy, intelligent, and creative children—these differences are also facts that must depend upon the organization of the human brain. In principle, therefore, we can account for the ways in which culture defines us within the context of neuroscience and psychology. The more we understand ourselves at the level of the brain, the more we will see that there are right and wrong answers to questions of human values.

Of course, we will have to confront some ancient disagreements about the status of moral truth: people who draw their worldview from religion generally believe that moral truth exists, but only because God has woven it into the very fabric of reality; while those who lack such faith tend to think that notions of "good" and "evil" must be the products of evolutionary pressure and cultural invention. On the first account, to speak of "moral truth" is, of necessity, to invoke God; on the second, it is merely to give voice to one's apish urges, cultural biases, and philosophical confusion. My purpose is to persuade you that both sides in this debate are wrong. The goal of this book is to begin a conversation about how moral truth can be understood in the context of science.

While the argument I make in this book is bound to be controversial, it rests on a very simple premise: human well-being entirely depends on events in the world and on states of the human brain. Consequently, there must be scientific truths to be known about it. A more detailed understanding of these truths will force us to draw clear distinctions between different ways of living in society with one another, judging some to be better or worse, more or less true to the facts, and more or less ethical. Clearly, such insights could help us to improve the quality of human life—and this is where academic debate ends and choices affecting the lives of millions of people begin.

I am not suggesting that we are guaranteed to resolve every moral controversy through science. Differences of opinion will remain—but opinions will be increasingly constrained by facts. And it is important to realize that our inability to answer a question says nothing about whether the question itself has an answer. Exactly how many people were bitten by mosquitoes in the last sixty seconds? How many of these people will contract malaria? How many will die as a result? Given the technical challenges involved, no team of scientists could possibly respond to such questions. And yet we know that they admit of simple numerical answers. Does our inability to gather the relevant data oblige us to respect all opinions equally? Of course not. In the same way, the fact that we may not be able to resolve specific moral dilemmas does not suggest that all competing responses to them are equally valid. In my experience, mistaking *no answers in practice* for *no answers in principle* is a great source of moral confusion.

There are, for instance, twenty-one U.S. states that still allow corporal punishment in their schools. These are places where it is actually legal for a teacher to beat a child with a wooden board hard enough to raise large bruises and even to break the skin. Hundreds of thousands of children are subjected to this violence each year, almost exclusively in the South. Needless to say, the rationale for this behavior is explicitly religious: for the Creator of the Universe Himself has told us not to spare the rod, lest we spoil the child (Proverbs 13:24, 20:30, and 23:13–14). However, if we are actually concerned about human well-being, and would treat children in such a way as to promote it, we might wonder whether it is generally wise to subject little boys and girls to pain, terror, and public humiliation as a means of encouraging their cognitive and emotional development. Is there any doubt that this question *has* an answer? Is there any doubt that it matters that we get it right? In fact, all the research indicates that corporal punishment is a disastrous practice, leading to more violence and social pathology—and, perversely, to greater support for corporal punishment.[4]

But the deeper point is that there simply must be answers to questions of this kind, whether we know them or not. And these are not areas where we can afford to simply respect the "traditions" of others and agree to disagree. Why will science increasingly decide such questions? Because the discrepant answers people give to them—along with the consequences that follow in terms of human relationships, states of mind, acts of violence, entanglements with the law, etc.—translate into differences in our brains, in the brains of others, and in the world at large. I hope to show that when talking about values, we are actually talking about an interdependent world of facts.

There are facts to be understood about how thoughts and intentions arise in the human brain; there are facts to be learned about how these mental states translate into behavior; there are further facts to be known about how these behaviors influence the world and the experience of other conscious beings. We will see that facts of this sort exhaust what we can reasonably mean by terms like "good" and "evil." They will also increasingly fall within the purview of science and run far deeper than a person's religious affiliation. Just as there is no such thing as Christian physics or Muslim algebra, we will see that there is no such thing as Christian or Muslim morality. Indeed, I will argue that morality should be considered an undeveloped branch of science.

Since the publication of my first book, *The End of Faith,* I have had a privileged view of the "culture wars"—both in the United States, between secular liberals and Christian conservatives, and in Europe, between largely irreligious societies and their growing Muslim populations. Having received tens of thousands of letters and emails from people at every point on the continuum between faith and doubt, I can say with some confidence that a shared belief in the limitations of reason lies at the bottom of these cultural divides. Both sides believe that reason is powerless to answer the most important questions in human life. And how a person perceives the gulf between facts and values seems to influence his views on almost every issue of social importance—from the fighting of wars to the education of children.

This rupture in our thinking has different consequences at each end of the political spectrum: religious conservatives tend to believe that there are right answers to questions of meaning and morality, but only because the God of Abraham deems it so.[5] They concede that ordinary facts can be discovered through rational inquiry, but they believe that values must come from a voice in a whirlwind. Scriptural literalism, intolerance of diversity, mistrust of science, disregard for the real causes of human and animal suffering—too often, this is how the division between facts and values expresses itself on the religious right.

Secular liberals, on the other hand, tend to imagine that no objective answers to moral questions exist. While John Stuart Mill might conform to *our* cultural ideal of goodness better than Osama bin Laden does, most secularists suspect that Mill's ideas about right and wrong reach no closer to the Truth. Multiculturalism, moral relativism, political correctness, tolerance even of *intolerance*—these are the familiar consequences of separating facts and values on the left.

It should concern us that these two orientations are not equally empowering. Increasingly, secular democracies are left supine before the unreasoning zeal of old-time religion. The juxtaposition of conservative dogmatism and liberal doubt accounts for the decade that has been lost in the United States to a ban on federal funding for embryonic stem-cell research; it explains the years of political distraction we have suffered, and will continue to suffer, over issues like abortion and gay marriage; it lies at the bottom of current efforts to pass antiblasphemy laws at the United Nations (which would make it illegal for the citizens of member states to criticize religion); it has hobbled the West in its generational war against radical Islam; and it may yet refashion the societies of Europe into a new Caliphate.[6] Knowing what the Creator of the Universe believes about right and wrong inspires religious conservatives to enforce this vision in the public sphere at almost any cost; not knowing what is right—or that anything can ever be *truly* right—often leads secular liberals to surrender their intellectual standards and political freedoms with both hands.

The scientific community is predominantly secular and liberal—and the concessions that scientists have made to religious dogmatism have been breathtaking. As we will see, the problem reaches as high as the National Academies of Science and the National Institutes of Health. Even the journal *Nature,* the most influential scientific publication on earth, has been unable to reliably police the boundary between reasoned discourse and pious fiction. I recently reviewed every appearance of the term "religion" in the journal going back ten years and found that *Nature*'s editors have generally accepted Stephen J. Gould's doomed notion of "nonoverlapping magisteria"—the idea that science and religion, properly construed, cannot be in conflict because they constitute different domains of expertise.[7] As one editorial put it, problems arise only when these disciplines "stray onto each other's territories and stir up trouble."[8] The underlying claim is that while science is the best authority on the workings of the physical universe, religion is the best authority on meaning, values, morality, and the good life. I hope to persuade you that this is not only untrue, it could not possibly be true. Meaning, values, morality, and the good life must relate to facts about the well-being of conscious creatures—and, in our case, must lawfully depend upon events in the world and upon states of the human brain. Rational, open-ended, honest inquiry has always been the true source of insight into such processes. Faith, if it is ever right about anything, is right by accident.

The scientific community's reluctance to take a stand on moral issues has come at a price. It has made science appear divorced, in principle, from the most important questions of human life. From the point of view of popular culture, science often seems like little more than a hatchery for technology. While most educated people will concede that the scientific method has delivered centuries of fresh embarrassment to religion on matters of fact, it is now an article of almost unquestioned certainty, both inside and outside scientific circles, that science has nothing to say about what constitutes a good life. Religious thinkers in all faiths, and on both ends of the political spectrum, are united on precisely this point; the defense one most often hears for belief in God is not that there is compelling evidence for His existence, but that faith in Him

is the only reliable source of meaning and moral guidance. Mu
incompatible religious traditions now take refuge behind the same non sequitur.

It seems inevitable, however, that science will gradually encompass life's deepest questions—and this is guaranteed to provoke a backlash. How we respond to the resulting collision of worldviews will influence the progress of science, of course, but it may also determine whether we succeed in building a global civilization based on shared values. The question of how human beings should live in the twenty-first century has many competing answers—and most of them are surely wrong. Only a rational understanding of human well-being will allow billions of us to coexist peacefully, converging on the same social, political, economic, and environmental goals. A science of human flourishing may seem a long way off, but to achieve it, we must first acknowledge that the intellectual terrain actually exists.[9]

Throughout this book I make reference to a hypothetical space that I call "the moral landscape"—a space of real and potential outcomes whose peaks correspond to the heights of potential well-being and whose valleys represent the deepest possible suffering. Different ways of thinking and behaving—different cultural practices, ethical codes, modes of government, etc.—will translate into movements across this landscape and, therefore, into different degrees of human flourishing. I'm not suggesting that we will necessarily discover one right answer to every moral question or a single best way for human beings to live. Some questions may admit of many answers, each more or less equivalent. However, the existence of multiple peaks on the moral landscape does not make them any less real or worthy of discovery. Nor would it make the difference between being on a peak and being stuck deep in a valley any less clear or consequential.

To see that multiple answers to moral questions need not pose a problem for us, consider how we currently think about food: no one would argue that there must be *one* right food to eat. And yet there is still an objective difference between healthy food and poison. There are exceptions—some people will die if they eat peanuts, for instance—but we can account for these within the context of a rational discussion about chemistry, biology, and human health. The world's profusion of foods never tempts us to say that there are no facts to be known about human nutrition or that all culinary styles must be equally healthy in principle.

Movement across the moral landscape can be analyzed on many levels—ranging from biochemistry to economics—but where human beings are concerned, change will necessarily depend upon states and capacities of the human brain. While I fully support the notion of "consilience" in science[10]—and, therefore, view the boundaries between scientific specialties as primarily a function of university architecture and limitations on how much any one person can learn in a lifetime—the primacy of neuroscience and the other sciences of mind on questions of human experience cannot be denied. Human experience shows every sign of being determined by, and realized in, states of the human brain.

Many people seem to think that a universal conception of morality requires that we find moral principles that admit of no exceptions. If, for instance, it is truly wrong to lie, it must *always* be wrong to lie—and if one can find a single exception, any notion of moral truth must be abandoned. But the existence of moral truth—that is, the connection between how we think and behave and our well-being—does not require that we define morality in terms of unvarying moral precepts. Morality could be a lot like chess: there are surely principles that generally apply, but they might admit of important exceptions. If you want to play good chess, a principle like "Don't lose your Queen" is almost always worth following. But it admits of exceptions: sometimes sacrificing your Queen is a brilliant thing to do; occasionally, it is the *only* thing you can do. It remains a fact, however, that from any position in a game of chess there will be a range of objectively good moves and objectively bad ones. If there are objective truths to be known about human well-being—if kindness, for instance, is generally more conducive to happiness than cruelty is—then science should one day be able to make very precise claims about which of our behaviors and uses of attention are morally good, which are neutral, and which are worth abandoning.

While it is too early to say that we have a full understanding of how human beings flourish, a piecemeal account is emerging. Consider, for instance, the connection between early childhood experience, emotional bonding, and a person's ability to form healthy relationships later in life. We know, of course, that emotional neglect and abuse are not good for us, psychologically or socially. We also know that the effects of early childhood experience must be realized in the brain. Research on rodents suggests that parental care, social attachment, and stress regulation are governed, in part, by the hormones vasopressin and oxytocin,[11] because they influence activity in the brain's reward system. When asking why early childhood neglect is harmful to our psychological and social development, it seems reasonable to think that it might result from a disturbance in this same system.

While it would be unethical to deprive young children of normal care for the purposes of experiment, society inadvertently performs such experiments every day. To study the effects of emotional deprivation in early childhood, one group of researchers measured the blood concentrations of oxytocin and vasopressin in two populations: children raised in traditional homes and children who spent their first years in an orphanage.[12] As you might expect, children raised by the State generally do not receive normal levels of nurturing. They also tend to have social and emotional difficulties later in life. As predicted, these children failed to show a normal surge of oxytocin and vasopressin in response to physical contact with their adoptive mothers.

The relevant neuroscience is in its infancy, but we know that our emotions, social interactions, and moral intuitions mutually influence one another. We grow attuned to our fellow human beings through these systems, creating culture in the process. Culture becomes a mechanism for further social, emotional, and moral development. There is simply no doubt that the human brain is the nexus of these influences. Cultural norms influence our thinking and behavior by altering the structure and function of our brains. Do you feel that sons are more desirable than daughters? Is obedience to parental authority more important than honest inquiry? Would you cease to love your child if you learned that he or she was gay? The ways parents view such questions, and the subsequent effects in the lives of their children, must translate into facts about their brains.

My goal is to convince you that human knowledge and human values can no longer be kept apart. The world of measurement and the world of meaning must eventually be reconciled. And science and religion—being antithetical ways of thinking about the same reality—will never come to terms. As with all matters of fact, differences of opinion on moral questions merely reveal the incompleteness of our knowledge; they do not oblige us to respect a diversity of views indefinitely.

Facts and Values

The eighteenth-century Scottish philosopher David Hume famously argued that no description of the way the world is (facts) can tell us how we ought to behave (morality).[13] Following Hume, the philosopher G. E. Moore declared that any attempt to locate moral truths in the natural world was to commit a "naturalistic fallacy."[14] Moore argued that goodness could not be equated with any property of human experience (e.g., pleasure, happiness, evolutionary fitness) because it would always be appropriate to ask whether the property on offer was itself *good*. If, for instance, we were to say that goodness is synonymous with whatever gives people pleasure, it would still be possible to worry whether a specific instance of pleasure is actually *good*. This is known as Moore's "open question argument." And while I think this verbal trap is easily avoided when we focus on human well-being, most scientists and public intellectuals appear to have fallen into it. Other influential philosophers, including Karl Popper,[15] have echoed Hume and Moore on this point, and the effect has been to create a firewall between facts and values throughout our intellectual discourse.[16]

While psychologists and neuroscientists now routinely study human happiness, positive emotions, and moral reasoning, they rarely draw conclusions about how human beings ought to think or behave in light of their findings. In fact, it seems to be generally considered intellectually disreputable, even vaguely authoritarian, for a scientist to suggest that his or her work offers some guidance about how people should live. The philosopher and psychologist Jerry Fodor crystallizes the view:

> Science is about facts, not norms; it might tell us how we are, but it couldn't tell us what is wrong with how we are. There couldn't be a science of the human condition.[17]

While it is rarely stated this clearly, this faith in the intrinsic limits of reason is now the received opinion in intellectual circles.

Despite the reticence of most scientists on the subject of good and evil, the scientific study of morality and human happiness is well underway. This research is bound to bring science into conflict with religious orthodoxy and popular opinion—just as our growing understanding of evolution has—because the divide between facts and values is illusory in at least three senses: (1) whatever can be known about maximizing the well-being of conscious creatures—which is, I will argue, the only thing we can reasonably value—must at some point translate into facts about brains and their interaction with the world at large; (2) the very idea of "objective" knowledge (i.e., knowledge acquired through honest observation and reasoning) has values built into it, as every effort we make to discuss facts depends upon principles that we must first value (e.g., logical consistency, reliance on evidence, parsimony, etc.); (3) beliefs about facts and beliefs about values seem to arise from similar processes at the level of the brain: it appears that we have a common system for judging truth and falsity in both domains. I will discuss each of these points in greater detail below. Both in terms of what there is to know about the world and the brain mechanisms that allow us to know it, we will see that a clear boundary between facts and values simply does not exist.

Many readers might wonder how can we base our values on something as difficult to define as "well-being"? It seems to me, however, that the concept of well-being is like the concept of physical health: it resists precise definition, and yet it is indispensable.[18] In fact, the meanings of both terms seem likely to remain perpetually open to revision as we make progress in science. Today, a person can consider himself physically healthy if he is free of detectable disease, able to exercise, and destined to live into his eighties without suffering obvious decrepitude. But this standard may change. If the biogerontologist Aubrey de Grey is correct in viewing aging as an engineering problem that admits of a full solution,[19] being able to walk a mile on your hundredth birthday will not always constitute "health." There may come a time when not being able to run a marathon at age five hundred will be considered a profound disability. Such a radical transformation of our view of human health would not suggest that current notions of health and sickness are arbitrary, merely subjective, or culturally constructed. Indeed, the difference between a healthy person and a dead one is about as clear and consequential a distinction as we ever make in science. The differences between the heights of human fulfillment and the depths of human misery are no less clear, even if new frontiers await us in both directions.

If we define "good" as that which supports well-being, as I will argue we must, the regress initiated by Moore's "open question argument" really does stop. While I agree with Moore that it is reasonable to wonder whether maximizing pleasure in any given instance is "good," it makes no sense at all to ask whether maximizing well-being is "good." It seems clear that what we are really asking when we wonder whether a certain state of pleasure is "good," is whether it is conducive to, or obstructive of, some deeper form of well-being. This question is perfectly coherent; it surely has an answer (whether or not we are in a position to answer it); and yet, it keeps notions of goodness anchored to the experience of sentient beings.[20]

Defining goodness in this way does not resolve all questions of value; it merely directs our attention to what values actually are—the set of attitudes, choices, and behaviors that potentially affect our well-being, as well as that of other conscious minds. While this leaves the question of what constitutes well-being genuinely open, there is every reason to think that this question has a finite range of answers. Given that change in the well-being of conscious creatures is bound to be a product of natural laws, we must expect that this space of possibilities—the moral landscape—will increasingly be illuminated by science.

It is important to emphasize that a scientific account of human values—i.e., one that places them squarely within the web of influences that link states of the world and states of the human brain—is not the same as an *evolutionary* account. Most of what constitutes human well-being at this moment escapes any narrow Darwinian calculus. While the possibilities of human experience must be realized in the brains that evolution has built for us, our brains were not designed with a view to our ultimate fulfillment. Evolution could never have foreseen the wisdom or necessity of creating stable democracies, mitigating climate change, saving other species from extinction, containing the spread of nuclear weapons, or of doing much else that is now crucial to our happiness in this century.

As the psychologist Steven Pinker has observed,[21] if conforming to the dictates of evolution were the foundation of subjective well-being, most men would discover no higher calling in life than to make daily contributions to their local sperm bank. After all, from the perspective of a man's genes, there could be nothing more fulfilling than spawning thousands of children without incurring any associated costs or responsibilities. But our minds do not merely conform to the logic of natural selection. In fact, anyone who wears eyeglasses or uses sunscreen has confessed his disinclination to live the life that his genes have made for him. While we have inherited a multitude of yearnings that probably helped our ancestors survive and reproduce in small bands of hunter-gatherers, much of our inner life is frankly incompatible with our finding happiness in today's world. The temptation to start each day with several glazed donuts and to end it with an extramarital affair might be difficult for some people to resist, for reasons that are easily understood in evolutionary terms, but there are surely better ways to maximize one's long-term well-being. I hope it is clear that the view of "good" and "bad" I am advocating, while fully constrained by our current biology (as well as by its future possibilities), cannot be directly reduced to instinctual drives and evolutionary imperatives. As with mathematics, science, art, and almost everything else that interests us, our modern concerns about meaning and morality have flown the perch built by evolution.

The Importance of Belief

The human brain is an engine of belief. Our minds continually consume, produce, and attempt to integrate ideas about ourselves and the world that purport to be true: *Iran is developing nuclear weapons; the seasonal flu can be spread through casual contact; I actually look better with gray hair.* What must we do to believe such statements? What, in other words, must a brain do to accept such propositions as *true*? This question marks the intersection of many fields: psychology, neuroscience, philosophy, economics, political science, and even jurisprudence.[22]

Belief also bridges the gap between facts and values. We form beliefs about facts: and belief in this sense constitutes most of what we know about the world—through science, history, journalism, etc. But we also form beliefs about values: judgments about morality, meaning, personal goals, and life's larger purpose. While they might differ in certain respects, beliefs in these two domains share very important features. Both types of belief make tacit claims about right and wrong: claims not merely about how we think and behave, but about how we *should* think and behave. Factual beliefs like "water is two parts hydrogen and one part oxygen" and ethical beliefs like "cruelty is wrong" are not expressions of mere preference. To *really* believe either proposition is also to believe that you have accepted it for legitimate reasons. It is, therefore, to believe that you are in compliance with certain norms—that you are sane, rational, not lying to yourself, not confused, not overly biased, etc. When we believe that something is factually true or morally good, we also believe that another person, similarly placed, should share our belief. This seems unlikely to change. In chapter 3, we will see that both the logical and neurological properties of belief further suggest that the divide between facts and values is illusory.

The Bad Life and the Good Life

For my argument about the moral landscape to hold, I think one need only grant two points: (1) some people have better lives than others, and (2) these differences relate, in some lawful and not entirely arbitrary way, to states of the human brain and to states of the world. To make these premises less abstract, consider two generic lives that lie somewhere near the extremes on this continuum:

> *The Bad Life*
> You are a young widow who has lived her entire life in the midst of civil war. Today, your seven-year-old daughter was raped and dismembered before your eyes. Worse still, the perpetrator was your fourteen-year-old son, who was goaded to this evil at the point of a machete by a press gang of drug-addled soldiers. You are now running barefoot through the jungle with killers in pursuit. While this is the worst day of your life, it is not entirely out of character with the other days of your life: since the moment you were born, your world has been a theater of cruelty and violence. You have never learned to read, taken a hot shower, or traveled beyond the green hell of the jungle. Even the luckiest people you have known have experienced little more than an occasional respite from chronic hunger, fear, apathy, and confusion. Unfortunately, you've been very unlucky, even by these bleak standards. Your life has been one long emergency, and now it is nearly over.
>
> *The Good Life*
> You are married to the most loving, intelligent, and charismatic person you have ever met. Both of you have careers that are intellectually stimulating and financially rewarding. For decades, your wealth and social connections have allowed you to devote yourself to activities that bring you immense personal satisfaction. One of your greatest sources of happiness has been to find creative ways to help people who have not had your good fortune in life. In fact, you have just won a billion-dollar grant to

> benefit children in the developing world. If asked, you would say that you could not imagine how your time on earth could be better spent. Due to a combination of good genes and optimal circumstances, you and your closest friends and family will live very long, healthy lives, untouched by crime, sudden bereavements, and other misfortunes.

The examples I have picked, while generic, are nonetheless real—in that they represent lives that some human beings are likely to be leading at this moment. While there are surely ways in which this spectrum of suffering and happiness might be extended, I think these cases indicate the general range of experience that is accessible, in principle, to most of us. I also think it is indisputable that most of what we do with our lives is predicated on there being nothing more important, at least for ourselves and for those closest to us, than the difference between the Bad Life and the Good Life.

Let me simply concede that if you don't see a distinction between these two lives that is worth valuing (premise 1 above), there may be nothing I can say that will attract you to my view of the moral landscape. Likewise, if you admit that these lives are different, and that one is surely better than the other, but you believe these differences have no lawful relationship to human behavior, societal conditions, or states of the brain (premise 2), then you will also fail to see the point of my argument. While I don't see how either premise 1 or 2 can be reasonably doubted, my experience discussing these issues suggests that I should address such skepticism, however far-fetched it may seem.

There are actually people who claim to be unimpressed by the difference between the Bad Life and the Good Life. I have even met people who will go so far as to deny that any difference exists. While they will acknowledge that we habitually speak and act *as if* there were a continuum of experience that can be described by words like "misery," "terror," "agony," "madness," etc., on one end and "well-being," "happiness," "peace," "bliss," etc., on the other, when the conversation turns to philosophical and scientific matters, such people will say learned things like, "but, of course, that is just how we play our particular language game. It doesn't mean there is a difference *in reality*." One hopes that these people take life's difficulties in stride. They also use words like "love" and "happiness," from time to time, but we should wonder what these terms could signify that does not entail a preference for the Good Life over the Bad Life. Anyone who claims to see no difference between these two states of being (and their concomitant worlds), should be just as likely to consign himself and those he "loves" to one or the other at random and call the result "happiness."

Ask yourself, if the difference between the Bad Life and the Good Life doesn't matter to a person, what could possibly matter to him? Is it conceivable that something might matter *more* than this difference, expressed on the widest possible scale? What would we think of a person who said, "Well, I could have delivered all seven billion of us into the Good Life, but I had other priorities." Would it be *possible* to have other priorities? Wouldn't any real priority be best served amid the freedom and opportunity afforded by the Good Life? Even if you happen to be a masochist who fancies an occasional taunting with a machete, wouldn't this desire be best satisfied in the context of the Good Life?

Imagine someone who spends all his energy trying to move as many people as possible toward the Bad Life, while another person is equally committed to undoing this damage and moving people in the opposite direction: Is it conceivable that you or anyone you know could overlook the differences between these two projects? Is there any possibility of confusing them or their underlying motivations? And won't there necessarily be objective conditions for these differences? If, for instance, one's goal were to place a whole population securely in the Good Life, wouldn't there be more and less effective ways of doing this? How would forcing boys to rape and murder their female relatives fit into the picture?

I do not mean to belabor the point, but the point is crucial—and there is a pervasive assumption among educated people that either such differences don't exist, or that they are too variable, complex, or culturally idiosyncratic to admit of general value judgments. However, the moment one grants there is a difference between the Bad Life and the

Good Life that lawfully relates to states of the human brain, to human behavior, and to states of the world, one has admitted that there are right and wrong answers to questions of morality. To make sure this point is nailed down, permit me to consider a few more objections:

> *What if, seen in some larger context, the Bad Life is actually better than the Good Life—e.g., what if all those child soldiers will be happier in some afterlife, because they have been purified of sin or have learned to call God by the right name, while the people in the Good Life will get tortured in some physical hell for eternity?*

If the universe is really organized this way, much of what I believe will stand corrected on the Day of Judgment. However, my basic claim about the connection between facts and values would remain unchallenged. The rewards and punishments of an afterlife would simply alter the temporal characteristics of the moral landscape. If the Bad Life is actually better over the long run than the Good Life—because it wins you endless happiness, while the Good Life represents a mere dollop of pleasure presaging an eternity of suffering—then the Bad Life would surely be better than the Good Life. If this were the way the universe worked, we would be morally obligated to engineer an appropriately pious Bad Life for as many people as possible. Under such a scheme, there would still be right and wrong answers to questions of morality, and these would still be assessed according to the experience of conscious beings. The only thing left to be decided is how reasonable it is to worry that the universe might be structured in so bizarre a way. It is not reasonable at all, I think—but that is a different discussion.

> *What if certain people would actually prefer the Bad Life to the Good Life? Perhaps there are psychopaths and sadists who can expect to thrive in the context of the Bad Life and would enjoy nothing more than killing other people with machetes.*

Worries like this merely raise the question of how we should value dissenting opinions. Jeffrey Dahmer's idea of a life well lived was to kill young men, have sex with their corpses, dismember them, and keep their body parts as souvenirs. We will confront the problem of psychopathy in greater detail in chapter 3. For the moment, it seems sufficient to notice that in any domain of knowledge, we are free to say that certain opinions do not count. In fact, we *must* say this for knowledge or expertise to count at all. Why should it be any different on the subject of human well-being?

Anyone who doesn't see that the Good Life is preferable to the Bad Life is unlikely to have anything to contribute to a discussion about human well-being. Must we really argue that beneficence, trust, creativity, etc., enjoyed in the context of a prosperous civil society are better than the horrors of civil war endured in a steaming jungle filled with aggressive insects carrying dangerous pathogens? I don't think so. In the next chapter, I will argue that anyone who would seriously maintain that the opposite is the case—or even that it *might* be the case—is either misusing words or not taking the time to consider the details.

If we were to discover a new tribe in the Amazon tomorrow, there is not a scientist alive who would assume *a priori* that these people must enjoy optimal physical health and material prosperity. Rather, we would ask questions about this tribe's average lifespan, daily calorie intake, the percentage of women dying in childbirth, the prevalence of infectious disease, the presence of material culture, etc. Such questions would have answers, and they would likely reveal that life in the Stone Age entails a few compromises. And yet news that these jolly people enjoy sacrificing their firstborn children to imaginary gods would prompt many (even most) anthropologists to say that this tribe was in possession of an alternate moral code every bit as valid and impervious to refutation as our own. However, the moment one draws the link between morality and well-being, one sees that this is tantamount to saying that the members of this tribe must be as fulfilled, psychologically and socially, as any people on earth. The disparity between how we think about physical health and mental/societal health reveals a bizarre double standard: one that is predicated on our not knowing—or, rather, on our *pretending* not to know—anything at all about human well-being.

Of course, some anthropologists have refused to follow their colleagues over the cliff. Robert Edgerton performed a book-length exorcism on the myth of the "noble savage," detailing the ways in which the most influential anthropologists of the 1920s and 1930s—such as Franz Boas, Margaret Mead, and Ruth Benedict—systematically exaggerated the harmony of folk societies and ignored their all too frequent barbarism or reflexively attributed it to the malign influence of colonialists, traders, missionaries, and the like.[23] Edgerton details how this romance with mere difference set the course for the entire field. Thereafter, to compare societies in moral terms was deemed impossible. Rather, it was believed that one could only hope to understand and accept a culture on its own terms. Such cultural relativism became so entrenched that by 1939 one prominent Harvard anthropologist wrote that this suspension of judgment was "probably the most meaningful contribution which anthropological studies have made to general knowledge."[24] Let's hope not. In any case, it is a contribution from which we are still struggling to awaken.

Many social scientists incorrectly believe that all long-standing human practices must be evolutionarily adaptive: for how else could they persist? Thus, even the most bizarre and unproductive behaviors—female genital excision, blood feuds, infanticide, the torture of animals, scarification, foot binding, cannibalism, ceremonial rape, human sacrifice, dangerous male initiations, restricting the diet of pregnant and lactating mothers, slavery, potlatch, the killing of the elderly, sati, irrational dietary and agricultural taboos attended by chronic hunger and malnourishment, the use of heavy metals to treat illness, etc.—have been rationalized, or even idealized, in the fire-lit scribblings of one or another dazzled ethnographer. But the mere endurance of a belief system or custom does not suggest that it is adaptive, much less wise. It merely suggests that it hasn't led directly to a society's collapse or killed its practitioners outright.

The obvious difference between genes and *memes* (e.g., beliefs, ideas, cultural practices) is also important to keep in view. The latter are *communicated;* they do not travel with the gametes of their human hosts. The survival of memes, therefore, is not dependent on their conferring some actual benefit (reproductive or otherwise) on individuals or groups. It is quite possible for people to traffic in ideas and other cultural products that diminish their well-being for centuries on end.

Clearly, people can adopt a form of life that needlessly undermines their physical health—as the average lifespan in many primitive societies is scarcely a third of what it has been in the developed world since the middle of the twentieth century.[25] Why isn't it equally obvious that an ignorant and isolated people might undermine their psychological well-being or that their social institutions could become engines of pointless cruelty, despair, and superstition? Why is it even slightly controversial to imagine that some tribe or society could harbor beliefs about reality that are not only false but demonstrably harmful?

Every society that has ever existed has had to channel and subdue certain aspects of human nature—envy, territorial violence, avarice, deceit, laziness, cheating, etc.—through social mechanisms and institutions. It would be a miracle if all societies—irrespective of size, geographical location, their place in history, or the genomes of their members—had done this equally well. And yet the prevailing bias of cultural relativism assumes that such a miracle has occurred not just once, but always.

Let's take a moment to get our bearings. From a factual point of view, is it possible for a person to believe the wrong things? Yes. It is possible for a person to *value* the wrong things (that is, to believe the wrong things about human well-being)? I am arguing that the answer to this question is an equally emphatic "yes" and, therefore, that science should increasingly inform our values. Is it possible that certain people are incapable of wanting what they should want? Of course—just as there will always be people who are unable to grasp specific facts or believe certain true propositions. As with every other description of a mental capacity or incapacity, these are ultimately statements about the human brain.

Can Suffering Be Good?

It seems clear that ascending the slopes of the moral landscape may sometimes require suffering. It may also require negative social emotions, like guilt and indignation. Again, the analogy with physical health seems useful: we must occasionally experience some unpleasantness—medication, surgery, etc.—in order to avoid greater suffering or death. This principle seems to apply throughout our lives. Merely learning to read or to play a new sport can produce feelings of deep frustration. And yet there is little question that acquiring such skills generally improves our lives. Even periods of depression may lead to better life decisions and to creative insights.[26] This seems to be the way our minds work. So be it.

Of course, this principle also applies to civilization as a whole. Merely making necessary improvements to a city's infrastructure greatly inconveniences millions of people. And unintended effects are always possible. For instance, the most dangerous road on earth now appears to be a two-lane highway between Kabul and Jalalabad. When it was unpaved, cratered, and strewn with boulders, it was comparatively safe. But once some helpful Western contractors improved it, the driving skills of the local Afghans were finally liberated from the laws of physics. Many now have a habit of passing slow-moving trucks on blind curves, only to find themselves suddenly granted a lethally unimpeded view of a thousand-foot gorge.[27] Are there lessons to be learned from such missteps in the name of progress? Of course. But they do not negate the reality of progress. Again, the difference between the Good Life and the Bad Life could not be clearer: the question, for both individuals and groups, is how can we most reliably move in one direction and avoid moving in the other?

The Problem of Religion

Anyone who wants to understand the world should be open to new facts and new arguments, even on subjects where his or her views are very well established. Similarly, anyone truly interested in morality—in the principles of behavior that allow people to flourish—should be open to new evidence and new arguments that bear upon questions of happiness and suffering. Clearly, the chief enemy of open conversation is dogmatism in all its forms. Dogmatism is a well-recognized obstacle to scientific reasoning; and yet, because scientists have been reluctant even to imagine that they might have something prescriptive to say about values, dogmatism is still granted remarkable scope on questions of both truth and goodness under the banner of religion.

In the fall of 2006, I participated in a three-day conference at the Salk Institute entitled Beyond Belief: Science, Religion, Reason, and Survival. This event was organized by Roger Bingham and conducted as a town-hall meeting before an audience of invited guests. Speakers included Steven Weinberg, Harold Kroto, Richard Dawkins, and many other scientists and philosophers who have been, and remain, energetic opponents of religious dogmatism and superstition. It was a room full of highly intelligent, scientifically literate people—molecular biologists, anthropologists, physicists, and engineers—and yet, to my amazement, three days were insufficient to force agreement on the simple question of whether there is *any conflict at all* between religion and science. Imagine a meeting of mountaineers unable to agree about whether their sport ever entails walking uphill, and you will get a sense of how bizarre our deliberations began to seem.

While at Salk, I witnessed scientists giving voice to some of the most dishonest religious apologies I have ever heard. It is one thing to be told that the pope is a peerless champion of reason and that his opposition to embryonic stem-cell research is both morally principled and completely uncontaminated by religious dogmatism; it is quite another to be told this by a Stanford physician who sits on the President's Council on Bioethics.[28] Over the course of the conference, I had the pleasure of hearing that Hitler, Stalin, and Mao were examples of secular reason run amok, that the Islamic doctrines of martyrdom and jihad are not the cause of Islamic terrorism, that people can never be argued out of their beliefs because we live in an irrational world, that science has made no important contributions to our ethical lives (and cannot), and that it is not the job of scientists to undermine ancient mythologies and, thereby, "take away people's hope"—all from *atheist* scientists who, while insisting on their own skeptical hardheadedness, were equally adamant that there was something feckless and foolhardy, even indecent, about criticizing religious belief. There were several moments during our panel discussions that brought to mind the final scene of *Invasion of the Body Snatchers:* people who looked like scientists, had published as scientists, and would soon be returning to their labs, nevertheless gave voice to the alien hiss of religious obscurantism at the slightest prodding. I had previously imagined that the front lines in our culture wars were to be found at the entrance to a megachurch. I now realized that we have considerable work to do in a nearer trench.

I have made the case elsewhere that religion and science are in a zero-sum conflict with respect to facts.[29] Here, I have begun to argue that the division between facts and values is intellectually unsustainable, especially from the perspective of neuroscience. Consequently, it should come as no surprise that I see very little room for compromise between faith and reason on questions of morality. While religion is not the primary focus of this book, any discussion about the relationship between facts and values, the nature of belief, and the role of science in public discourse must continually labor under the burden of religious opinion. I will, therefore, examine the conflict between religion and science in greater depth in chapter 4.

But there is no mystery why many scientists feel that they must *pretend* that religion and science are compatible. We have recently emerged—some of us leaping, some shuffling, others crawling—out of many dark centuries of religious bewilderment and persecution, into an age when mainstream science is still occasionally treated with overt hostility by the general public and even by governments.[30] While few scientists living in the West now fear torture or death at the hands of religious fanatics, many will voice concerns about losing their funding if they give offense to religion, particularly in the United States. It also seems that, given the relative poverty of science, wealthy organizations like the Templeton Foundation (whose endowment currently stands at $1.5 billion) have managed to convince some scientists and science journalists that it is wise to split the difference between intellectual integrity and the fantasies of a prior age.

Because there are no easy remedies for social inequality, many scientists and public intellectuals also believe that the great masses of humanity are best kept sedated by pious delusions. Many assert that, while they can get along just fine without an imaginary friend, most human beings will always need to believe in God. In my experience, people holding this opinion never seem to notice how condescending, unimaginative, and pessimistic a view it is of the rest of humanity—and of generations to come.

There are social, economic, environmental, and geopolitical costs to this strategy of benign neglect—ranging from personal hypocrisy to public policies that needlessly undermine the health and safety of millions. Nevertheless, many scientists seem to worry that subjecting people's religious beliefs to criticism will start a war of ideas that science cannot win. I believe that they are wrong. More important, I am confident that we will eventually have no choice in the matter. Zero-sum conflicts have a way of becoming explicit.

Here is our situation: if the basic claims of religion are true, the scientific worldview is so blinkered and susceptible to supernatural modification as to be rendered nearly ridiculous; if the basic claims of religion are false, most people are profoundly confused about the nature of reality, confounded by irrational hopes and fears, and tending to waste precious time and attention—often with tragic results. Is this really a dichotomy about which science can claim to be neutral?

The deference and condescension of most scientists on these subjects is part of a larger problem in public discourse: people tend not to speak honestly about the nature of belief, about the invidious gulf between science and religion as modes of thought, or about the real sources of moral progress. Whatever is true about us, ethically and spiritually, is discoverable in the present and can be talked about in terms that are not an outright affront to our growing understanding of the world. It makes no sense at all to have the most important features of our lives anchored to divisive claims about the unique sanctity of ancient books or to rumors of ancient miracles. There is simply no question that how we speak about human values—and how we study or fail to study the relevant phenomena at the level of the brain—will profoundly influence our collective future.

Chapter 1

MORAL TRUTH

Many people believe that something in the last few centuries of intellectual progress prevents us from speaking in terms of "moral truth" and, therefore, from making cross-cultural moral judgments—or moral judgments at all. Having discussed this subject in a variety of public forums, I have heard from literally thousands of highly educated men and women that morality is a myth, that statements about human values are without truth conditions (and are, therefore, nonsensical), and that concepts like well-being and misery are so poorly defined, or so susceptible to personal whim and cultural influence, that it is impossible to know anything about them.[1]

Many of these people also claim that a scientific foundation for morality would serve no purpose in any case. They think we can combat human evil all the while knowing that our notions of "good" and "evil" are completely unwarranted. It is always amusing when these same people then hesitate to condemn specific instances of patently abominable behavior. I don't think one has fully enjoyed the life of the mind until one has seen a celebrated scholar defend the "contextual" legitimacy of the burqa, or of female genital mutilation, a mere thirty seconds after announcing that moral relativism does nothing to diminish a person's commitment to making the world a better place.[2]

And so it is obvious that before we can make any progress toward a science of morality, we will have to clear some philosophical brush. In this chapter, I attempt to do this within the limits of what I imagine to be most readers' tolerance for such projects. Those who leave this section with their doubts intact are encouraged to consult the endnotes.

First, I want to be very clear about my general thesis: I am not suggesting that science can give us an evolutionary or neurobiological account of what people do in the name of "morality." Nor am I merely saying that science can help us get what we want out of life. These would be quite banal claims to make—unless one happens to doubt the truth of evolution, the mind's dependency on the brain, or the general utility of science. Rather I am arguing that science can, in principle, help us understand what we *should* do and *should* want—and, therefore, what *other people* should do and should want in order to live the best lives possible. My claim is that there are right and wrong answers to moral questions, just as there are right and wrong answers to questions of physics, and such answers may one day fall within reach of the maturing sciences of mind.

Once we see that a concern for well-being (defined as deeply and as inclusively as possible) is the only intelligible basis for morality and values, we will see that there *must* be a science of morality, whether or not we ever succeed in developing it: because the well-being of conscious creatures depends upon how the universe is, altogether. Given that changes in the physical universe and in our experience of it can be understood, science should increasingly enable us to answer specific moral questions. For instance, would it be better to spend our next billion dollars eradicating racism or malaria? Which is generally more harmful to our personal relationships, "white" lies or gossip? Such questions may seem impossible to get a hold of at this moment, but they may not stay that way forever. As we come to understand how human beings can best collaborate and thrive in this world, science can help us find a path leading away from the lowest depths of misery and toward the heights of happiness for the greatest number of people. Of course, there will be practical impediments to evaluating the consequences of certain actions, and different paths through life may be morally equivalent (i.e., there may be many peaks on the moral landscape), but I am arguing that there are no obstacles, in principle, to our speaking about *moral truth.*

It seems to me, however, that most educated, secular people (and this includes most scientists, academics, and journalists) believe that there is no such thing as moral truth—only moral preference, moral opinion, and emotional reactions that we mistake for genuine knowledge of right and wrong. While we can understand how human beings think and behave in the name of "morality," it is widely imagined that there are no right answers to moral questions for science to discover.

Some people maintain this view by defining "science" in exceedingly narrow terms, as though it were synonymous with mathematical modeling or immediate access to experimental data. However, this is to mistake science for a few of its tools. Science simply represents our best effort to understand what is going on in this universe, and the boundary between it and the rest of rational thought cannot always be drawn. There are many tools one must get in hand to think scientifically—ideas about cause and effect, respect for evidence and logical coherence, a dash of curiosity and intellectual honesty, the inclination to make falsifiable predictions, etc.—and these must be put to use long before one starts worrying about mathematical models or specific data.

Many people are also confused about what it means to speak with scientific "objectivity" about the human condition. As the philosopher John Searle once pointed out, there are two very different senses of the terms "objective" and "subjective."[3] The first sense relates to how we know (i.e., epistemology), the second to what there is to know (i.e., ontology). When we say that we are reasoning or speaking "objectively," we generally mean that we are free of obvious bias, open to counterarguments, cognizant of the relevant facts, and so on. This is to make a claim about *how* we are thinking. In this sense, there is no impediment to our studying *subjective* (i.e., first-person) facts "objectively."

For instance, it is true to say that I am experiencing tinnitus (ringing in my ear) at this moment. This is a subjective fact about me, but in stating this fact, I am being entirely objective: I am not lying; I am not exaggerating for effect; I am not expressing a mere preference or personal bias. I am simply stating a fact about what I am hearing at this moment. I have also been to an otologist and had the associated hearing loss in my right ear confirmed. No doubt, my experience of tinnitus must have an objective (third-person) cause that could be discovered (likely, damage to my cochlea). There is simply no question that I can speak about my tinnitus in the spirit of scientific objectivity—and, indeed, the sciences of mind are largely predicated on our being able to correlate first-person reports of subjective experience with third-person states of the brain. This is the only way to study a phenomenon like depression: the underlying brain states must be distinguished with reference to a person's subjective experience.

However, many people seem to think that because moral facts relate to our experience (and are, therefore, ontologically "subjective"), all talk of morality must be "subjective" in the epistemological sense (i.e., biased, merely personal, etc.). This is simply untrue. I hope it is clear that when I speak about "objective" moral truths, or about the "objective" causes of human well-being, I am not denying the necessarily *subjective* (i.e., experiential) component of the facts under discussion. I am certainly not claiming that moral truths exist *independent* of the experience of conscious beings—like the Platonic Form of the Good[4]—or that certain actions are *intrinsically* wrong.[5] I am simply saying that, given that there are facts—*real* facts—to be known about how conscious creatures can experience the worst possible misery and the greatest possible well-being, it is objectively true to say that there are right and wrong answers to moral questions, whether or not we can always answer these questions in practice.

And, as I have said, people consistently fail to distinguish between there being *answers in practice* and *answers in principle* to specific questions about the nature of reality. When thinking about the application of science to questions of human well-being, it is crucial that we not lose sight of this distinction. After all, there are countless phenomena that are subjectively real, which we can discuss objectively (i.e., honestly and rationally), but which remain impossible to describe with precision. Consider the complete set of "birthday wishes" corresponding to every conscious hope that people have entertained silently while blowing out candles on birthday cakes. Will we ever be able to retrieve these unspoken thoughts? Of course not. Many of us would be hard-pressed to recall even one of our own birthday wishes. Does this mean that these wishes never existed or that we can't make true or false statements about them? What if I were to say that every one of these wishes was phrased in Latin, focused on improvements in solar panel technology, and produced by the activity of exactly 10,000 neurons in each person's brain? Is this a vacuous assertion? No, it is quite precise and surely wrong. But only a lunatic could believe such a thing about his fellow human beings. Clearly, we can make true or false claims about human (and animal) subjectivity, and we can often evaluate these claims without having access to the facts in question. This is a perfectly reasonable, scientific, and often necessary thing to do. And yet many scientists will say that moral truths do not exist, simply because certain facts about human experience cannot be readily known, or may never be known. As I hope to show, this misunderstanding has created tremendous confusion about the relationship between human knowledge and human values.

Another thing that makes the idea of moral truth difficult to discuss is that people often employ a double standard when thinking about consensus: most people take scientific consensus to mean that scientific truths exist, and they consider scientific controversy to be merely a sign that further work remains to be done; and yet many of these same people believe that moral controversy *proves* that there can be no such thing as moral truth, while moral consensus shows only that human beings often harbor the same biases. Clearly, this double standard rigs the game against a universal conception of morality.[6]

The deeper issue, however, is that truth has nothing, in principle, to do with consensus: one person can be right, and everyone else can be wrong. Consensus is a guide to discovering what is going on in the world, but that is all that it is. Its presence or absence in no way constrains what may or may not be true.[7] There are surely physical, chemical, and biological facts about which we are ignorant or mistaken. In speaking of "moral truth," I am saying that there must be facts regarding human and animal well-being about which we can also be ignorant or mistaken. In both cases, science—and rational thought generally—is the tool we can use to uncover these facts.

And here is where the real controversy begins, for many people strongly object to my claim that morality and values relate to facts about the well-being of conscious creatures. My critics seem to think that consciousness holds no special place where values are concerned, or that any state of consciousness stands the same chance of being valued as any other. The most common objection to my argument is some version of the following:

> But you haven't said *why* the well-being of conscious beings *ought* to matter to us. If someone wants to torture all conscious beings to the point of madness, what is to say that he isn't just as "moral" as you are?

While I do not think anyone sincerely believes that this kind of moral skepticism makes sense, there is no shortage of people who will press this point with a ferocity that often passes for sincerity.

Let us begin with the fact of consciousness: I think we can know, through reason alone, that consciousness is the only intelligible domain of value. What is the alternative? I invite you to try to think of a source of value that has absolutely nothing to do with the (actual or potential) experience of conscious beings. Take a moment to think about what this would entail: whatever this alternative is, it cannot affect the experience of any creature (in this life or in any other). Put this thing in a box, and what you have in that box is—it would seem, *by definition*—the least interesting thing in the universe.

So how much time should we spend worrying about such a transcendent source of value? I think the time I will spend typing this sentence is already too much. All other notions of value *will* bear some relationship to the actual or potential experience of conscious beings. So my claim that consciousness is the basis of human values and morality is not an arbitrary starting point.[8]

Now that we have consciousness on the table, my further claim is that the concept of "well-being" captures all that we can intelligibly value. And "morality"—whatever people's associations with this term happen to be—*really* relates to the intentions and behaviors that affect the well-being of conscious creatures.

On this point, religious conceptions of moral law are often put forward as counterexamples: for when asked why it is important to follow God's law, many people will cannily say, "for its own sake." Of course, it is possible to *say* this, but this seems neither an honest nor a coherent claim. What if a more powerful God would punish us for eternity for following Yahweh's law? Would it then make sense to follow Yahweh's law "for its own sake"? The inescapable fact is that religious people are as eager to find happiness and to avoid misery as anyone else: many of them just happen to believe that the most important changes in conscious experience occur after death (i.e., in heaven or in hell). And while Judaism is sometimes held up as an exception—because it tends not to focus on the afterlife—the Hebrew Bible makes it absolutely clear that Jews should follow Yahweh's law *out of concern for the negative consequences of not following it.* People who do not believe in God or an afterlife, and yet still think it important to subscribe to a religious tradition, only believe this because living this way seems to make some positive contribution to their well-being or to the well-being of others.[9]

Religious notions of morality, therefore, are not exceptions to our common concern for well-being. And all other philosophical efforts to describe morality in terms of duty, fairness, justice, or some other principle that is not explicitly tied to the well-being of conscious creatures, draw upon some conception of well-being in the end.[10]

The doubts that immediately erupt on this point invariably depend upon bizarre and restrictive notions of what the term "well-being" might mean.[11] I think there is little doubt that most of what matters to the average person—like fairness, justice, compassion, and a general awareness of terrestrial reality—will be integral to our creating a thriving global civilization and, therefore, to the greater well-being of humanity.[12] And, as I have said, there may be many different ways for individuals and communities to thrive—many peaks on the moral landscape—so if there is real diversity in how people can be deeply fulfilled in this life, such diversity can be accounted for and honored in the context of science. The concept of "well-being," like the concept of "health," is truly open for revision and discovery. Just how fulfilled is it possible for us to be, personally and collectively? What are the conditions—ranging from changes in the genome to changes in economic systems—that will produce such happiness? We simply do not know.

But what if certain people insist that their "values" or "morality" have nothing to do with well-being? Or, more realistically, what if their conception of well-being is so idiosyncratic and circumscribed as to be hostile, in principle, to the well-being of all others? For instance, what if a man like Jeffrey Dahmer says, "The only peaks on the moral landscape that interest me are ones where I get to murder young men and have sex with their corpses." This possibility—the prospect of radically different moral commitments—is at the heart of many people's doubts about moral truth.

Again, we should observe the double standard in place regarding the significance of consensus: those who do not share our scientific goals have no influence on scientific discourse whatsoever; but, for some reason, people who do not share our moral goals render us incapable of even speaking about moral truth. It is, perhaps, worth remembering that there are trained "scientists" who are Biblical Creationists, and their "scientific" thinking is purposed toward interpreting the data of science to fit the Book of Genesis. Such people claim to be doing "science," of course, but real scientists are free, and indeed obligated, to point out that they are misusing the term. Similarly, there are people who claim to be highly concerned about "morality" and "human values," but when we see that their beliefs cause tremendous misery, nothing need prevent us from saying that they are misusing the term "morality" or that their values are distorted. How have we convinced ourselves that, on the most important questions in human life, all views must count equally?

Consider the Catholic Church: an organization which advertises itself as the greatest force for good and as the only true bulwark against evil in the universe. Even among non-Catholics, its doctrines are widely associated with the concepts of "morality" and "human values." However, the Vatican is an organization that excommunicates women for attempting to become priests[13] but does not excommunicate male priests for raping children.[14] It excommunicates doctors who perform abortions to save a mother's life—even if the mother is a *nine-year-old girl raped by her stepfather and pregnant with twins*[15]—but it did not excommunicate a single member of the Third Reich for committing genocide. Are we really obliged to consider such a diabolical inversion of priorities to be evidence of an alternative "moral" framework? No. It seems clear that the Catholic Church is as misguided in speaking about the "moral" peril of contraception, for instance, as it would be in speaking about the "physics" of Transubstantiation. In both domains, it is true to say that the Church is grotesquely confused about which things in this world are worth paying attention to.

However, many people will continue to insist that we cannot speak about moral truth, or anchor morality to a deeper concern for well-being, because concepts like "morality" and "well-being" must be defined with reference to specific goals and other criteria—and nothing prevents people from disagreeing about these definitions. I might claim that morality is really about maximizing well-being and that well-being entails a wide range of psychological virtues and wholesome pleasures, but someone else will be free to say that morality depends upon worshipping the gods of the Aztecs and that well-being, if it matters at all, entails always having a terrified person locked in one's basement, waiting to be sacrificed.

Of course, goals and conceptual definitions matter. But this holds for all phenomena and for every method we might use to study them. My father, for instance, has been dead for twenty-five years. What do I mean by "dead"? Do I mean "dead" with reference to specific *goals?* Well, if you must, yes—goals like respiration, energy metabolism, responsiveness to stimuli, etc. The definition of "life" remains, to this day, difficult to pin down. Does this mean we can't study life scientifically? No. The science of biology thrives despite such ambiguities. Again, the concept of "health" is looser still: it, too, must be defined with reference to specific goals—not suffering chronic pain, not always vomiting, etc.—and these goals are continually changing. Our notion of "health" may one day be defined by goals that we cannot currently entertain with a straight face (like the goal of spontaneously regenerating a lost limb). Does this mean we can't study health scientifically?

I wonder if there is anyone on earth who would be tempted to attack the philosophical underpinnings of medicine with questions like: "What about all the people who don't share your goal of avoiding disease and early death? Who is to say that living a long life free of pain and debilitating illness is 'healthy'? What makes you think that you could convince a person suffering from fatal gangrene that he is not as healthy as you are?" And yet these are precisely the kinds of objections I face when I speak about morality in terms of human and animal well-being. Is it possible to voice such doubts in human speech? Yes. But that doesn't mean we should take them seriously.

One of my critics put the concern this way: "Morals are relative to the time and place in which they appear. If you do not already accept well-being as a value, then there seems to be no argument for why one *should* promote well-being." As proof of this assertion, he observed that I would be unable to convince the Taliban that they value the wrong things. By this standard, however, the truths of science are also "relative to the time and place in which they appear," and there is no way to convince someone who does not value empirical evidence that he *should* value it.[16] Despite 150 years of working at it, we still can't convince a majority of Americans that evolution is a fact. Does this mean biology isn't a proper science?

Everyone has an intuitive "physics," but much of our intuitive physics is wrong (with respect to the goal of describing the behavior of matter). Only physicists have a deep understanding of the laws that govern the behavior of matter in our universe. I am arguing that everyone also has an intuitive "morality," but much of our intuitive morality is clearly wrong (with respect to the goal of maximizing personal and collective well-being). And only genuine moral experts would have a deep understanding of the causes and conditions of human and animal well-being.[17] Yes, we must have a goal to define what counts as "right" or "wrong" when speaking about physics or morality, but this criterion visits us equally in both domains. And yes, I think it is quite clear that members of the Taliban are seeking well-being in this world (as well as hoping for it in the next). But their religious beliefs have led them to create a culture that is almost perfectly hostile to human flourishing. Whatever they *think* they want out of life—like keeping all women and girls subjugated and illiterate—they simply do not understand how much better life would be for them if they had different priorities.

Science cannot tell us why, *scientifically,* we should value health. But once we admit that health is the proper concern of medicine, we can then study and promote it through science. Medicine can resolve specific questions about human health—and it can do this even while the very definition of "health" continues to change. Indeed, the science of medicine can make marvelous progress without knowing how much its own progress will alter our conception of health in the future.

I think our concern for well-being is even less in need of justification than our concern for health is—as health is merely one of its many facets. And once we begin thinking seriously about human well-being, we will find that science can resolve specific questions about morality and human values, even while our conception of "well-being" evolves.

It is essential to see that the demand for *radical* justification leveled by the moral skeptic could not be met by any branch of science. Science is defined with reference to the goal of understanding the processes at work in the universe. Can we justify this goal scientifically? Of course not. Does this make science itself *unscientific*? If so, we appear to have pulled ourselves *down* by our bootstraps.

It would be impossible to prove that our definition of science is correct, because our standards of proof will be built into any proof we would offer. What evidence could prove that we should value evidence? What logic could demonstrate the importance of logic?[18] We might observe that standard science is better at predicting the behavior of matter than Creationist "science" is. But what could we say to a "scientist" whose only goal is to authenticate the Word of God? Here, we seem to reach an impasse. And yet, no one thinks that the failure of standard science to silence all possible dissent has any significance whatsoever; why should we demand more of a science of morality?[19]

Many moral skeptics piously cite Hume's is/ought distinction as though it were well known to be the last word on the subject of morality until the end of the world.[20] They insist that notions of what we ought to do or value can be justified only in terms of other "oughts," never in terms of facts about the way the world is. After all, in a world of physics and chemistry, how could things like moral obligations or values really exist? How could it be objectively true, for instance, that we *ought* to be kind to children?

But this notion of "ought" is an artificial and needlessly confusing way to think about moral choice. In fact, it seems to be another dismal product of Abrahamic religion—which, strangely enough, now constrains the thinking of even atheists. If this notion of "ought" means anything we can possibly care about, it must translate into a concern about the actual or potential experience of conscious beings (either in this life or in some other). For instance, to say that we *ought* to treat children with kindness seems identical to saying that everyone will tend to be better off if we do. The person who claims that he does not want to be better off is either wrong about what he does, in fact, want (i.e., he doesn't know what he's missing), or he is lying, or he is not making sense. The person who insists that he is committed to treating children with kindness for reasons that have nothing to do with anyone's well-being is also not making sense. It is worth noting in this context that the God of Abraham never told us to treat children with kindness, but He did tell us to kill them for talking back to us (Exodus 21:15, Leviticus 20:9, Deuteronomy 21:18–21, Mark 7:9–13, and Matthew 15:4–7). And yet everyone finds this "moral" imperative perfectly insane. Which is to say that no one—not even fundamentalist Christians and orthodox Jews—can so fully ignore the link between morality and human well-being as to be truly bound by God's law.[21]

The Worst Possible Misery for Everyone

I have argued that values only exist relative to actual and potential changes in the well-being of conscious creatures. However, as I have said, many people seem to have strange associations with the concept of "well-being"—imagining that it must be at odds with principles like justice, autonomy, fairness, scientific curiosity, etc., when it simply isn't. They also worry that the concept of "well-being" is poorly defined. Again, I have indicated why I do not think this is a problem (just as it's not a problem with concepts like "life" and "health"). However, it is also useful to notice that a universal morality can be defined with reference to the negative end of the spectrum of conscious experience: I refer to this extreme as "the worst possible misery for everyone."

Even if each conscious being has a unique nadir on the moral landscape, we can still conceive of a state of the universe in which everyone suffers as much as he or she (or it) possibly can. If you think we cannot say this would be "bad," then I don't know what you could mean by the word "bad" (and I don't think you know what you mean by it either). Once we conceive of "the worst possible misery for everyone," then we can talk about taking incremental steps toward this abyss: What could it mean for life on earth to get worse for all human beings simultaneously? Notice that this need have nothing to do with people enforcing their culturally conditioned moral precepts. Perhaps a neurotoxic dust could fall to earth from space and make everyone extremely uncomfortable. All we need imagine is a scenario in which everyone loses a little, or a lot, without there being compensatory gains (i.e., no one learns any important lessons, no one profits from others' losses, etc.). It seems uncontroversial to say that a change that leaves everyone worse off, by any rational standard, can be reasonably called "bad," if this word is to have any meaning at all.

We simply must stand somewhere. I am arguing that, in the moral sphere, it is safe to begin with the premise that it is good to avoid behaving in such a way as to produce the worst possible misery for everyone. I am not claiming that most of us personally care about the experience of all conscious beings; I am saying that a universe in which all conscious beings suffer the worst possible misery is worse than a universe in which they experience well-being. This is all we need to speak about "moral truth" in the context of science. Once we admit that the extremes of absolute misery and absolute flourishing—whatever these states amount to for each particular being in the end—are different and dependent on facts about the universe, then we have admitted that there are right and wrong answers to questions of morality.[22]

Granted, genuine ethical difficulties arise when we ask questions like, "How much should I care about other people's children? How much should I be willing to sacrifice, or demand that my own children sacrifice, in order to help other people in need?" We are not, by nature, impartial—and much of our moral reasoning must be applied to situations in which there is tension between our concern for ourselves, or for those closest to us, and our sense that it would be better to be more committed to helping others. And yet "better" must still refer, in this context, to positive changes in the experience of sentient creatures.

Imagine if there were only two people living on earth: we can call them Adam and Eve. Clearly, we can ask how these two people might maximize their well-being. Are there wrong answers to this question? Of course. (Wrong answer number 1: smash each other in the face with a large rock.) And while there are ways for their personal interests to be in conflict, most solutions to the problem of how two people can thrive on earth will not be zero-sum. Surely the *best* solutions will not be zero-sum. Yes, both of these people could be blind to the deeper possibilities of collaboration: each might attempt to kill and eat the other, for instance. Would they be *wrong* to behave this way? Yes, if by "wrong" we mean that they would be forsaking far deeper and more durable sources of satisfaction. It seems uncontroversial to say that a man and woman alone on earth would be better off if they recognized their common interests—like getting food, building shelter, and defending themselves against larger predators. If Adam and Eve were industrious enough, they might realize the benefits of exploring the world, begetting future generations of humanity, and creating technology, art, and medicine. Are there good and bad paths to take across this landscape of possibilities? Of course. In fact, there are, by definition, paths that lead to the worst misery and paths that lead to the greatest fulfillment possible for these two people—given the structure of their respective brains, the immediate facts of their environment, and the laws of Nature. The underlying facts here are the facts of physics, chemistry, and biology as they bear on the experience of the only two people in existence. Unless the human mind is fully separable from the principles of physics, chemistry, and biology, any fact about Adam and Eve's subjective experience (morally salient or not) is a fact about (part of) the universe.[23]

In talking about the causes of Adam and Eve's first-person experience, we are talking about an extraordinarily complex interplay between brain states and environmental stimuli. However complex these processes are, it is clearly possible to understand them to a greater or lesser degree (i.e., there are right and wrong answers to questions about Adam's and Eve's well-being). Even if there are a thousand different ways for these two people to thrive, there will be many ways for them not to thrive—and the differences between luxuriating on a peak of well-being and languishing in a valley of internecine horror will translate into facts that can be scientifically understood. Why would the difference between right and wrong answers suddenly disappear once we add 6.7 billion more people to this experiment?

Grounding our values in a continuum of conscious states—one that has *the worst possible misery for everyone* at its depths and differing degrees of well-being at all other points—seems like the only legitimate context in which to conceive of values and moral norms. Of course, anyone who has an alternative set of moral axioms is free to put them forward, just as they are free to define "science" any way they want. But some definitions will be useless, or worse—and many current definitions of "morality" are so bad that we can know, far in advance of any breakthrough in the sciences of mind, that they have no place in a serious conversation about how we should live in this world. The Knights of the Ku Klux Klan have nothing meaningful to say about particle physics, cell physiology, epidemiology, linguistics, economic policy, etc. How is their ignorance any less obvious on the subject of human well-being?[24]

The moment we admit that consciousness is the context in which any discussion of values makes sense, we must admit that there are facts to be known about how the experience of conscious creatures can change. Human and animal well-being are natural phenomena. As such, they can be studied, in principle, with the tools of science and spoken about with greater or lesser precision. Do pigs suffer more than cows do when being led to slaughter? Would humanity suffer more or less, on balance, if the United States unilaterally gave up all its nuclear weapons? Questions like these are very difficult to answer. But this does not mean that they don't have answers.

The fact that it could be difficult or impossible to know exactly how to maximize human well-being does not mean that there are no right or wrong ways to do this—nor does it mean that we cannot exclude certain answers as obviously bad. For instance, there is often a tension between the autonomy of the individual and the common good, and many moral problems turn on just how to prioritize these competing values. However, autonomy brings obvious benefit to people and is, therefore, an important component of the common good. The fact that it might be difficult to decide *exactly* how to balance individual rights against collective interests, or that there might be a thousand equivalent ways of doing this, does not mean that there aren't objectively *terrible* ways of doing this. The difficulty of getting precise answers to certain moral questions does not mean that we must hesitate to condemn the morality of the Taliban—not just personally, but *from the point of view of science.* The moment we admit that we know anything about human well-being scientifically, we must admit that certain individuals or cultures can be absolutely wrong about it.

Moral Blindness in the Name of "Tolerance"

There are very practical concerns that follow from the glib idea that anyone is free to value anything—the most consequential being that it is precisely what allows highly educated, secular, and otherwise well-intentioned people to pause thoughtfully, and often interminably, before condemning practices like compulsory veiling, genital excision, bride burning, forced marriage, and the other cheerful products of alternative "morality" found elsewhere in the world. Fanciers of Hume's is/ought distinction never seem to realize what the stakes are, and they do not see how abject failures of compassion are enabled by this intellectual "tolerance" of moral difference. While much of the debate on these issues must be had in academic terms, this is not merely an academic debate. There are girls getting their faces burned off with acid at this moment for daring to learn to read, or for not consenting to marry men they have never met, or even for the "crime" of getting raped. The amazing thing is that some Western intellectuals won't even blink when asked to defend these practices on philosophical grounds. I once spoke at an academic conference on themes similar to those discussed here. Near the end of my lecture, I made what I thought would be a quite incontestable assertion: We already have good reason to believe that certain cultures are less suited to maximizing well-being than others. I cited the ruthless misogyny and religious bamboozlement of the Taliban as an example of a worldview that seems less than perfectly conducive to human flourishing.

As it turns out, to denigrate the Taliban at a scientific meeting is to court controversy. At the conclusion of my talk, I fell into debate with another invited speaker, who seemed, at first glance, to be very well positioned to reason effectively about the implications of science for our understanding of morality. In fact, this person has since been appointed to the President's Commission for the Study of Bioethical Issues and is now one of only thirteen people who will advise President Obama on "issues that may emerge from advances in biomedicine and related areas of science and technology" in order to ensure that "scientific research, health care delivery, and technological innovation are conducted in an ethically responsible manner."[25] Here is a snippet of our conversation, more or less verbatim:

She: What makes you think that science will ever be able to say that forcing women to wear burqas is wrong?

Me: Because I think that right and wrong are a matter of increasing or decreasing well-being—and it is obvious that forcing half the population to live in cloth bags, and beating or killing them if they refuse, is not a good strategy for maximizing human well-being.

She: But that's only your opinion.

Me: Okay . . . Let's make it even simpler. What if we found a culture that ritually blinded every third child by literally plucking out his or her eyes at birth, would you then agree that we had found a culture that was needlessly diminishing human well-being?

She: It would depend on why they were doing it.

Me *[slowly returning my eyebrows from the back of my head]:* Let's say they were doing it on the basis of religious superstition. In their scripture, God says, "Every third must walk in darkness."

She: Then you could never say that they were wrong.

Such opinions are not uncommon in the Ivory Tower. I was talking to a woman (it's hard not to feel that her gender makes her views all the more disconcerting) who had just delivered an entirely lucid lecture on some of the moral implications of recent advances in neuroscience. She was concerned that our intelligence services might one day use neuroimaging technology for the purposes of lie detection, which she considered a likely violation of cognitive liberty. She was especially exercised over rumors that our government might have exposed captured terrorists to aerosols containing the hormone oxytocin in an effort to make them more cooperative.[26] Though she did not say it, I suspect that she would even have opposed subjecting these prisoners to the smell of freshly baked bread, which has been shown to have a similar effect.[27] While listening to her talk, as yet unaware of her liberal views on compulsory veiling and ritual enucleation, I thought her slightly overcautious, but a basically sane and eloquent authority on scientific ethics. I confess that once we did speak, and I peered into the terrible gulf that separated us on these issues, I found that I could not utter another word to her. In fact, our conversation ended with my blindly enacting two neurological clichés: my jaw quite literally dropped open, and I spun on my heels before walking away.

While human beings have different moral codes, each competing view presumes its own universality. This seems to be true even of moral relativism. While few philosophers have ever answered to the name of "moral relativist," it is by no means uncommon to find local eruptions of this view whenever scientists and other academics encounter moral diversity. Forcing women and girls to wear burqas may be wrong in Boston or Palo Alto, so the argument will run, but we cannot say that it is wrong for Muslims in Kabul. To demand that the proud denizens of an ancient culture conform to our view of gender equality would be culturally imperialistic and philosophically naïve. This is a surprisingly common view, especially among anthropologists.[28]

Moral relativism, however, tends to be self-contradictory. Relativists may say that moral truths exist only relative to a specific cultural framework—but *this* claim about the status of moral truth purports to be true across all possible frameworks. In practice, relativism almost always amounts to the claim that we should be tolerant of moral difference because no moral truth can supersede any other. And yet this commitment to tolerance is not put forward as simply one relative preference among others deemed equally valid. Rather, tolerance is held to be more in line with the (universal) truth about morality than intolerance is. The contradiction here is unsurprising. Given how deeply disposed we are to make universal moral claims, I think one can reasonably doubt whether any consistent moral relativist has ever existed.

Moral relativism is clearly an attempt to pay intellectual reparations for the crimes of Western colonialism, ethnocentrism, and racism. This is, I think, the only charitable thing to be said about it. I hope it is clear that I am not defending the idiosyncrasies of the West as any more enlightened, in principle, than those of any other culture. Rather, I am arguing that the most basic facts about human flourishing must transcend culture, just as most other facts do. And if there are facts that are truly a matter of cultural construction—if, for instance, learning a specific language or tattooing your face fundamentally alters the possibilities of human experience—well, then these facts also arise from (neurophysiological) processes that transcend culture.

In his wonderful book *The Blank Slate,* Steven Pinker includes a quotation from the anthropologist Donald Symons that captures the problem of multiculturalism especially well:

> If only one person in the world held down a terrified, struggling, screaming little girl, cut off her genitals with a septic blade, and sewed her back up, leaving only a tiny hole for urine and menstrual flow, the only question would be how severely that person should be punished, and whether the death penalty would be a sufficiently severe sanction. But when millions of people do this, instead of the enormity being magnified millions-fold, suddenly it becomes "culture," and thereby magically becomes less, rather than more, horrible, and is even defended by some Western "moral thinkers," including feminists.[29]

It is precisely such instances of learned confusion (one is tempted to say "learned psychopathy") that lend credence to the claim that a universal morality requires the support of faith-based religion. The categorical distinction between facts and values has opened a sinkhole beneath secular liberalism—leading to moral relativism and masochistic depths of political correctness. Think of the champions of "tolerance" who reflexively blamed Salman Rushdie for his fatwa, or Ayaan Hirsi Ali for her ongoing security concerns, or the Danish cartoonists for their "controversy," and you will understand what happens when educated liberals think there is no universal foundation for human values. Among conservatives in the West, the same skepticism about the power of reason leads, more often than not, directly to the feet of Jesus Christ, Savior of the Universe. The purpose of this book is to help cut a third path through this wilderness.

Moral Science

Charges of "scientism" cannot be long in coming. No doubt, there are still some people who will reject any description of human nature that was not first communicated in iambic pentameter. Many readers may also fear that the case I am making is vaguely, or even explicitly, utopian. It isn't, as should become clear in due course.

However, other doubts about the authority of science are even more fundamental. There are academics who have built entire careers on the allegation that the foundations of science are rotten with bias—sexist, racist, imperialist, Northern, etc. Sandra Harding, a feminist philosopher of science, is probably the most famous proponent of this view. On her account, these prejudices have driven science into an epistemological cul-de-sac called "weak objectivity." To remedy this dire situation, Harding recommends that scientists immediately give "feminist" and "multicultural" epistemologies their due.[30]

First, let's be careful not to confuse this quite crazy claim for its sane cousin: There is no question that scientists have occasionally demonstrated sexist and racist biases. The composition of some branches of science is still disproportionately white and male (though some are now disproportionately female), and one can reasonably wonder whether bias is the cause. There are also legitimate questions to be asked about the direction and application of science: in medicine, for instance, it seems clear that women's health issues have been sometimes neglected because the prototypical human being has been considered male. One can also argue that the contributions of women and minority groups to science have occasionally been ignored or undervalued: the case of Rosalind Franklin standing in the shadows of Crick and Watson might be an example of this. But none of these facts, alone or in combination, or however multiplied, remotely suggests that our notions of scientific objectivity are vitiated by racism or sexism.

Is there really such a thing as a feminist or multicultural epistemology? Harding's case is not helped when she finally divulges that there is not just one feminist epistemology, but many. On this view, why was Hitler's notion of "Jewish physics" (or Stalin's idea of "capitalist biology") anything less than a thrilling insight into the richness of epistemology? Should we now consider the possibility of not only Jewish physics, but of Jewish *women's* physics? How could such a balkanization of science be a step toward "strong objectivity"? And if political inclusiveness is our primary concern, where could such efforts to broaden our conception of scientific truth possibly end? Physicists tend to have an unusual aptitude for complex mathematics, and anyone who doesn't cannot expect to make much of a contribution to the field. Why not remedy this situation as well? Why not create an epistemology for physicists who failed calculus? Why not be bolder still and establish a branch of physics for people suffering from debilitating brain injuries? Who could reasonably expect that such efforts at inclusiveness would increase our understanding of a phenomenon like gravity?[31] As Steven Weinberg once said regarding similar doubts about the objectivity of science, "You have to be very learned to be that wrong."[32] Indeed, one does—and many are.

There is no denying, however, that the effort to reduce all human values to biology can produce howlers. For instance, when the entomologist E. O. Wilson (in collaboration with the philosopher Michael Ruse) wrote that "morality, or more strictly our belief in morality, is merely an adaptation put in place to further our reproductive ends," the philosopher Daniel Dennett rightly dismissed it as "nonsense."[33] The fact that our moral intuitions probably conferred some adaptive advantage upon our ancestors does not mean that the *present* purpose of morality is successful reproduction, or that "our belief in morality" is just a useful delusion. (Is the purpose of astronomy successful reproduction? What about the practice of contraception? Is that all about reproduction, too?) Nor does it mean that our notion of "morality" cannot grow deeper and more refined as our understanding of ourselves develops.

Many universal features of human life need not have been selected for at all; they may simply be, as Dennett says, "good tricks" communicated by culture or "forced moves" that naturally emerge out of the regularities in our world. As Dennett says, it is doubtful that there is a gene for knowing that you should throw a spear "pointy end first." And it is, likewise, doubtful that our ancestors had to spend much time imparting this knowledge to each successive generation.[34]

We have good reason to believe that much of what we do in the name of "morality"—decrying sexual infidelity, punishing cheaters, valuing cooperation, etc.—is borne of unconscious processes that were shaped by natural selection.[35] But this does not mean that evolution designed us to lead deeply fulfilling lives. Again, in talking about a science of morality, I am not referring to an evolutionary account of all the cognitive and emotional processes that govern what people do when they say they are being "moral"; I am referring to the totality of scientific facts that govern the range of conscious experiences that are possible for us. To say that there are truths about morality and human values is simply to say that there are facts about well-being that await our discovery—regardless of our evolutionary history. While such facts necessarily relate to the experience of conscious beings, they cannot be the mere invention of any person or culture.

It seems to me, therefore, that there are at least three projects that we should not confuse:

1. We can explain why people tend to follow certain patterns of thought and behavior (many of them demonstrably silly and harmful) in the name of "morality."
2. We can think more clearly about the nature of moral truth and determine which patterns of thought and behavior we *should* follow in the name of "morality."
3. We can convince people who are committed to silly and harmful patterns of thought and behavior in the name of "morality" to break these commitments and to live better lives.

These are distinct and independently worthy endeavors. Most scientists who study morality in evolutionary, psychological, or neurobiological terms are exclusively devoted to the first project: their goal is to describe and understand how people think and behave in light of morally salient emotions like anger, disgust, empathy, love, guilt, humiliation, etc. This research is fascinating, of course, but it is not my focus. And while our common evolutionary origins and resultant physiological similarity to one another suggest that human well-being will admit of general principles that can be scientifically understood, I consider this first project all but irrelevant to projects 2 and 3. In the past, I have found myself in conflict with some of the leaders in this field because many of them, like the psychologist Jonathan Haidt, believe that this first project represents the only legitimate point of contact between science and morality.

I happen to believe that the third project—changing people's ethical commitments—is the most important task facing humanity in the twenty-first century. Nearly every other important goal—from combating climate change, to fighting terrorism, to curing cancer, to saving the whales—falls within its purview. Of course, moral persuasion is a difficult business, but it strikes me as especially difficult if we haven't figured out in what sense moral truths exist. Hence, my main focus is on project 2.

To see the difference between these three projects, it is best to consider specific examples: we can, for instance, give a plausible evolutionary account of why human societies have tended to treat women as the property of men (1); it is, however, quite another thing to give a scientific account of whether, why, and to what degree human societies change for the better when they outgrow this tendency (2); it is yet another thing altogether to decide how best to change people's attitudes at this moment in history and to empower women on a global scale (3).

It is easy to see why the study of the evolutionary origins of "morality" might lead to the conclusion that morality has nothing at all to do with Truth. If morality is simply an adaptive means of organizing human social behavior and mitigating conflict, there would be no reason to think that our current sense of right and wrong would reflect any deeper understanding about the nature of reality. Hence, a narrow focus explaining why people think and behave as they do can lead a person to find the idea of "moral truth" literally unintelligible.

But notice that the first two projects give quite different accounts of how "morality" fits into the natural world. In 1, "morality" is the collection of impulses and behaviors (along with their cultural expressions and neurobiological underpinnings) that have been hammered into us by evolution. In 2, "morality" refers to the impulses and behaviors we can follow so as to maximize our well-being in the future.

To give a concrete example: Imagine that a handsome stranger tries to seduce another man's wife at the gym. When the woman politely informs her admirer that she is married, the cad persists, as though a happy marriage could be no impediment to his charms. The woman breaks off the conversation soon thereafter, but far less abruptly than might have been compatible with the laws of physics.

I write now, in the rude glare of recent experience. I can say that when my wife reported these events to me yesterday, they immediately struck me as morally salient. In fact, she had not completed her third sentence before the dark fluids of moral indignation began coursing through my brain—jealousy, embarrassment, anger, etc.—albeit only at a trickle. First, I was annoyed by the man's behavior—and had I been present to witness it, I suspect that my annoyance would have been far greater. If this Don Juan had been as dismissive of me in my presence as he was in my absence, I could imagine how such an encounter could result in physical violence.

No evolutionary psychologist would find it difficult to account for my response to this situation—and almost all scientists who study "morality" would confine their attention to this set of facts: my inner ape had swung into view, and any thoughts I might entertain about "moral truth" would be linguistic effluvium masking far more zoological concerns. I am the product of an evolutionary history in which every male of the species has had to guard against squandering his resources on another man's offspring. Had we scanned my brain and correlated my subjective feelings with changes in my neurophysiology, the scientific description of these events would be nearly complete. So ends project 1.

But there are many different ways for an ape to respond to the fact that other apes find his wife desirable. Had this happened in a traditional honor culture, the jealous husband might beat his wife, drag her to the gym, and force her to identify her suitor so that he could put a bullet in his brain. In fact, in an honor society, the employees of the gym might sympathize with this project and help to organize a proper duel. Or perhaps the husband would be satisfied to act more obliquely, killing one of his rival's relatives and initiating a classic blood feud. In either case, assuming he didn't get himself killed in the process, he might then murder his wife for emphasis, leaving his children motherless. There are many communities on earth where men commonly behave this way, and hundreds of millions of boys are beginning to run this ancient software on their brains even now.

However, my own mind shows some precarious traces of civilization: one being that I view the emotion of jealously with suspicion. What is more, I happen to love my wife and genuinely want her to be happy, and this entails a certain empathetic understanding of her point of view. Given a moment to think about it, I can feel glad that her self-esteem received a boost from this man's attention; I can also feel compassion for the fact that, after recently having our first child, her self-esteem needed any boost at all. I also know that she would not want to be rude, and that this probably made her somewhat slow to extricate herself from a conversation that had taken a wrong turn. And I am under no illusions that I am the only man on earth whom she will find attractive, or momentarily distracting, nor do I imagine that her devotion to me should consist in this impossible narrowing of her focus. And how do I feel about the man? Well, I still find his behavior objectionable—because I cannot sympathize with his effort to break up a marriage, and I know that I would not behave as he did—but I sympathize with everything else he must have felt, because I also happen to think that my wife is beautiful, and I know what it's like to be a single ape in the jungle.

Most important, however, I value my own well-being, as well as that of my wife and daughter, and I want to live in a society that maximizes the possibility of human well-being generally. Here begins project 2: Are there right and wrong answers to the question of how to maximize well-being? How would my life have been affected if I had killed my wife in response to this episode? We do not need a completed neuroscience to know that my happiness, as well as that of many other people, would have been profoundly diminished. And what about the collective well-being of people in an honor society that might support such behavior? It seems to me that members of these societies are obviously worse off. If I am wrong about this, however, and there are ways to organize an honor culture that allow for precisely the same level of human flourishing enjoyed elsewhere—then so be it. This would represent another peak on the moral landscape. Again, the existence of multiple peaks would not render the truths of morality merely subjective.

The framework of a moral landscape guarantees that many people will have flawed conceptions of morality, just as many people have flawed conceptions of physics. Some people think "physics" includes (or validates) practices like astrology, voodoo, and homeopathy. These people are, by all appearances, simply wrong about physics. In the United States, a majority of people (57 percent) believe that preventing homosexuals from marrying is a "moral" imperative.[36] However, if this belief rests on a flawed sense of how we can maximize our well-being, such people may simply be wrong about morality. And the fact that millions of people use the term "morality" as a synonym for religious dogmatism, racism, sexism, or other failures of insight and compassion should not oblige us to merely accept their terminology until the end of time.

What will it mean for us to acquire a deep, consistent, and fully scientific understanding of the human mind? While many of the details remain unclear, the challenge is for us to begin speaking sensibly about right and wrong, and good and evil, given what we already know about our world. Such a conversation seems bound to shape our morality and public policy in the years to come.[37]

Chapter 2

GOOD AND EVIL

There may be nothing more important than human cooperation. Whenever more pressing concerns seem to arise—like the threat of a deadly pandemic, an asteroid impact, or some other global catastrophe—human cooperation is the only remedy (if a remedy exists). Cooperation is the stuff of which meaningful human lives and viable societies are made. Consequently, few topics will be more relevant to a maturing science of human well-being.

Open a newspaper, today or any day for the rest of your life, and you will witness failures of human cooperation, great and small, announced from every corner of the world. The results of these failures are no less tragic for being utterly commonplace: deception, theft, violence, and their associated miseries arise in a continuous flux of misspent human energy. When one considers the proportion of our limited time and resources that must be squandered merely to guard against theft and violence (to say nothing of addressing their effects), the problem of human cooperation seems almost the only problem worth thinking about.[1] "Ethics" and "morality" (I use these terms interchangeably) are the names we give to our deliberate thinking on these matters.[2] Clearly, few subjects have greater bearing upon the question of human well-being.

As we better understand the brain, we will increasingly understand all of the forces—kindness, reciprocity, trust, openness to argument, respect for evidence, intuitions of fairness, impulse control, the mitigation of aggression, etc.—that allow friends and strangers to collaborate successfully on the common projects of civilization. Understanding ourselves in this way, and using this knowledge to improve human life, will be among the most important challenges to science in the decades to come.

Many people imagine that the theory of evolution entails selfishness as a biological imperative. This popular misconception has been very harmful to the reputation of science. In truth, human cooperation and its attendant moral emotions are fully compatible with biological evolution. Selection pressure at the level of "selfish" genes would surely incline creatures like ourselves to make sacrifices for our relatives, for the simple reason that one's relatives can be counted on to share one's genes: while this truth might not be obvious through introspection, your brother's or sister's reproductive success is, in part, your own. This phenomenon, known as *kin selection,* was not given a formal analysis until the 1960s in the work of William Hamilton,[3] but it was at least implicit in the understanding of earlier biologists. Legend has it that J. B. S. Haldane was once asked if he would risk his life to save a drowning brother, to which he quipped, "No, but I would save two brothers or eight cousins."[4]

The work of evolutionary biologist Robert Trivers on *reciprocal altruism* has gone a long way toward explaining cooperation among unrelated friends and strangers.[5] Trivers's model incorporates many of the psychological and social factors related to altruism and reciprocity, including: friendship, moralistic aggression (i.e., the punishment of cheaters), guilt, sympathy, and gratitude, along with a tendency to deceive others by mimicking these states. As first suggested by Darwin, and recently elaborated by the psychologist Geoffrey Miller, *sexual selection* may have further encouraged the development of moral behavior. Because moral virtue is attractive to both sexes, it might function as a kind of peacock's tail: costly to produce and maintain, but beneficial to one's genes in the end.[6]

Clearly, our selfish and selfless interests do not always conflict. In fact, the well-being of others, especially those closest to us, is one of our primary (and, indeed, most *selfish*) interests. While much remains to be understood about the biology of our moral impulses, kin selection, reciprocal altruism, and sexual selection explain how we have evolved to be, not merely atomized selves in thrall to our self-interest, but social selves disposed to serve a common interest with others.[7]

Certain biological traits appear to have been shaped by, and to have further enhanced, the human capacity for cooperation. For instance, unlike the rest of the earth's creatures, including our fellow primates, the sclera of our eyes (the region surrounding the colored iris) is white and exposed. This makes the direction of the human gaze very easy to detect, allowing us to notice even the subtlest shifts in one another's visual attention. The psychologist Michael Tomasello suggests the following adaptive logic:

> If I am, in effect, advertising the direction of my eyes, I must be in a social environment full of others who are not often inclined to take advantage of this to my detriment—by, say, beating me to the food or escaping aggression before me. Indeed, I must be in a cooperative social environment in which others following the direction of my eyes somehow benefits me.[8]

Tomasello has found that even twelve-month old children will follow a person's gaze, while chimpanzees tend to be interested only in head movements. He suggests that our unique sensitivity to gaze direction facilitated human cooperation and language development.

While each of us is selfish, we are not merely so. Our own happiness requires that we extend the circle of our self-interest to others—to family, friends, and even to perfect strangers whose pleasures and pains matter to us. While few thinkers have placed greater focus on the role that competing self-interests play in society, even Adam Smith recognized that each of us cares deeply about the happiness of others.[9] He also recognized, however, that our ability to care about others has its limits and that these limits are themselves the object of our personal and collective concern:

> Let us suppose that the great empire of China, with all its myriads of inhabitants, was suddenly swallowed up by an earthquake, and let us consider how a man of humanity in Europe, who had no sort of connection with that part of the world, would be affected upon receiving intelligence of this dreadful calamity. He would, I imagine, first of all, express very strongly his sorrow for the misfortune of that unhappy people, he would make many melancholy reflections upon the precariousness of human life, and the vanity of all the labours of man, which could thus be annihilated in a moment. He would too, perhaps, if he was a man of speculation, enter into many reasonings concerning the effects which this disaster might produce upon the commerce of Europe, and the trade and business of the world in general. And when all this fine philosophy was over, when all these humane sentiments had been once fairly expressed, he would pursue his business or his pleasure, take his repose or his diversion, with the same ease and tranquility, as if no such accident had happened. The most frivolous disaster which could befall himself would occasion a more real disturbance. If he was to lose his little finger to-morrow, he would not sleep to-night; but, provided he never saw them, he will snore with the most profound security over the ruin of a hundred millions of his brethren, and the destruction of that immense multitude seems plainly an object less interesting to him, than this paltry misfortune of his own. To prevent, therefore, this paltry misfortune to himself, would a man of humanity be willing to sacrifice the lives of a hundred millions of his brethren, provided he had never seen them? Human nature startles with horror at the thought, and the world, in its greatest depravity and corruption, never produced such a villain as could be capable of entertaining it. But what makes this difference?[10]

Smith captures the tension between our reflexive selfishness and our broader moral intuitions about as well as anyone can here. The truth about us is plain to see: most of us are powerfully absorbed by selfish desires almost every moment of our lives; our attention to our own pains and pleasures could scarcely be more acute; only the most piercing cries of anonymous suffering capture our interest, and then fleetingly. And yet, when we consciously reflect on what we *should* do, an angel of beneficence and impartiality seems to spread its wings within us: we genuinely want fair and just societies; we want others to have their hopes realized; we want to leave the world better than we found it.

Questions of human well-being run deeper than any explicit code of morality. Morality—in terms of consciously held precepts, social contracts, notions of justice, etc.—is a relatively recent development. Such conventions require, at a minimum, complex language and a willingness to cooperate with strangers, and this takes us a stride or two beyond the Hobbesian "state of nature." However, any biological changes that served to mitigate the internecine misery of our ancestors would fall within the scope of an analysis of morality as a guide to personal and collective well-being. To simplify matters enormously:

1. Genetic changes in the brain gave rise to social emotions, moral intuitions, and language . . .
2. These allowed for increasingly complex cooperative behavior, the keeping of promises, concern about one's reputation, etc. . . .
3. Which became the basis for cultural norms, laws, and social institutions whose purpose has been to render this growing system of cooperation durable in the face of countervailing forces.

Some version of this progression has occurred in our case, and each step represents an undeniable enhancement of our personal and collective well-being. To be sure, catastrophic regressions are always possible. We could, either by design or negligence, employ the hard-won fruits of civilization, and the emotional and social leverage wrought of millennia of biological and cultural evolution, to immiserate ourselves more fully than unaided Nature ever could. Imagine a global North Korea, where the better part of a starving humanity serve as slaves to a lunatic with bouffant hair: this might be worse than a world filled merely with warring australopithecines. What would "worse" mean in this context? Just what our intuitions suggest: more painful, less satisfying, more conducive to terror and despair, and so on. While it may never be feasible to compare such counterfactual states of the world, this does not mean that there are no experiential truths to be compared. Once again, there is a difference between *answers in practice* and *answers in principle.*

The moment one begins thinking about morality in terms of well-being, it becomes remarkably easy to discern a moral hierarchy across human societies. Consider the following account of the Dobu islanders from Ruth Benedict:

> Life in Dobu fosters extreme forms of animosity and malignancy which most societies have minimized by their institutions. Dobuan institutions, on the other hand, exalt them to the highest degree. The Dobuan lives out without repression man's worst nightmares of the ill-will of the universe, and according to his view of life virtue consists in selecting a victim upon whom he can vent the malignancy he attributes alike to human society and to the powers of nature. All existence appears to him as a cut-throat struggle in which deadly antagonists are pitted against one another in contest for each one of the goods of life. Suspicion and cruelty are his trusted weapons in the strife and he gives no mercy, as he asks none.[11]

The Dobu appear to have been as blind to the possibility of true cooperation as they were to the truths of modern science. While innumerable things would have been worthy of their attention—the Dobu were, after all, extremely poor and mightily ignorant—their main preoccupation seems to have been malicious sorcery. Every Dobuan's primary interest was to cast spells on other members of the tribe in an effort to sicken or kill them and in the hopes of magically appropriating their crops. The relevant spells were generally passed down from a maternal uncle and became every Dobuan's most important possessions. Needless to say, those who received no such inheritance were believed to be at a terrible disadvantage. Spells could be purchased, however, and the economic life of the Dobu was almost entirely devoted to trade in these fantastical commodities.

Certain members of the tribe were understood to have a monopoly over both the causes and cures for specific illnesses. Such people were greatly feared and ceaselessly propitiated. In fact, the conscious application of magic was believed necessary for the most mundane tasks. Even the work of gravity had to be supplemented by relentless wizardry: absent the right spell, a man's vegetables were expected to rise out of the soil and vanish under their own power.

To make matters worse, the Dobu imagined that good fortune conformed to a rigid law of thermodynamics: if one man succeeded in growing more yams than his neighbor, his surplus crop must have been pilfered through sorcery. As all Dobu continuously endeavored to steal one another's crops by such methods, the lucky gardener is likely to have viewed his surplus in precisely these terms. A good harvest, therefore, was tantamount to "a confession of theft."

This strange marriage of covetousness and magical thinking created a perfect obsession with secrecy in Dobu society. Whatever possibility of love and real friendship remained seems to have been fully extinguished by a final doctrine: the power of sorcery was believed to grow in proportion to one's intimacy with the intended victim. This belief gave every Dobuan an incandescent mistrust of all others, which burned brightest on those closest. Therefore, if a man fell seriously ill or died, his misfortune was immediately blamed on his wife, and vice versa. The picture is of a society completely in thrall to antisocial delusions.

Did the Dobu love their friends and family as much as we love ours? Many people seem to think that the answer to such a question must, in principle, be "yes," or that the question itself is vacuous. I think it is clear, however, that the question is well posed and easily answered. The answer is "no." Being fellow *Homo sapiens*, we must presume that the Dobu islanders had brains sufficiently similar to our own to invite comparison. Is there any doubt that the selfishness and general malevolence of the Dobu would have been expressed at the level of their brains? Only if you think the brain does nothing more than filter oxygen and glucose out of the blood. Once we more fully understand the neurophysiology of states like love, compassion, and trust, it will be possible to spell out the differences between ourselves and people like the Dobu in greater detail. But we need not await any breakthroughs in neuroscience to bring the general principle in view: just as it is possible for individuals and groups to be wrong about how best to maintain their physical health, it is possible for them to be wrong about how to maximize their personal and social well-being.

I believe that we will increasingly understand good and evil, right and wrong, in scientific terms, because moral concerns translate into facts about how our thoughts and behaviors affect the well-being of conscious creatures like ourselves. If there are facts to be known about the well-being of such creatures—and there are—then there must be right and wrong answers to moral questions. Students of philosophy will notice that this commits me to some form of moral realism (viz. moral claims can really be true or false) and some form of consequentialism (viz. the rightness of an act depends on how it impacts the well-being of conscious creatures). While moral realism and consequentialism have both come under pressure in philosophical circles, they have the virtue of corresponding to many of our intuitions about how the world works.[12]

Here is my (consequentialist) starting point: all questions of value (right and wrong, good and evil, etc.) depend upon the possibility of experiencing such value. Without potential consequences at the level of experience—happiness, suffering, joy, despair, etc.—all talk of value is empty. Therefore, to say that an act is morally necessary, or evil, or blameless, is to make (tacit) claims about its consequences in the lives of conscious creatures (whether actual or potential). I am unaware of any interesting exception to this rule. Needless to say, if one is worried about pleasing God or His angels, this assumes that such invisible entities are conscious (in some sense) and cognizant of human behavior. It also generally assumes that it is possible to suffer their wrath or enjoy their approval, either in this world or the world to come. Even within religion, therefore, consequences and conscious states remain the foundation of all values.

Consider the thinking of a Muslim suicide bomber who decides to obliterate himself along with a crowd of infidels: this would appear to be a perfect repudiation of the consequentialist attitude. And yet, when we look at the rationale for seeking martyrdom within Islam, we see that the consequences of such actions, both real and imagined, are entirely the point. Aspiring martyrs expect to please God and experience an eternity of happiness after death. If one fully accepts the metaphysical presuppositions of traditional Islam, martyrdom must be viewed as the ultimate attempt at career advancement. The martyr is also the greatest of altruists: for not only does he secure a place for himself in Paradise, he wins admittance for seventy of his closest relatives as well. Aspiring martyrs also believe that they are furthering God's work here on earth, with desirable consequences for the living. We know quite a lot about how such people think—indeed, they advertise their views and intentions ceaselessly—and it has everything to do with their belief that God has told them, in the Qur'an and the *hadith,* precisely what the consequences of certain thoughts and actions will be. Of course, it seems profoundly unlikely that our universe has been designed to reward individual primates for killing one another while believing in the divine origin of a specific book. The fact that would-be martyrs are almost surely wrong about the consequences of their behavior is precisely what renders it such an astounding and immoral misuse of human life.

Because most religions conceive of morality as a matter of being obedient to the word of God (generally for the sake of receiving a supernatural reward), their precepts often have nothing to do with maximizing well-being in *this* world. Religious believers can, therefore, assert the immorality of contraception, masturbation, homosexuality, etc., without ever feeling obliged to argue that these practices actually cause suffering. They can also pursue aims that are flagrantly immoral, in that they needlessly perpetuate human misery, while believing that these actions are morally obligatory. This pious uncoupling of moral concern from the reality of human and animal suffering has caused tremendous harm.

Clearly, there are mental states and capacities that contribute to our general well-being (happiness, compassion, kindness, etc.) as well as mental states and incapacities that diminish it (cruelty, hatred, terror, etc.). It is, therefore, meaningful to ask whether a specific action or way of thinking will affect a person's well-being and/or the well-being of others, and there is much that we might eventually learn about the biology of such effects. Where a person finds himself on this continuum of possible states will be determined by many factors—genetic, environmental, social, cognitive, political, economic, etc.—and while our understanding of such influences may never be complete, their effects are realized at the level of the human brain. Our growing understanding of the brain, therefore, will have increasing relevance for any claims we make about how thoughts and actions affect the welfare of human beings.

Notice that I do not mention morality in the preceding paragraph, and perhaps I need not. I began this book by arguing that, despite a century of timidity on the part of scientists and philosophers, morality can be linked directly to facts about the happiness and suffering of conscious creatures. However, it is interesting to consider what would happen if we simply ignored this step and merely spoke about "well-being." What would our world be like if we ceased to worry about "right" and "wrong," or "good" and "evil," and simply acted so as to maximize well-being, our own and that of others? Would we lose anything important? And if important, wouldn't it be, by definition, a matter of *someone's* well-being?

Can We Ever Be "Right" About Right and Wrong?

The philosopher and neuroscientist Joshua Greene has done some of the most influential neuroimaging research on morality.[13] While Greene wants to understand the brain processes that govern our moral lives, he believes that we should be skeptical of moral realism on metaphysical grounds. For Greene, the question is not, "How can you know for sure that your moral beliefs are true?" but rather, "How could it *be* that any-

one's moral beliefs are true?" In other words, what is it about the world that could make a moral claim true or false?[14] He appears to believe that the answer to this question is "nothing."

However, it seems to me that this question is easily answered. Moral view A is truer than moral view B, if A entails a more accurate understanding of the connections between human thoughts/intentions/behavior and human well-being. Does forcing women and girls to wear burqas make a net positive contribution to human well-being? Does it produce happier boys and girls? Does it produce more compassionate men or more contented women? Does it make for better relationships between men and women, between boys and their mothers, or between girls and their fathers? I would bet my life that the answer to each of these questions is "no." So, I think, would many scientists. And yet, as we have seen, most scientists have been trained to think that such judgments are mere expressions of cultural bias—and, thus, unscientific in principle. Very few of us seem willing to admit that such simple, moral truths increasingly fall within the scope of our scientific worldview. Greene articulates the prevailing skepticism quite well:

> Moral judgment is, for the most part, driven not by moral reasoning, but by moral intuitions of an emotional nature. Our capacity for moral judgment is a complex evolutionary adaptation to an intensely social life. We are, in fact, so well adapted to making moral judgments that our making them is, from our point of view, rather easy, a part of "common sense." And like many of our common sense abilities, our ability to make moral judgments feels to us like a perceptual ability, an ability, in this case, to discern immediately and reliably mind-independent moral facts. As a result, we are naturally inclined toward a mistaken belief in moral realism. The psychological tendencies that encourage this false belief serve an important biological purpose, and that explains why we should find moral realism so attractive even though it is false. Moral realism is, once again, a mistake we were born to make.[15]

Greene alleges that moral realism assumes that "there is sufficient uniformity in people's underlying moral outlooks to warrant speaking as if there is a fact of the matter about what's 'right' or 'wrong,' 'just' or 'unjust.'"[16] But do we really need to assume such uniformity for there to be right answers to moral questions? Is physical or biological realism predicated on "sufficient uniformity in people's underlying [physical or biological] outlooks"? Taking humanity as a whole, I am quite certain that there is a greater consensus that cruelty is wrong (a common moral precept) than the passage of time varies with velocity (special relativity) or that humans and lobsters share a common ancestor (evolution). Should we doubt whether there is a "fact of the matter" with respect to these physical and biological truth claims? Does the general ignorance about the special theory of relativity or the pervasive disinclination of Americans to accept the scientific consensus on evolution put our scientific worldview, even slightly, in question?[17]

Greene notes that it is often difficult to get people to agree about moral truth, or to even get an individual to agree with himself in different contexts. These tensions lead him to the following conclusion:

> [M]oral theorizing fails because our intuitions do not reflect a coherent set of moral truths and were not designed by natural selection or anything else to behave as if they were . . . If you want to make sense of your moral sense, turn to biology, psychology, and sociology—not normative ethics.[18]

This objection to moral realism may seem reasonable, until one notices that it can be applied, with the same leveling effect, to any domain of human knowledge. For instance, it is just as true to say that our logical, mathematical, and physical intuitions have not been designed by natural selection to track the Truth.[19] Does this mean that we must cease to be realists with respect to physical reality? We need not look far in science to find ideas and opinions that defy easy synthesis. There are many scientific frameworks (and levels of description) that resist integration and which divide our discourse into areas of specialization, even pitting Nobel laureates in the same discipline against one another. Does this mean that we can never hope to understand what is really going on in the world? No. It means the conversation must continue.[20]

Total uniformity in the moral sphere—either interpersonally or intrapersonally—may be hopeless. So what? This is precisely the lack of closure we face in all areas of human knowledge. Full consensus as a scientific goal only exists in the limit, at a hypothetical end of inquiry. Why not tolerate the same open-endedness in our thinking about human well-being?

Again, this does not mean that all opinions about morality are justified. To the contrary—the moment we accept that there are right and wrong answers to questions of human well-being, we must admit that many people are simply wrong about morality. The eunuchs who tended the royal family in China's Forbidden City, dynasty after dynasty, seem to have felt generally well compensated for their lives of arrested development and isolation by the influence they achieved at court—as well as by the knowledge that their genitalia, which had been preserved in jars all the while, would be buried with them after their deaths, ensuring them rebirth as human beings. When confronted with such an exotic point of view, a moral realist would like to say we are witnessing more than a mere difference of opinion: we are in the presence of moral error. It seems to me that we can be reasonably confident that it is bad for parents to sell their sons into the service of a government that intends to cut off their genitalia "using only hot chili sauce as a local anesthetic."[21] This would mean that Sun Yaoting, the emperor's last eunuch, who died in 1996 at the age of ninety-four, was wrong to harbor, as his greatest regret, "the fall of the imperial system he had aspired to serve." Most scientists seem to believe that no matter how maladaptive or masochistic a person's moral commitments, it is impossible to say that he is ever mistaken about what constitutes a good life.

Moral Paradox

One of the problems with consequentialism in practice is that we cannot always determine whether the effects of an action will be bad or good. In fact, it can be surprisingly difficult to decide this even in retrospect.

Dennett has dubbed this problem "the Three Mile Island Effect."[22] Was the meltdown at Three Mile Island a bad outcome or a good one? At first glance, it surely *seems* bad, but it might have also put us on a path toward greater nuclear safety, thereby saving many lives. Or it might have caused us to grow dependent on more polluting technologies, contributing to higher rates of cancer and to global climate change. Or it might have produced a multitude of effects, some mutually reinforcing, and some mutually canceling. If we cannot determine the net result of even such a well-analyzed event, how can we judge the likely consequences of the countless decisions we must make throughout our lives?

One difficulty we face in determining the moral valence of an event is that it often seems impossible to determine whose well-being should most concern us. People have competing interests, mutually incompatible notions of happiness, and there are many well-known paradoxes that leap into our path the moment we begin thinking about the welfare of whole populations. As we are about to see, population ethics is a notorious engine of paradox, and no one, to my knowledge, has come up with a way of assessing collective well-being that conserves all of our intuitions. As the philosopher Patricia Churchland puts it, "no one has the slightest idea how to compare the mild headache of five million against the broken legs of two, or the needs of one's own two children against the needs of a hundred unrelated brain-damaged children in Serbia."[23]

Such puzzles may seem of mere academic interest, until we realize that population ethics governs the most important decisions societies ever make. What are our moral responsibilities in times of war, when diseases spread, when millions suffer famine, or when global resources are scarce? These are moments in which we have to assess changes in collective welfare in ways that purport to be rational and ethical. Just how motivated should we be to act when 250,000 people die in an earthquake on the island of Haiti? Whether we know it or not, intuitions about the welfare of whole populations determine our thinking on these matters.

Except, that is, when we simply ignore population ethics—as, it seems, we are psychologically disposed to do. The work of the psychologist Paul Slovic and colleagues has uncovered some rather startling limitations on our capacity for moral reasoning when thinking about large groups of people—or, indeed, about groups larger than one.[24] As Slovic observes, when human life is threatened, it seems both rational and moral for our concern to increase with the number of lives at stake. And if we think that losing many lives might have some additional negative consequences (like the collapse of civilization), the curve of our concern should grow steeper still. But this is not how we characteristically respond to the suffering of other human beings.

Slovic's experimental work suggests that we intuitively care most about a single, identifiable human life, less about two, and we grow more callous as the body count rises. Slovic believes that this "psychic numbing" explains the widely lamented fact that we are generally more distressed by the suffering of single child (or even a single animal) than by a proper genocide. What Slovic has termed "genocide neglect"—our reliable failure to respond, both practically and emotionally, to the most horrific instances of unnecessary human suffering—represents one of the more perplexing and consequential failures of our moral intuition.

Slovic found that when given a chance to donate money in support of needy children, subjects give most generously and feel the greatest empathy when told only about a *single* child's suffering. When presented with two needy cases, their compassion wanes. And this diabolical trend continues: the greater the need, the less people are emotionally affected and the less they are inclined to give.

Of course, charities have long understood that putting a face on the data will connect their constituents to the reality of human suffering and increase donations. Slovic's work has confirmed this suspicion, which is now known as the "identifiable victim effect."[25] Amazingly, however, adding information about the scope of a problem to these personal appeals proves to be counterproductive. Slovic has shown that setting the story of a single needy person in the context of wider human need reliably diminishes altruism.

The fact that people seem to be reliably *less* concerned when faced with an increase in human suffering represents an obvious violation of moral norms. The important point, however, is that we immediately recognize how indefensible this allocation of emotional and material resources is once it is brought to our attention. What makes these experimental findings so striking is that they are patently inconsistent: if you care about what happens to one little girl, and you care about what happens to her brother, you must, at the very least, care as much about their combined fate. Your concern should be (in some sense) cumulative.[26] When your violation of this principle is revealed, you will feel that you have committed a moral error. This explains why results of this kind can only be obtained *between* subjects (where one group is asked to donate to help one child and another group is asked to support two); we can be sure that if we presented both questions to each participant in the study, the effect would disappear (unless subjects could be prevented from noticing when they were violating the norms of moral reasoning).

Clearly, one of the great tasks of civilization is to create cultural mechanisms that protect us from the moment-to-moment failures of our ethical intuitions. We must build our better selves into our laws, tax codes, and institutions. Knowing that we are generally incapable of valuing two children more than either child alone, we must build a structure that reflects and enforces our deeper understanding of human well-being. This is where a science of morality could be indispensable to us: the more we understand the causes and constituents of human fulfillment, and the more we know about the experiences of our fellow human beings, the more we will be able to make intelligent decisions about which social policies to adopt.

For instance, there are an estimated 90,000 people living on the streets of Los Angeles. Why are they homeless? How many of these people are mentally ill? How many are addicted to drugs or alcohol? How many have simply fallen through the cracks in our economy? Such questions have answers. And each of these problems admits of a range of responses, as well as false solutions and neglect. Are there policies we could adopt that would make it easy for every person in the United States to help alleviate the problem of homelessness in their own communities? Is there some brilliant idea that no one has thought of that would make people *want* to alleviate the problem of homelessness more than they want to watch television or play video games?

Would it be possible to design a video game that could help solve the problem of homelessness in the real world?[27] Again, such questions open onto a world of facts, whether or not we can bring the relevant facts into view.

Clearly, morality is shaped by cultural norms to a great degree, and it can be difficult to do what one believes to be right on one's own. A friend's four-year-old daughter recently observed the role that social support plays in making moral decisions:

> "It's so sad to eat baby lambies," she said as she gnawed greedily on a lamb chop.
>
> "So, why don't you stop eating them?" her father asked.
>
> "Why would they kill such a soft animal? Why wouldn't they kill some other kind of animal?"
>
> "Because," her father said, "people like to eat the meat. Like you are, right now."
>
> His daughter reflected for a moment—still chewing her lamb—and then replied:
>
> "It's not good. But I can't stop eating them if they keeping killing them."

And the practical difficulties for consequentialism do not end here. When thinking about maximizing the well-being of a population, are we thinking in terms of total or average well-being? The philosopher Derek Parfit has shown that both bases of calculation lead to troubling paradoxes.[28] If we are concerned only about total welfare, we should prefer a world with hundreds of billions of people whose lives are just barely worth living to a world in which 7 billion of us live in perfect ecstasy. This is the result of Parfit's famous argument known as "The Repugnant Conclusion."[29] If, on the other hand, we are concerned about the average welfare of a population, we should prefer a world containing a single, happy inhabitant to a world of billions who are only slightly less happy; it would even suggest that we might want to painlessly kill many of the least happy people currently alive, thereby increasing the average of human well-being. Privileging average welfare would also lead us to prefer a world in which billions live under the misery of constant torture to a world in which only one person is tortured ever-so-slightly more. It could also render the morality of an action dependent upon the experience of unaffected people. As Parfit points out, if we care about the average over time, we might deem it morally wrong to have a child today whose life, while eminently worth living, would not compare favorably to the lives of the ancient Egyptians. Parfit has even devised scenarios in which everyone alive could have a *lower* quality of life than they otherwise would and yet the average quality of life will have increased.[30] Clearly, this proves that we cannot rely on a simple summation or averaging of welfare as our only metric. And yet, at the extremes, we can see that human welfare must aggregate in *some* way: it really is better for all of us to be deeply fulfilled than it is for everyone to live in absolute agony.

Placing only consequences in our moral balance also leads to indelicate questions. For instance, do we have a moral obligation to come to the aid of wealthy, healthy, and intelligent hostages before poor, sickly, and slow-witted ones? After all, the former are more likely to make a positive contribution to society upon their release. And what about remaining partial to one's friends and family? Is it wrong for me to save the life of my only child if, in the process, I neglect to save a stranger's brood of eight? Wrestling with such questions has convinced many people that morality does not obey the simple laws of arithmetic.

However, such puzzles merely suggest that certain moral questions could be difficult or impossible to answer in practice; they do not suggest that morality depends upon something other than the consequences of our actions and intentions. This is a frequent source of confusion: consequentialism is less a method of answering moral questions than it is a claim about the status of moral truth. Our assessment of consequences in the moral domain must proceed as it does in all others: under the shadow of uncertainty, guided by theory, data, and honest conversation. The fact that it may often be difficult, or even impossible, to know what the consequences of our thoughts and actions will be does not mean that there is some other basis for human values that is worth worrying about.

Such difficulties notwithstanding, it seems to me quite possible that we will one day resolve moral questions that are often thought to be unanswerable. For instance, we might agree that having a preference for one's intimates is better (in that it increases general welfare) than being fully disinterested as to how consequences accrue. Which is to say that there may be some forms of love and happiness that are best served by each of us being specially connected to a subset of humanity. This certainly appears to be descriptively true of us at present. Communal experiments that ignore parents' special attachment to their own children, for instance, do not seem to work very well. The Israeli *kibbutzim* learned this the hard way: after discovering that raising children communally made both parents and children less happy, they reinstated the nuclear family.[31] Most people may be happier in a world in which a natural bias toward one's own children is conserved—presumably in the context of laws and social norms that disregard this bias. When I take my daughter to the hospital, I am naturally more concerned about her than I am about the other children in the lobby. I do not, however, expect the hospital staff to share my bias. In fact, given time to reflect about it, I realize that I would not want them to. How could such a denial of my self-interest actually be in the service of my self-interest? Well, first, there are many more ways for a system to be biased against me than in my favor, and I know that I will benefit from a fair system far more than I will from one that can be easily corrupted. I also happen to care about other people, and this experience of empathy deeply matters to me. I feel better as a person valuing fairness, and I want my daughter to become a person who shares this value. And how would I feel if the physician attending my daughter actually shared my bias for her and viewed her as far more important than the other patients under his care? Frankly, it would give me the creeps.

But perhaps there are two possible worlds that maximize the well-being of their inhabitants to precisely the same degree: in world X everyone is focused on the welfare of all others without bias, while in world Y everyone shows some degree of moral preference for their friends and family. Perhaps these worlds are equally good, in that their inhabitants enjoy precisely the same level of well-being. These could be thought of as two peaks on the moral landscape. Perhaps there are others. Does this pose a threat to moral realism or to consequentialism? No, because there would still be right and wrong ways to move from our current position on the moral landscape toward one peak or the other, and movement would still be a matter of increasing well-being in the end.

To bring the discussion back to the especially low-hanging fruit of conservative Islam: there is absolutely no reason to think that demonizing homosexuals, stoning adulterers, veiling women, soliciting the murder of artists and intellectuals, and celebrating the exploits of suicide bombers will move humanity toward a peak on the moral landscape. This is, I think, as *objective* a claim as we ever make in science.

Consider the Danish cartoon controversy: an eruption of religious insanity that still flows to this day. Kurt Westergaard, the cartoonist who drew what was arguably the most inflammatory of these utterly benign cartoons has lived in hiding since pious Muslims first began calling for his murder in 2006. A few weeks ago—more than three years after the controversy first began—a Somali man broke into Westergaard's home with an axe. Only the construction of a specially designed "safe room" allowed Westergaard to escape being slaughtered for the glory of God (his five-year-old granddaughter also witnessed the attack). Westergaard now lives with continuous police protection—as do the other eighty-seven men in Denmark who have the misfortune of being named "Kurt Westergaard."[32]

The peculiar concerns of Islam have created communities in almost every society on earth that grow so unhinged in the face of criticism that they will reliably riot, burn embassies, and seek to kill peaceful people, over *cartoons*. This is something they will not do, incidentally, in protest over the continuous atrocities committed against them by their fellow Muslims. The reasons why such a terrifying inversion of priorities does not tend to maximize human happiness are susceptible to many levels of analysis—ranging from biochemistry to economics. But do we need further information in this case? It seems to me that we already know enough about the human condition to know that killing cartoonists for blasphemy does not lead anywhere worth going on the moral landscape.

There are other results in psychology and behavioral economics that make it difficult to assess changes in human well-being. For instance, people tend to consider losses to be far more significant than forsaken gains, even when the net result is the same. For instance, when presented with a wager where they stand a 50 percent chance of losing $100, most people will consider anything less than a potential gain of $200 to be unattractive. This bias relates to what has come to be known as "the endowment effect": people demand more money in exchange for an object that has been given to them than they would spend to acquire the object in the first place. In psychologist Daniel Kahneman's words, "a good is worth more when it is considered as something that could be lost or given up than when it is evaluated as a potential gain."[33] This aversion to loss causes human beings to generally err on the side of maintaining the status quo. It is also an important impediment to conflict resolution through negotiation: for if each party values his opponent's concessions as gains and his own as losses, each is bound to perceive his sacrifice as being greater.[34]

Loss aversion has been studied with functional magnetic resonance imaging (fMRI). If this bias were the result of negative feelings associated with potential loss, we would expect brain regions known to govern negative emotion to be involved. However, researchers have not found increased activity in any areas of the brain as losses increase. Instead, those regions that represent gains show decreasing activity as the size of the potential losses increases. In fact, these brain structures themselves exhibit a pattern of "neural loss aversion": their activity decreases at a steeper rate in the face of potential losses than they increase for potential gains.[35]

There are clearly cases in which such biases seem to produce moral illusions—where a person's view of right and wrong will depend on whether an outcome is described in terms of gains or losses. Some of these illusions might not be susceptible to full correction. As with many perceptual illusions, it may be impossible to "see" two circumstances as morally equivalent, even while "knowing" that they are. In such cases, it may be ethical to ignore how things seem. Or it may be that the path we take to arrive at identical outcomes really does matter to us—and, therefore, that losses and gains will remain incommensurable.

Imagine, for instance, that you are empaneled as the member of a jury in a civil trial and asked to determine how much a hospital should pay in damages to the parents of children who received substandard care in their facility. There are two scenarios to consider:

> Couple A learned that their three-year-old daughter was inadvertently given a neurotoxin by the hospital staff. Before being admitted, their daughter was a musical prodigy with an IQ of 195. She has since lost all her intellectual gifts. She can no longer play music with any facility and her IQ is now a perfectly average 100.

> Couple B learned that the hospital neglected to give their three-year-old daughter, who has an IQ of 100, a perfectly safe and inexpensive genetic enhancement that would have given her remarkable musical talent and nearly doubled her IQ. Their daughter's intelligence remains average, and she lacks any noticeable musical gifts. The critical period for giving this enhancement has passed.

Obviously the end result under either scenario is the same. But what if the mental suffering associated with loss is simply bound to be greater than that associated with forsaken gains? If so, it may be appropriate to take this difference into account, even when we cannot give a rational explanation of why it is worse to lose something than not to gain it. This is another source of difficulty in the moral domain: unlike dilemmas in behavioral economics, it is often difficult to establish the criteria by which two outcomes can be judged equivalent.[36] There is probably another principle at work in this example, however: people tend to view sins of commission more harshly than sins of omission. It is not clear how we should account for this bias either. But, once again, to say that there are right answers to questions of how to maximize human well-being is not to say that we will always be in a position to answer such questions. There will be peaks and valleys on the moral landscape, and movement between them is clearly possible, whether or not we always know which way is up.

There are many other features of our subjectivity that have implications for morality. For instance, people tend to evaluate an experience based on its peak intensity (whether positive or negative) and the quality of its final moments. In psychology, this is known as the "peak/end rule." Testing this rule in a clinical environment, one group found that patients undergoing colonoscopies (in the days when this procedure was done without anesthetic) could have their perception of suffering markedly reduced, and their likelihood of returning for a follow-up exam increased, if their physician needlessly prolonged the procedure at its lowest level of discomfort by leaving the colonoscope inserted for a few extra minutes.[37] The same principle seems to hold for aversive sounds[38] and for exposure to cold.[39] Such findings suggest that, under certain conditions, it is compassionate to *prolong a person's pain unnecessarily* so as to reduce his memory of suffering later on. Indeed, it might be unethical to do otherwise. Needless to say, this is a profoundly counter-intuitive result. But this is precisely what is so important about science: it allows us to investigate the world, and our place within it, in ways that get behind first appearances. Why shouldn't we do this with morality and human values generally?

Fairness and Hierarchy

It is widely believed that focusing on the consequences of a person's actions is merely one of several approaches to ethics—one that is beset by paradox and often impossible to implement. Imagined alternatives are either highly rational, as in the work of a modern philosopher like John Rawls,[40] or decidedly otherwise, as we see in the disparate and often contradictory precepts that issue from the world's major religions.

My reasons for dismissing revealed religion as a source of moral guidance have been spelled out elsewhere,[41] so I will not ride this hobbyhorse here, apart from pointing out the obvious: (1) there are many revealed religions available to us, and they offer mutually incompatible doctrines; (2) the scriptures of many religions, including the most well subscribed (i.e., Christianity and Islam), countenance patently unethical practices like slavery; (3) the faculty we use to validate religious precepts, judging the Golden Rule to be wise and the murder of apostates to be foolish, is something we bring *to* scripture; it does not, therefore, come *from* scripture; (4) the reasons for believing that any of the world's religions were "revealed" to our ancestors (rather than merely invented by men and women who did not have the benefit of a twenty-first-century education) are either risible or nonexistent—and the idea that each of these mutually contradictory doctrines is inerrant remains a logical impossibility. Here we can take refuge in Bertrand Russell's famous remark that even if we could be certain that one of the world's religions was perfectly true, given the sheer number of conflicting faiths on offer, every believer should expect damnation purely as a matter of probability.

Among the rational challenges to consequentialism, the "contractualism" of John Rawls has been the most influential in recent decades. In his book *A Theory of Justice* Rawls offered an approach to building a fair society that he considered an alternative to the aim of maximizing human welfare.[42] His primary method, for which this work is duly famous, was to ask how reasonable people would structure a society, guided by their self-interest, if they couldn't know what sort of person they would be in it. Rawls called this novel starting point "the original position," from which each person must judge the fairness of every law and social arrangement from behind a "veil of ignorance." In other words, we can design any society we like as long as we do not presume to know, in advance, whether we will be black or white, male or female, young or old, healthy or sick, of high or low intelligence, beautiful or ugly, etc.

As a method for judging questions of fairness, this thought experiment is undeniably brilliant. But is it really an alternative to thinking about the actual consequences of our behavior? How would we feel if, after structuring our ideal society from behind a veil of ignorance, we were told by an omniscient being that we had made a few choices that, though eminently fair, would lead to the unnecessary misery of millions, while parameters that were ever-so-slightly less fair would entail no such suffering? Could we be indifferent to this information? The moment we conceive of justice as being *fully* separable from human well-being, we are faced with the prospect of there being morally "right" actions and social systems that are, on balance, detrimental to the welfare of everyone affected by them. To simply bite the bullet on this point, as Rawls seemed to do, saying "there is no reason to think that just institutions will maximize the good"[43] seems a mere embrace of moral and philosophical defeat.

Some people worry that a commitment to maximizing a society's welfare could lead us to sacrifice the rights and liberties of the few wherever these losses would be offset by the greater gains of the many. Why not have a society in which a few slaves are continually worked to death for the pleasure of the rest? The worry is that a focus on collective welfare does not seem to respect people as ends in themselves. And whose welfare should we care about? The pleasure that a racist takes in abusing some minority group, for instance, seems on all fours with the pleasure a saint takes in risking his life to help a stranger. If there are more racists than saints, it seems the racists will win, and we will be obliged to build a society that maximizes the pleasure of unjust men.

But such concerns clearly rest on an incomplete picture of human well-being. To the degree that treating people as ends in themselves is a good way to safeguard human well-being, it is precisely what we should do. Fairness is not merely an abstract principle—it is a felt experience. We all know this from the inside, of course, but neuroimaging has also shown that fairness drives reward-related activity in the brain, while accepting unfair proposals requires the regulation of negative emotion.[44] Taking others' interests into account, making impartial decisions (and knowing that others will make them), rendering help to the needy—these are experiences that contribute to our psychological and social well-being. It seems perfectly reasonable, within a consequentialist framework, for each of us to submit to a system of justice in which our immediate, selfish interests will often be superseded by considerations of fairness. It is only reasonable, however, on the assumption that everyone will tend to be better off under such a system. As, it seems, they will.[45]

While each individual's search for happiness may not be compatible in every instance with our efforts to build a just society, we should not lose sight of the fact that societies do not suffer; people do. The only thing wrong with injustice is that it is, on some level, actually or potentially bad for people.[46] Injustice makes its victims demonstrably less happy, and it could be easily argued that it tends to make its perpetrators less happy than they would be if they cared about the well-being of others. Injustice also destroys trust, making it difficult for strangers to cooperate. Of course, here we are talking about the nature of conscious experience, and so we are, of necessity, talking about processes at work in the brains of human beings. The neuroscience of morality and social emotions is only just beginning, but there seems no question that it will one day deliver morally relevant insights regarding the material causes of our happiness and suffering. While there may be some surprises in store for us down this path, there is every reason to expect that kindness, compassion, fairness, and other classically "good" traits will be vindicated neuroscientifically—which is to say that we will only discover further reasons to believe that they are good for us, in that they generally enhance our lives.

We have already begun to see that morality, like rationality, implies the existence of certain norms—that is, it does not merely describe how we tend to think and behave; it tells us how we *should* think and behave. One norm that morality and rationality share is the interchangeability of perspective.[47] The solution to a problem should not depend on whether you are the husband or the wife, the employer or employee, the creditor or debtor, etc. This is why one cannot argue for the rightness of one's views on the basis of mere preference. In the moral sphere, this requirement lies at the core of what we mean by "fairness." It also reveals why it is generally not a good thing to have a different ethical code for friends and strangers.

We have all met people who behave quite differently in business than in their personal lives. While they would never lie to their friends, they might lie without a qualm to their clients or customers. Why is this a moral failing? At the very least, it is vulnerable to what could be called the *principle of the unpleasant surprise*. Consider what happens to such a person when he discovers that one of his customers is actually a friend: "Oh, why didn't you say you were Jennifer's sister! Uh . . . Okay, don't buy that model; this one is a much better deal." Such moments expose a rift in a person's ethics that is always unflattering. People with two ethical codes are perpetually susceptible to embarrassments of this kind. They are also less trustworthy—and trust is a measure of how much a person can be relied upon to safeguard other people's well-being. Even if you happen to be a close friend of such a person—that is, on the right side of his ethics—you can't trust him to interact with others you may care about ("I didn't know she was *your* daughter. Sorry about that").

Or consider the position of a Nazi living under the Third Reich, having fully committed himself to exterminating the world's Jews, only to learn, as many did, that he was Jewish himself. Unless some compelling argument for the moral necessity of his suicide were forthcoming, we can imagine that it would be difficult for our protagonist to square his Nazi ethics with his actual identity. Clearly, his sense of right and wrong was predicated on a false belief about his own genealogy. A genuine ethics should not be vulnerable to such unpleasant surprises. This seems another way of arriving at Rawls's "original position." That which is right cannot be dependent upon one's being a member of a certain tribe—if for no other reason than one can be mistaken about the fact of one's membership.

Kant's "categorical imperative," perhaps the most famous prescription in all of moral philosophy, captures some of these same concerns:

> Hence there is only one categorical imperative and it is this: "Act only according to that maxim whereby you can at the same time will that it should become a universal law."[48]

While Kant believed that this criterion of universal applicability was the product of pure reason, it appeals to us because it relies on basic intuitions about fairness and justification.[49] One cannot claim to be "right" about anything—whether as a matter of reason or a matter of ethics—unless one's views can be generalized to others.[50]

Is Being Good Just Too Difficult?

Most of us spend some time over the course of our lives deciding how (or whether) to respond to the fact that other people on earth needlessly starve to death. Most of us also spend some time deciding which delightful foods we want to consume at home and in our favorite restaurants. Which of these projects absorbs more of your time and material resources on a yearly basis? If you are like most people living in the developed world, such a comparison will not recommend you for sainthood. Can the disparity between our commitment to fulfilling our selfish desires and our commitment to alleviating the unnecessary misery and death of millions be morally justified? Of course not. These failures of ethical consistency are often considered a strike against consequentialism. They shouldn't be. Who ever said that being truly good, or even ethically consistent, must be easy?

I have no doubt that I am less good than I could be. Which is to say, I am not living in a way that truly maximizes the well-being of others. I am nearly as sure, however, that I am also failing to live in a way that maximizes my own well-being. This is one of the paradoxes of human psychology: we often fail to do what we ostensibly want to do and what is most in our self-interest to do. We often fail to do what we *most want* to do—or, at the very least, we fail to do what, at the end of the day (or year, or lifetime) we will most wish we had done.

Just think of the heroic struggles many people must endure simply to quit smoking or lose weight. The right course of action is generally obvious: if you are smoking two packs of cigarettes a day or are fifty pounds overweight, you are surely not maximizing your well-being. Perhaps this isn't so clear to you now, but imagine: if you could successfully stop smoking or lose weight, what are the chances that you would regret this decision a year hence? Probably zero. And yet, if you are like most people, you will find it extraordinarily difficult to make the simple behavioral changes required to get what you want.[51]

Most of us are in this predicament in moral terms. I know that helping people who are starving is far more important than most of what I do. I also have no doubt that doing what is most important would give me more pleasure and emotional satisfaction than I get from most of what I do by way of seeking pleasure and emotional satisfaction. But this knowledge does not change me. I still want to do what I do for pleasure more than I want to help the starving. I strongly believe that I would be happier if I wanted to help the starving more—and I have no doubt that they would be happier if I spent more time and money helping them—but these beliefs are not sufficient to change me. I know that I would be happier and the world would be a (marginally) better place if I were different in these respects. I am, therefore, virtually certain that I am neither as moral, nor as happy, as I could be.[52] I know all of these things, and I want to maximize my happiness, but I am generally not moved to do what I believe will make me happier than I now am.

At bottom, these are claims both about the architecture of my mind and about the social architecture of our world. It is quite clear to me that given the current state of my mind—that is, given how my actions and uses of attention affect my life—I would be happier if I were less selfish. This means I would be more wisely and effectively selfish if I were less selfish. This is not a paradox.

What if I could change the architecture of my mind? On some level, this has always been possible, as everything we devote attention to, every discipline we adopt, or piece of knowledge we acquire changes our minds. Each of us also now has access to a swelling armamentarium of drugs that regulate mood, attention, and wakefulness. And the possibility of far more sweeping (as well as more precise) changes to our mental capacities may be within reach. Would it be good to make changes to our minds that affect our sense of right and wrong? And would our ability to alter our moral sense undercut the case I am making for moral realism? What if, for instance, I could rewire my brain so that eating ice cream was not only extremely pleasurable, but also felt like the most *important* thing I could do?

Despite the ready availability of ice cream, it seems that my new disposition would present certain challenges to self-actualization. I would gain weight. I would ignore social obligations and intellectual pursuits. No doubt, I would soon scandalize others with my skewed priorities. But what if advances in neuroscience eventually allow us to change the way every brain responds to morally relevant experiences? What if we could program the entire species to hate fairness, to admire cheating, to love cruelty, to despise compassion, etc. Would this be morally good? Again, the devil is in the details. Is this really a world of equivalent and genuine well-being, where the concept of "well-being" is susceptible to ongoing examination and refinement as it is in our world? If so, so be it. What could be more important than *genuine* well-being? But, given all that the concept of "well-being" entails in our world, it is very difficult to imagine that its properties could be entirely fungible as we move across the moral landscape.

A miniature version of this dilemma is surely on the horizon: increasingly, we will need to consider the ethics of using medications to mitigate mental suffering. For instance, would it be good for a person to take a drug that made her indifferent to the death of her child? Surely not while she still had responsibilities as a parent. But what if a mother lost her only child and was thereafter inconsolable? How much better than inconsolable should her doctor make her feel? How much better should she *want* to feel? Would any of us want to feel perfectly happy in this circumstance? Given a choice—and this choice, in some form, is surely coming—I think that most of us will want our mental states to be coupled, however loosely, to the reality of our lives. How else could our bonds with one another be maintained? How, for instance, can we love our children and yet be totally indifferent to their suffering and death? I suspect we cannot. But what will we do once our pharmacies begin stocking a genuine antidote to grief?

If we cannot always resolve such conundrums, how should we proceed? We cannot perfectly measure or reconcile the competing needs of billions of creatures. We often cannot effectively prioritize our own competing needs. What we can do is try, within practical limits, to follow a path that seems likely to maximize both our own well-being and the well-being of others. This is what it means to live wisely and ethically. As we will see, we have already begun to discover which regions of the brain allow us to do this. A fuller understanding of what moral life entails, however, would require a science of morality.

Bewildered by Diversity

The psychologist Jonathan Haidt has put forward a very influential thesis about moral judgment known as the "social-intuitionist model." In a widely referenced article entitled "The Emotional Dog and Its Rational Tail," Haidt summarizes our predicament this way:

> [O]ur moral life is plagued by two illusions. The first illusion can be called the "wag-the-dog" illusion: We believe that our own moral judgment (the dog) is driven by our own moral reasoning (the tail). The second illusion can be called the "wag-the-other-dog's-tail" illusion: In a moral argument, we expect the successful rebuttal of our opponents' arguments to change our opponents' minds. Such a belief is analogous to believing that forcing a dog's tail to wag by moving it with your hand should make the dog happy.[53]

Haidt does not go so far as to say that reasoning *never* produces moral judgments; he simply argues that this happens far less often than people think. Haidt is pessimistic about our ever making realistic claims about right and wrong, or good and evil, because he has observed that human beings tend to make moral decisions on the basis of emotion, justify these decisions with post hoc reasoning, and stick to their guns even when their reasoning demonstrably fails. He notes that when asked to justify their responses to specific moral (and pseudo-moral) dilemmas, people are often "morally dumbfounded." His experimental subjects would "stutter, laugh, and express surprise at their inability to find supporting reasons, yet they would not change their initial judgments . . ."

The same can be said, however, about our failures to reason effectively. Consider the Monty Hall Problem (based on the television game show *Let's Make a Deal*). Imagine that you are a contestant on a game show and presented with three closed doors: behind one sits a new car; the other two conceal goats. Pick the correct door, and the car is yours.

The game proceeds this way: Assume that you have chosen Door #1. Your host then opens Door #2, revealing a goat. He now gives you a chance to switch your bet from Door #1 to the remaining Door #3. Should you switch? The correct answer is "yes." But most people find this answer very perplexing, as it violates the common intuition that, with two unopened doors remaining, the odds must be 1 in 2 that the car will be behind either one of them. If you stick with your initial choice, however, your odds of winning are actually 1 in 3. If you switch, your odds increase to 2 in 3.[54]

It would be fair to say that the Monty Hall problem leaves many of its victims "logically dumbfounded." Even when people understand conceptually why they should switch doors, they can't shake their initial intuition that each door represents a 1/2 chance of success. This reliable failure of human reasoning is just that—a *failure* of reasoning. It does not suggest that there is no correct answer to the Monty Hall problem.

And yet scientists like Joshua Greene and Jonathan Haidt seem to think that the very existence of moral controversy nullifies the possibility of moral truth. In their opinion, all we can do is study what human beings do in the name of "morality." Thus, if religious conservatives find the prospect of gay marriage abhorrent, and secular liberals find it perfectly acceptable, we are confronted by a mere difference of moral preference—not a difference that relates to any deeper truths about human life.

In opposition to the liberal notion of morality as being a system of "prescriptive judgments of justice, rights, and welfare pertaining to how people ought to relate to each other," Haidt asks us to ponder mysteries of the following sort:

> [I]f morality is about how we treat each other, then why did so many ancient texts devote so much space to rules about menstruation, who can eat what, and who can have sex with whom?[55]

Interesting question. Are these the same ancient texts that view slavery as morally unproblematic? Perhaps slavery has no moral implications after all—otherwise, surely these ancient texts would have something of substance to say against it. Could abolition have been the ultimate instance of liberal bias? Or, following Haidt's logic, why not ask, "if physics is just a system of laws that explains the structure of the universe in terms of mass and energy, why do so many ancient texts devote so much space to immaterial influences and miraculous acts of God?" Why indeed.

Haidt appears to consider it an intellectual virtue to accept, uncritically, the moral categories of his subjects. But where is it written that everything that people do or decide in the name of "morality" deserves to be considered part of its subject matter? A majority of Americans believe that the Bible provides an accurate account of the ancient world. Many millions of Americans also believe that a principal cause of cancer is "repressed anger." Happily, we do not allow these opinions to anchor us when it comes time to have serious discussions about history and oncology. It seems abundantly clear that many people are simply wrong about morality—just as many people are wrong about physics, biology, history, and everything else worth understanding. What scientific purpose is served by averting our eyes from this fact? If morality is a system of thinking about (and maximizing) the well-being of conscious creatures like ourselves, many people's moral concerns must be immoral.

Moral skeptics like Haidt generally emphasize the intractability of moral disagreements:

> The bitterness, futility, and self-righteousness of most moral arguments can now be explicated. In a debate about abortion, politics, consensual incest, or what my friend did to your friend, both sides believe that their positions are based on reasoning about the facts and issues involved (the wag-the-dog illusion). Both sides present what they take to be excellent arguments in support of their positions. Both sides expect the other side to be responsive to such reasons (the wag-the-other-dog's-tail illusion). When the other side fails to be affected by such good reasons, each side concludes that the other side must be closed minded or insincere. In this way the culture wars over issues such as homosexuality and abortion can generate morally motivated players on both sides who believe that their opponents are not morally motivated.[56]

But the dynamic Haidt describes will be familiar to anyone who has ever entered into a debate on any subject. Such failures of persuasion do not suggest that both sides of every controversy are equally credible. For instance, the above passage perfectly captures my occasional collisions with 9/11 conspiracy theorists. A nationwide poll conducted by the Scripps Survey Research Center at Ohio University found that more than a third of Americans suspect that the federal government "assisted in the 9/11 terrorist attacks or took no action to stop them so the United States could go to war in the Middle East" and 16 percent believe that this proposition is "very likely" to be true.[57] Many of these people believe that the Twin Towers collapsed not because fully fueled passenger jets smashed into them but because agents of the Bush administration had secretly rigged these buildings to explode (6 percent of all respondents judged this "very likely," 10 percent judged it "somewhat likely"). Whenever I encounter people harboring these convictions, the impasse that Haidt describes is well in place: both sides "present what they take to be excellent arguments in support of their positions. Both sides expect the other side to be responsive to such reasons (the wag-the-other-dog's-tail illusion). When the other side fails to be affected by such good reasons, each side concludes that the other side must be closed minded or insincere." It is undeniable, however, that if one side in this debate is right about what actually happened on September 11, 2001, the other side must be absolutely wrong.

Of course, it is now well known that our feeling of reasoning objectively is often illusory.[58] This does not mean, however, that we cannot learn to reason more effectively, pay greater attention to evidence, and grow more mindful of the ever-present possibility of error. Haidt is right to notice that the brain's emotional circuitry often governs our moral intuitions, and the way in which feeling drives judgment is surely worthy of study. But it does not follow that there are no right and wrong answers to questions of morality. Just as people are often less than rational when claiming to be rational, they can be less than moral when claiming to be moral.

In describing the different forms of morality available to us, Haidt offers a choice between "contractual" and "beehive" approaches: the first is said to be the province of liberals, who care mainly about harm and fairness; the second represents the conservative (generally religious) social order, which incorporates further concerns about group loyalty, respect for authority, and religious purity. The opposition between these two conceptions of the good life may be worth discussing, and Haidt's data on the differences between liberals and conservatives is interesting, but is his interpretation correct? It seems possible, for instance, that his five foundations of morality are simply facets of a more general concern about harm.

What, after all, is the problem with desecrating a copy of the Qur'an? There would be no problem but for the fact that people believe that the Qur'an is a divinely authored text. Such people almost surely believe that some harm could come to them or to their tribe as a result of such sacrileges—if not in this world, then in the next. A more esoteric view might be that any person who desecrates scripture will have harmed himself directly: a lack of reverence might be its own punishment, dimming the eyes of faith. Whatever interpretation one favors, sacredness and respect for religious authority seem to reduce to a concern about harm just the same.

The same point can be made in the opposite direction: even a liberal like myself, enamored as I am of thinking in terms of harm and fairness, can readily see that my vision of the good life must be safeguarded from the aggressive tribalism of others. When I search my heart, I discover that I want to keep the barbarians beyond the city walls just as much as my conservative neighbors do, and I recognize that sacrifices of my own freedom may be warranted for this purpose. I expect that epiphanies of this sort could well multiply in the coming years. Just imagine, for instance, how liberals might be disposed to think about the threat of Islam after an incident of nuclear terrorism. Liberal hankering for happiness and freedom might one day produce some very strident calls for stricter laws and tribal loyalty. Will this mean that liberals have become religious conservatives pining for the beehive? Or is the liberal notion of avoiding harm flexible enough to encompass the need for order and differences between in-group and out-group?

There is also the question of whether conservatism contains an extra measure of cognitive bias—or outright hypocrisy—as the moral convictions of social conservatives are so regularly belied by their louche behavior. The most conservative regions of the United States tend to have the highest rates of divorce and teenage pregnancy, as well as the greatest appetite for pornography.[59] Of course, it could be argued that social conservatism is the consequence of so much ambient sinning. But this seems an unlikely explanation—especially in those cases where a high level of conservative moralism and a predilection for sin can be found in a single person. If one wants examples of such hypocrisy, Evangelical ministers and conservative politicians seem to rarely disappoint.

When is a belief system not only false but so encouraging of falsity and needless suffering as to be worthy of our condemnation? According to a recent poll, 36 percent of British Muslims (ages sixteen to twenty-four) think apostates should be put to death for their unbelief.[60] Are these people "morally motivated," in Haidt's sense, or just morally confused?

And what if certain cultures are found to harbor moral codes that look terrible no matter how we jigger Haidt's five variables of harm, fairness, group loyalty, respect for authority, and spiritual purity? What if we find a group of people who aren't especially sensitive to harm and fairness, or cognizant of the sacred, or morally astute in any other way? Would Haidt's conception of morality then allow us to stop these benighted people from abusing their children? Or would that be unscientific?

The Moral Brain

Imagine that you are having dinner in a restaurant and spot your best friend's wife seated some distance away. As you stand to say hello, you notice that the man seated across from her is not your best friend, but a handsome stranger. You hesitate. Is he a colleague of hers from work? Her brother from out of town? Something about the scene strikes you as illicit. While you cannot hear what they are saying, there is an unmistakable sexual chemistry between them. You now recall that your best friend is away at a conference. Is his wife having an affair? What should you do?

Several regions of the brain will contribute to this impression of moral salience and to the subsequent stirrings of moral emotion. There are many separate strands of cognition and feeling that intersect here: sensitivity to context, reasoning about other people's beliefs, the interpretation of facial expressions and body language, suspicion, indignation, impulse control, etc. At what point do these disparate processes constitute an instance of moral cognition? It is difficult to say. At a minimum, we know that we have entered moral territory once thoughts about morally relevant events (e.g., the possibility of a friend's betrayal) have been consciously entertained. For the purposes of this discussion, we need draw the line no more precisely than this.

The brain regions involved in moral cognition span many areas of the prefrontal cortex and the temporal lobes. The neuroscientists Jorge Moll, Ricardo de Oliveira-Souza, and colleagues have written the most comprehensive reviews of this research.[61] They divide human actions into four categories:

1. Self-serving actions that do not affect others
2. Self-serving actions that negatively affect others

3. Actions that are beneficial to others, with a high probability of reciprocation ("reciprocal altruism")
4. Actions that are beneficial to others, with no direct personal benefits (material or reputation gains) and no expected reciprocation ("genuine altruism"). This includes altruistic helping as well as costly punishment of norm violators ("altruistic punishment")[62]

As Moll and colleagues point out, we share behaviors 1 through 3 with other social mammals, while 4 seems to be the special province of human beings. (We should probably add that this altruism must be intentional/conscious, so as to exclude the truly heroic self-sacrifice seen among eusocial insects like bees, ants, and termites.) While Moll et al. admit to ignoring the reward component of genuine altruism (often called the "warm glow" associated with cooperation), we know from neuroimaging studies that cooperation is associated with heightened activity in the brain's reward regions.[63] Here, once again, the traditional opposition between selfish and selfless motivation seems to break down. If helping others can be rewarding, rather than merely painful, it should be thought of as serving the self in another mode.

It is easy to see the role that negative and positive motivations play in the moral domain: we feel contempt/anger for the moral transgressions of others, guilt/shame over our own moral failings, and the warm glow of reward when we find ourselves playing nicely with other people. Without the engagement of such motivational mechanisms, moral prescriptions (purely rational notions of "ought") would be very unlikely to translate into actual behaviors. The fact that motivation is a separate variable explains the conundrum briefly touched on above: we often know what would make us happy, or what would make the world a better place, and yet we find that we are not motivated to seek these ends; conversely, we are often motivated to behave in ways that we know we will later regret. Clearly, moral motivation can be uncoupled from the fruits of moral reasoning. A science of morality would, of necessity, require a deeper understanding of human motivation.

The regions of the brain that govern judgments of right and wrong include a broad network of cortical and subcortical structures. The contribution of these areas to moral thought and behavior differs with respect to emotional tone: lateral regions of the frontal lobes seem to govern the indignation associated with punishing transgressors, while medial frontal regions produce the feelings of reward associated with trust and reciprocation.[64] As we will see, there is also a distinction between personal and impersonal moral decisions. The resulting picture is complicated: factors like moral sensitivity, moral motivation, moral judgment, and moral reasoning rely on separable, mutually overlapping processes.

The medial prefrontal cortex (MPFC) is central to most discussions of morality and the brain. As discussed further in chapters 3 and 4, this region is involved in emotion, reward, and judgments of self-relevance. It also seems to register the difference between belief and disbelief. Injuries here have been associated with a variety of deficits including poor impulse control, emotional blunting, and the attenuation of social emotions like empathy, shame, embarrassment, and guilt. When frontal damage is limited to the MPFC, reasoning ability as well as the conceptual knowledge of moral norms are generally spared, but the ability to behave appropriately toward others tends to be disrupted.

Interestingly, patients suffering from MPFC damage are more inclined to consequentialist reasoning than normal subjects are when evaluating certain moral dilemmas—when, for instance, the means of sacrificing one person's life to save many others is personal rather than impersonal.[65] Consider the following two scenarios:

1. You are at the wheel of a runaway trolley quickly approaching a fork in the tracks. On the tracks extending to the left is a group of five railway workmen. On the tracks extending to the right is a single railway workman.

   If you do nothing the trolley will proceed to the left, causing the deaths of the five workmen. The only way to avoid the deaths of these workmen is to hit a switch on your dashboard that will cause the trolley to proceed to the right, causing the death of the single workman.

   Is it appropriate for you to hit the switch in order to avoid the deaths of the five workmen?

2. A runaway trolley is heading down the tracks toward five workmen who will be killed if the trolley proceeds on its present course. You are on a footbridge over the tracks, in between the approaching trolley and the five workmen. Next to you on this footbridge is a stranger who happens to be very large.

   The only way to save the lives of the five workmen is to push this stranger off the bridge and onto the tracks below where his large body will stop the trolley. The stranger will die if you do this, but the five workmen will be saved.

   Is it appropriate for you to push the stranger onto the tracks in order to save the five workmen?[66]

Most people strongly support sacrificing one person to save five in the first scenario, while considering such a sacrifice morally abhorrent in the second. This paradox has been well known in philosophical circles for years.[67] Joshua Greene and colleagues were the first to look at the brain's response to these dilemmas using fMRI.[68] They found that the personal forms of these dilemmas, like the one described in scenario two, more strongly activate brain regions associated with emotion. Another group has since found that the disparity between people's responses to the two scenarios can be modulated, however slightly, by emotional context. Subjects who spent a few minutes watching a pleasant video prior to confronting the footbridge dilemma were more apt to push the man to his death.[69]

The fact that patients suffering from MPFC injuries find it easier to sacrifice the one for the many is open to differing interpretations. Greene views this as evidence that emotional and cognitive processes often work in opposition.[70] There are reasons to worry, however, that mere opposition between consequentialist thinking and negative emotion does not adequately account for the data.[71]

I suspect that a more detailed understanding of the brain processes involved in making moral judgments of this type could affect our sense of right and wrong. And yet superficial differences between moral dilemmas may continue to play a role in our reasoning. If losses will always cause more suffering than forsaken gains, or if pushing a person to his death is guaranteed to traumatize us in a way that throwing a switch will not, these distinctions become variables that constrain how we can move across the moral landscape toward higher states of well-being. It seems to me, however, that a science of morality can absorb these details: scenarios that appear, on paper, to lead to the same outcome (e.g., one life lost, five lives saved), may actually have different consequences in the real world.

Psychopaths

In order to understand the relationship between the mind and the brain, it is often useful to study subjects who, whether through illness or injury, lack specific mental capacities. As luck would have it, Mother Nature has provided us with a nearly perfect dissection of conventional morality. The resulting persons are generally referred to as "psychopaths" or "sociopaths,"[72] and there seem to be many more of them living among us than most of us realize. Studying their brains has yielded considerable insight into the neural basis of conventional morality.

As a personality disorder, psychopathy has been so sensationalized in the media that it is difficult to research it without feeling that one is pandering, either to oneself or to one's audience. However, there is no question that psychopaths exist, and many of them speak openly about the pleasure they take in terrorizing and torturing innocent people. The extreme examples, which include serial killers and sexual sadists, seem to defy any sympathetic understanding on our parts. Indeed, if you immerse yourself in this literature, each case begins to seem more horrible and incomprehensible than the last. While I am reluctant to traffic in the details of these crimes, I fear that speaking in abstractions may obscure the underlying reality. Despite a steady diet of news, which provides a daily reminder of human evil, it can be difficult to remember that certain people truly lack the capacity to care about their fellow human beings. Consider the statement of a man who was convicted of repeatedly raping and torturing his nine-year-old stepson:

> After about two years of molesting my son, and all the pornography that I had been buying, renting, swapping, I had got my

> hands on some "bondage discipline" pornography with children involved. Some of the reading that I had done and the pictures that I had seen showed total submission. Forcing the children to do what I wanted.
>
> And I eventually started using some of this bondage discipline with my own son, and it had escalated to the point where I was putting a large Zip-loc bag over his head and taping it around his neck with black duct tape or black electrical tape and raping and molesting him . . . to the point where he would turn blue, pass out. At that point I would rip the bag off his head, not for fear of hurting him, but because of the excitement.
>
> I was extremely aroused by inflicting pain. And when I see him pass out and change colors, that was very arousing and heightening to me, and I would rip the bag off his head and then I'd jump on his chest and masturbate in his face and make him suck my penis while he . . . started to come back awake. While he was coughing and choking, I would rape him in the mouth.
>
> I used this same sadistic style of plastic bag and the tape two or three times a week, and it went on for I'd say a little over a year.[73]

I suspect that this brief glimpse of one man's private passions will suffice to make the point. Be assured that this is not the worst abuse a man or woman has ever inflicted upon a child just for the fun of it. And one remarkable feature of the literature on psychopaths is the extent to which even the worst people are able to find collaborators. For instance, the role played by violent pornography in these cases is difficult to overlook. Child pornography alone—which, as many have noted, is the visual record of an actual crime—is now a global, multibillion-dollar industry, involving kidnapping, "sex tourism," organized crime, and great technical sophistication in the use of the internet. Apparently, there are enough people who are eager to see children—and, increasingly, toddlers and infants—raped and tortured so as to create an entire subculture.[74]

While psychopaths are especially well represented in our prisons,[75] many live below the threshold of overt criminality. For every psychopath who murders a child, there are tens of thousands who are guilty of far more conventional mischief. Robert Hare, the creator of the standard diagnostic instrument to assess psychopathy, the Psychopathy Checklist–Revised (PCL–R), estimates that while there are probably no more than a hundred serial killers in the United States at any moment, there are probably 3 million psychopaths (about 1 percent of the population).[76] If Hare is correct, each of us crosses paths with such people all the time.

For instance, I recently met a man who took considerable pride in having arranged his life so as to cheat on his wife with impunity. In fact, he was also cheating on the many women with whom he was cheating—for each believed him to be faithful. All this gallantry involved aliases, fake businesses, and, needless to say, a blizzard of lies. While I can't say for certain this man was a psychopath, it was quite apparent that he lacked what most of us would consider a normal conscience. A life of continuous deception and selfish machination seemed to cause him no discomfort whatsoever.[77]

Psychopaths are distinguished by their extraordinary egocentricity and their total lack of concern for the suffering of others. A list of their most frequent characteristics reads like a personal ad from hell: they are said to be callous, manipulative, deceptive, impulsive, secretive, grandiose, thrill-seeking, sexually promiscuous, unfaithful, irresponsible, prone to both reactive and calculated aggression,[78] and lacking in emotional depth. They also show reduced emotional sensitivity to punishment (whether actual or anticipated). Most important, psychopaths do not experience a normal range of anxiety and fear, and this may account for their lack of conscience.

The first neuroimaging experiment done on psychopaths found that, when compared to nonpsychopathic criminals and noncriminal controls, they exhibit significantly less activity in regions of the brain that generally respond to emotional stimuli.[79] While anxiety and fear are emotions that most of us would prefer to live without, they serve as anchors to social and moral norms.[80] Without an ability to feel anxious about one's own transgressions, real or imagined, norms become nothing more than "rules that others make up."[81] The developmental literature also supports this interpretation: fearful children have been shown to display greater moral understanding.[82] It remains an open question, therefore, just how free of anxiety we can reasonably want to be. Again, this is something that only an empirical science of morality could decide. And as more effective remedies for anxiety appear on the horizon, this is an issue that we will have to confront in some form.

Further neuroimaging work suggests that psychopathy is also a product of pathological arousal and reward.[83] People scoring high on the psychopathic personality inventory show abnormally high activity in the reward regions of their brain (in particular, the nucleus accumbens) in response to amphetamine and while anticipating monetary gains. Hypersensitivity of this circuitry is especially linked to the impulsive-antisocial dimension of psychopathy, which leads to risky and predatory behavior. Researchers speculate that an excessive response to anticipated reward can prevent a person from learning from the negative emotions of others.

Unlike others who suffer from mental illness or mood disorders, psychopaths generally do not feel that anything is wrong with them. They also meet the legal definition of sanity, in that they possess an intellectual understanding of the difference between right and wrong. However, psychopaths generally fail to distinguish between conventional and moral transgressions. When asked "Would it be okay to eat at your desk if the teacher gave you permission?" vs. "Would it be okay to hit another student in the face if the teacher gave you permission?" normal children age thirty-nine months and above tend to see these questions as fundamentally distinct and consider the latter transgression intrinsically wrong. In this, they appear to be guided by an awareness of potential human suffering. Children at risk for psychopathy tend to view these questions as morally indistinguishable.

When asked to identify the mental states of other people on the basis of photographs of their eyes alone, psychopaths show no general impairment.[84] Their "theory of mind" processing (as the ability to understand the mental states of others is generally known) seems to be basically intact, with subtle deficits resulting from their simply not caring about how other people feel.[85] The one crucial exception, however, is that psychopaths are often unable to recognize expressions of fear and sadness in others.[86] And this may be the difference that makes all the difference.

Neuroscientist James Blair and colleagues suggest that psychopathy results from a failure of emotional learning due to genetic impairments of the amygdala and orbitofrontal cortex, regions vital to the processing of emotion.[87] The negative emotions of others, rather than parental punishment, may be what goad us to normal socialization. Psychopathy, therefore, could result from a failure to learn from the fear and sadness of other people.[88]

A child at risk for psychopathy, being emotionally blind to the suffering he causes, may increasingly resort to antisocial behavior in pursuit of his goals throughout adolescence and adulthood.[89] As Blair points out, parenting strategies that increase empathy tend to successfully mitigate antisocial behavior in healthy children; such strategies inevitably fail with children who present with the callousness/unemotional (CU) trait that is characteristic of psychopathy. While it may be difficult to accept, the research strongly suggests that some people cannot learn to care about others.[90] Perhaps we will one day develop interventions to change this. For the purposes of this discussion, however, it seems sufficient to point out that we are beginning to understand the kinds of brain pathologies that lead to the most extreme forms of human evil. And just as some people have obvious moral deficits, others must possess moral talent, moral expertise, and even moral genius. As with any human ability, these gradations must be expressed at the level of the brain.

Game theory suggests that evolution probably selected for two stable orientations toward human cooperation: *tit for tat* (often called "strong reciprocity") and *permanent defection.*[91] Tit for tat is generally what we see throughout society: you show me some kindness, and I am eager to return the favor; you do something rude or injurious, and the temptation to respond in kind becomes difficult to resist. But consider how permanent defection would appear at the level of human relationships:

the defector would probably engage in continuous cheating and manipulation, sham moralistic aggression (to provoke guilt and altruism in others), and strategic mimicry of positive social emotions like sympathy (as well as of negative emotions like guilt). This begins to sound like garden-variety psychopathy. The existence of psychopaths, while otherwise quite mysterious, would seem to be predicted by game theory. And yet, the psychopath who lives his entire life in a tiny village must be at a terrible disadvantage. The stability of permanent defection as a strategy would require that a defector be able to find people to fleece who are not yet aware of his terrible reputation. Needless to say, the growth of cities has made this way of life far more practicable than it has ever been.

Evil

When confronted with psychopathy at its most extreme, it is very difficult not to think in terms of good and evil. But what if we adopt a more naturalistic view? Consider the prospect of being locked in a cage with a wild grizzly: why would this be a problem? Well, clearly, wild grizzlies suffer some rather glaring cognitive and emotional deficits. Your new roommate will not be easy to reason with or placate; he is unlikely to recognize that you have interests analogous to his own, or that the two of you might have shared interests; and if he could understand such things, he would probably lack the emotional resources to care. From his point of view, you will be a distraction at best, a cowering annoyance, and something tender to probe with his teeth. We might say that a wild bear is, like a psychopath, morally insane. However, we are very unlikely to refer to his condition as a form of "evil."

Human evil is a natural phenomenon, and some level of predatory violence is innate in us. Humans and chimpanzees tend to display the same level of hostility toward outsiders, but chimps are far more aggressive than humans are within a group (by a factor of about 200).[92] Therefore, we seem to have prosocial abilities that chimps lack. And, despite appearances, human beings have grown steadily less violent. As Jared Diamond explains:

> It's true, of course, that twentieth-century state societies, having developed potent technologies of mass killing, have broken all historical records for violent deaths. But this is because they enjoy the advantage of having by far the largest populations of potential victims in human history; the actual percentage of the population that died violently was on the average higher in traditional pre-state societies than it was even in Poland during the Second World War or Cambodia under Pol Pot.[93]

We must continually remind ourselves that there is a difference between what is natural and what is actually good for us. Cancer is perfectly natural, and yet its eradication is a primary goal of modern medicine. Evolution may have selected for territorial violence, rape, and other patently unethical behaviors as strategies to propagate one's genes—but our collective well-being clearly depends on our opposing such natural tendencies.

Territorial violence might have even been necessary for the development of altruism. The economist Samuel Bowles has argued that lethal, "out-group" hostility and "in-group" altruism are two sides of the same coin.[94] His computer models suggest that altruism cannot emerge without some level of conflict between groups. If true, this is one of the many places where we must transcend evolutionary pressures through reason—because, barring an attack from outer space, we now lack a proper "out-group" to inspire us to further altruism.

In fact, Bowles's work has interesting implications for my account of the moral landscape. Consider the following from Patricia Churchland:

> Assuming our woodland ape ancestors as well as our own human ancestors engaged in out-group raids, as chimps and several South American tribes still do, can we be confident in moral condemnation of *their* behavior? I see no basis in reality for such a judgment. If, as Samuel Bowles argues, the altruism typical of modern humans plausibly co-evolved with lethal out-group competition, such a judgment will be problematic.[95]

Of course, the purpose of my argument is to suggest a "basis in reality" for universal judgments of value. However, as Churchland points out, if there was simply no other way for our ancestors to progress toward altruism without developing a penchant for out-group hostility, then so be it. Assuming that the development of altruism represents an extraordinarily important advance in moral terms (I believe it does), this would be analogous to our ancestors descending into an unpleasant valley on the moral landscape only to make progress toward a higher peak. But it is important to reiterate that such evolutionary constraints no longer hold. In fact, given recent developments in biology, we are now poised to consciously engineer our further evolution. Should we do this, and if so, in which ways? Only a scientific understanding of the possibilities of human well-being could guide us.

The Illusion of Free Will

Brains allow organisms to alter their behavior and internal states in response to changes in the environment. The evolution of these structures, tending toward increased size and complexity, has led to vast differences in how the earth's species live.

The human brain responds to information coming from several domains: from the external world, from internal states of the body, and, increasingly, from a sphere of meaning—which includes spoken and written language, social cues, cultural norms, rituals of interaction, assumptions about the rationality of others, judgments of taste and style, etc. Generally, these domains seem unified in our experience: You spot your best friend standing on the street corner looking strangely disheveled. You recognize that she is crying and frantically dialing her cell phone. Did someone assault her? You rush to her side, feeling an acute desire to help. Your "self" seems to stand at the intersection of these lines of input and output. From this point of view, you tend to feel that you are the source of your own thoughts and actions. *You* decide what to do and not to do. You seem to be an agent acting of your own free will. As we will see, however, this point of view cannot be reconciled with what we know about the human brain.

We are conscious of only a tiny fraction of the information that our brains process in each moment. While we continually notice changes in our experience—in thought, mood, perception, behavior, etc.—we are utterly unaware of the neural events that produce these changes. In fact, by merely glancing at your face or listening to your tone of voice, others are often more aware of your internal states and motivations than you are. And yet most of us still feel that we are the authors of our own thoughts and actions.

All of our behavior can be traced to biological events about which we have no conscious knowledge: this has always suggested that free will is an illusion. For instance, the physiologist Benjamin Libet famously demonstrated that activity in the brain's motor regions can be detected some 350 milliseconds before a person feels that he has decided to move.[96] Another lab recently used fMRI data to show that some "conscious" decisions can be predicted up to *10 seconds* before they enter awareness (long before the preparatory motor activity detected by Libet).[97] Clearly, findings of this kind are difficult to reconcile with the sense that one is the conscious source of one's actions. Notice that distinction between "higher" and "lower" systems in the brain gets us nowhere: for I no more initiate events in executive regions of my prefrontal cortex than I cause the creaturely outbursts of my limbic system. The truth seems inescapable: I, as the subject of my experience, cannot know what I will next think or do until a thought or intention arises; and thoughts and intentions are caused by physical events and mental stirrings of which I am not aware.

Many scientists and philosophers realized long ago that free will could not be squared with our growing understanding of the physical world.[98] Nevertheless, many still deny this fact.[99] The biologist Martin Heisenberg recently observed that some fundamental processes in the brain, like the opening and closing of ion channels and the release of synaptic vesicles, occur at random, and cannot, therefore, be determined by environmental stimuli. Thus, much of our behavior can be considered "self-generated," and therein, he imagines, lies a basis for free will.[100] But "self-generated" in this sense means only that these events originate in the brain. The same can be said for the brain states of a chicken.

If I were to learn that my decision to have a third cup of coffee this morning was due to a random release of neurotransmitters, how could the indeterminacy of the initiating event count as the free exercise of my will? Such indeterminacy, if it were generally effective throughout the brain, would obliterate any semblance of human agency. Imagine what your life would be like if all your actions, intentions, beliefs, and desires were "self-generated" in this way: you would scarcely seem to have a mind at all. You would live as one blown about by an internal wind. Actions, intentions, beliefs, and desires are the sorts of things that can exist only in a system that is significantly constrained by patterns of behavior and the laws of stimulus-response. In fact, the possibility of reasoning with other human beings—or, indeed, of finding their behaviors and utterances comprehensible at all—depends on the assumption that their thoughts and actions will obediently ride the rails of a shared reality. In the limit, Heisenberg's "self-generated" mental events would amount to utter madness.[101]

The problem is that no account of causality leaves room for free will. Thoughts, moods, and desires of every sort simply spring into view—and move us, or fail to move us, for reasons that are, from a subjective point of view, perfectly inscrutable. Why did I use the term "inscrutable" in the previous sentence? I must confess that I do not know. Was I free to do otherwise? What could such a claim possibly mean? Why, after all, didn't the word "opaque" come to mind? Well, it just didn't—and now that it vies for a place on the page, I find that I am still partial to my original choice. Am I free with respect to this preference? Am I free to feel that "opaque" is the better word, *when I just do not feel that it is the better word?* Am I free to change my mind? Of course not. It can only change *me.*

It means nothing to say that a person would have done otherwise had he chosen to do otherwise, because a person's "choices" merely appear in his mental stream as though sprung from the void. In this sense, each of us is like a phenomenological glockenspiel played by an unseen hand. From the perspective of your conscious mind, you are no more responsible for the next thing you think (and therefore *do*) than you are for the fact that you were born into this world.[102]

Our belief in free will arises from our moment-to-moment ignorance of specific prior causes. The phrase "free will" describes what it *feels like* to be identified with the content of each thought as it arises in consciousness. Trains of thought like, "What should I get my daughter for her birthday? I know, I'll take her to a pet store and have her pick out some tropical fish," convey the apparent reality of choices, freely made. But from a deeper perspective (speaking both subjectively and objectively), thoughts simply arise (what else could they do?) unauthored and yet author to our actions.

As Daniel Dennett has pointed out, many people confuse determinism with fatalism.[103] This gives rise to questions like, "If everything is determined, why should I do anything? Why not just sit back and see what happens?" But the fact that our choices depend on prior causes does not mean that they do not matter. If I had not decided to write this book, it wouldn't have written itself. My choice to write it was unquestionably the primary cause of its coming into being. Decisions, intentions, efforts, goals, willpower, etc., are causal states of the brain, leading to specific behaviors, and behaviors lead to outcomes in the world. Human choice, therefore, is as important as fanciers of free will believe. And to "just sit back and see what happens" is itself a choice that will produce its own consequences. It is also extremely difficult to do: just try staying in bed all day waiting for something to happen; you will find yourself assailed by the impulse to get up and do something, which will require increasingly heroic efforts to resist.

Of course, there is a distinction between voluntary and involuntary actions, but it does nothing to support the common idea of free will (nor does it depend upon it). The former are associated with felt intentions (desires, goals, expectations, etc.) while the latter are not. All of the conventional distinctions we like to make between degrees of intent—from the bizarre neurological complaint of *alien hand syndrome*[104] to the premeditated actions of a sniper—can be maintained: for they simply describe what else was arising in the mind at the time an action occurred. A voluntary action is accompanied by the felt intention to carry it out, while an involuntary action isn't. Where our intentions themselves come from, however, and what determines their character in every instant, remains perfectly mysterious in subjective terms. Our sense of free will arises from a failure to appreciate this fact: we do not know what we will intend to do until the intention itself arises. To see this is to realize that you are not the author of your thoughts and actions in the way that people generally suppose. This insight does not make social and political freedom any less important, however. The freedom to do what one intends, and not to do otherwise, is no less valuable than it ever was.

Moral Responsibility

The question of free will is no mere curio of philosophy seminars. The belief in free will underwrites both the religious notion of "sin" and our enduring commitment to retributive justice.[105] The Supreme Court has called free will a "universal and persistent" foundation for our system of law, distinct from "a deterministic view of human conduct that is inconsistent with the underlying precepts of our criminal justice system" (*United States v. Grayson,* 1978).[106] Any scientific developments that threatened our notion of free will would seem to put the ethics of punishing people for their bad behavior in question.[107]

But, of course, human goodness and human evil are the product of natural events. The great worry is that any honest discussion of the underlying causes of human behavior seems to erode the notion of moral responsibility. If we view people as neuronal weather patterns, how can we coherently speak about morality? And if we remain committed to seeing people as people, some who can be reasoned with and some who cannot, it seems that we must find some notion of personal responsibility that fits the facts.

What does it really mean to take responsibility for an action? For instance, yesterday I went to the market; as it turns out, I was fully clothed, did not steal anything, and did not buy anchovies. To say that I was responsible for my behavior is simply to say that what I did was sufficiently in keeping with my thoughts, intentions, beliefs, and desires to be considered an extension of them. If, on the other hand, I had found myself standing in the market naked, intent upon stealing as many tins of anchovies as I could carry, this behavior would be totally out of character; I would feel that I was not in my right mind, or that I was otherwise not responsible for my actions. Judgments of responsibility, therefore, depend upon the overall complexion of one's mind, not on the metaphysics of mental cause and effect.

Consider the following examples of human violence:

1. A four-year-old boy was playing with his father's gun and killed a young woman. The gun had been kept loaded and unsecured in a dresser drawer.
2. A twelve-year-old boy, who had been the victim of continuous physical and emotional abuse, took his father's gun and intentionally shot and killed a young woman because she was teasing him.
3. A twenty-five-year-old man, who had been the victim of continuous abuse as a child, intentionally shot and killed his girlfriend because she left him for another man.
4. A twenty-five-year-old man, who had been raised by wonderful parents and never abused, intentionally shot and killed a young woman he had never met "just for the fun of it."
5. A twenty-five-year-old man, who had been raised by wonderful parents and never abused, intentionally shot and killed a young woman he had never met "just for the fun of it." An MRI of the man's brain revealed a tumor the size of a golf ball in his medial prefrontal cortex (a region responsible for the control of emotion and behavioral impulses).

In each case a young woman has died, and in each case her death was the result of events arising in the brain of another human being. The degree of moral outrage we feel clearly depends on the background conditions described in each case. We suspect that a four-year-old child cannot truly intend to kill someone and that the intentions of a twelve-year-old do not run as deep as those of an adult. In both cases 1 and 2, we know that the brain of the killer has not fully matured and that all the responsibilities of personhood have not yet been conferred. The history of abuse and precipitating circumstance in example 3 seem to mitigate the man's guilt: this was a crime of passion committed by a person who had himself suffered at the hands of others. In 4, we have no abuse, and the motive brands the perpetrator a psychopath. In 5, we appear to have the same psychopathic behavior and motive, but a brain tumor somehow changes the moral calculus entirely: given its location in the MPFC, it seems to divest the killer of all responsibility. How can we make sense of these gradations of moral blame when brains and their background influences are, in every case, and to exactly the same degree, the real cause of a woman's death?

It seems to me that we need not have any illusions about a casual agent living within the human mind to condemn such a mind as unethical, negligent, or even evil, and therefore liable to occasion further harm. What we condemn in another person is the *intention to do harm*—and thus any condition or circumstance (e.g., accident, mental illness, youth) that makes it unlikely that a person could harbor such an intention would mitigate guilt, without any recourse to notions of free will. Likewise, degrees of guilt could be judged, as they are now, by reference to the facts of the case: the personality of the accused, his prior offenses, his patterns of association with others, his use of intoxicants, his confessed intentions with regard to the victim, etc. If a person's actions seem to have been entirely out of character, this will influence our sense of the risk he now poses to others. If the accused appears unrepentant and anxious to kill again, we need entertain no notions of free will to consider him a danger to society.

Of course, we hold one another accountable for more than those actions that we consciously plan, because most voluntary behavior comes about without explicit planning.[108] But why is the conscious decision to do another person harm particularly blameworthy? Because consciousness is, among other things, the context in which our intentions become completely available to us. What we do subsequent to conscious planning tends to most fully reflect the global properties of our minds—our beliefs, desires, goals, prejudices, etc. If, after weeks of deliberation, library research, and debate with your friends, you still decide to kill the king—well, then killing the king really reflects the sort of person you are. Consequently, it makes sense for the rest of society to worry about you.

While viewing human beings as forces of nature does not prevent us from thinking in terms of moral responsibility, it does call the logic of retribution into question. Clearly, we need to build prisons for people who are intent upon harming others. But if we could incarcerate earthquakes and hurricanes for their crimes, we would build prisons for them as well.[109] The men and women on death row have some combination of bad genes, bad parents, bad ideas, and bad luck—which of these quantities, exactly, were they responsible for? No human being stands as author to his own genes or his upbringing, and yet we have every reason to believe that these factors determine his character throughout life. Our system of justice should reflect our understanding that each of us could have been dealt a very different hand in life. In fact, it seems immoral not to recognize just how much luck is involved in morality itself.

Consider what would happen if we discovered a cure for human evil. Imagine, for the sake of argument, that every relevant change in the human brain can be made cheaply, painlessly, and safely. The cure for psychopathy can be put directly into the food supply like vitamin D. Evil is now nothing more than a nutritional deficiency.

If we imagine that a cure for evil exists, we can see that our retributive impulse is profoundly flawed. Consider, for instance, the prospect of *withholding* the cure for evil from a murderer as part of his punishment. Would this make any moral sense at all? What could it possibly mean to say that a person *deserves* to have this treatment withheld? What if the treatment had been available prior to the person's crime? Would he still be responsible for his actions? It seems far more likely that those who had been aware of his case would be indicted for negligence. Would it make any sense at all to deny surgery to the man in example 5 as a *punishment* if we knew the brain tumor was the proximate cause of his violence? Of course not. The urge for retribution, therefore, seems to depend upon our not seeing the underlying causes of human behavior.

Despite our attachment to notions of free will, most us know that disorders of the brain can trump the best intentions of the mind. This shift in understanding represents progress toward a deeper, more consistent, and more compassionate view of our common humanity—and we should note that this is progress away from religious metaphysics. It seems to me that few concepts have offered greater scope for human cruelty than the idea of an immortal soul that stands independent of all material influences, ranging from genes to economic systems.

And yet one of the fears surrounding our progress in neuroscience is that this knowledge will dehumanize us. Could thinking about the mind as the product of the physical brain diminish our compassion for one another? While it is reasonable to ask this question, it seems to me that, on balance, soul/body dualism has been the enemy of compassion. For instance, the moral stigma that still surrounds disorders of mood and cognition seems largely the result of viewing the mind as distinct from the brain. When the pancreas fails to produce insulin, there is no shame in taking synthetic insulin to compensate for its lost function. Many people do not feel the same way about regulating mood with antidepressants (for reasons that appear quite distinct from any concern about potential side effects). If this bias has diminished in recent years, it has been because of an increased appreciation of the brain as a physical organ.

However, the issue of retribution is a genuinely tricky one. In a fascinating article in *The New Yorker,* Jared Diamond recently wrote of the high price we often pay for leaving vengeance to the state.[110] He compares the experience of his friend Daniel, a New Guinea highlander, who avenged the death of a paternal uncle and felt exquisite relief, to the tragic experience of his late father-in-law, who had the opportunity to kill the man who murdered his family during the Holocaust but opted instead to turn him over to the police. After spending only a year in jail, the killer was released, and Diamond's father-in-law spent the last sixty years of his life "tormented by regret and guilt." While there is much to be said against the vendetta culture of the New Guinea Highlands, it is clear that the practice of taking vengeance answers to a common psychological need.

We are deeply disposed to perceive people as the authors of their actions, to hold them responsible for the wrongs they do us, and to feel that these debts must be repaid. Often, the only compensation that seems appropriate requires that the perpetrator of a crime suffer or forfeit his life. It remains to be seen how the best system of justice would steward these impulses. Clearly, a full account of the causes of human behavior should undermine our natural response to injustice, at least to some degree. It seems doubtful, for instance, that Diamond's father-in-law would have suffered the same pangs of unrequited vengeance if his family had been trampled by an elephant or laid low by cholera. Similarly, we can expect that his regret would have been significantly eased if he had learned that his family's killer had lived a flawlessly moral life until a virus began ravaging his medial prefrontal cortex.

It may be that a sham form of retribution could still be moral, if it led people to behave far better than they otherwise would. Whether it is useful to emphasize the punishment of certain criminals—rather than their containment or rehabilitation—is a question for social and psychological science. But it seems quite clear that a retributive impulse, based upon the idea that each person is the free author of his thoughts and actions, rests on a cognitive and emotional illusion—and perpetuates a moral one.

It is generally argued that our sense of free will presents a compelling mystery: on the one hand, it is impossible to make sense of it in causal terms; on the other, there is a powerful subjective sense that we are the authors of our own actions.[111] However, I think that this mystery is itself a symptom of our confusion. It is not that free will is simply an illusion: our experience is not merely delivering a distorted view of reality; rather, we are mistaken about the nature of our experience. We do not feel as free as we think we feel. Our sense of our own freedom results from our not paying attention to what it is actually like to be what we are. The moment we do pay attention, we begin to see that free will is nowhere to be found, and our subjectivity is perfectly compatible with this truth. Thoughts and intentions simply arise in the mind. What else could they do? The truth about us is stranger than many suppose: *The illusion of free will is itself an illusion.*

Chapter 3

BELIEF

A candidate for the presidency of the United States once met a group of potential supporters at the home of a wealthy benefactor. After brief introductions, he spotted a bowl of potpourri on the table beside him. Mistaking it for a bowl of trail mix, he scooped up a fistful of this decorative debris—which consisted of tree bark, incense, flowers, pinecones, and other inedible bits of woodland—and delivered it greedily into his mouth.

What our hero did next went unreported (suffice it to say that he did not become the next president of the United States). We can imagine the psychology of the scene, however: the candidate wide-eyed in ambush, caught between the look of horror on his host's face and the panic of his own tongue, having to quickly decide whether to swallow the vile material or disgorge it in full view of his audience. We can see the celebrities and movie producers feigning not to notice the great man's gaffe and taking a sudden interest in the walls, ceiling, and floorboards of the room. Some were surely less discreet. We can imagine their faces from the candidate's point of view: a pageant of ill-concealed emotion, ranging from amazement to schadenfreude.

All such responses, their personal and social significance, and their moment-to-moment physiological effects, arise from mental capacities that are distinctly human: the recognition of another's intentions and state of mind, the representation of the self in both physical and social space, the impulse to save face (or to help others to save it), etc.

While such mental states undoubtedly have analogs in the lives of other animals, we human beings experience them with a special poignancy. There may be many reasons for this, but one is clearly paramount: we alone, among all earth's creatures, possess the ability to think and communicate with complex language.

The work of archeologists, paleoanthropologists, geneticists, and neuroscientists—not to mention the relative taciturnity of our primate cousins—suggests that human language is a very recent adaptation.[1] Our species diverged from its common ancestor with the chimpanzees only 6.3 million years ago. And it now seems that the split with chimps may have been less than decisive, as comparisons between the two genomes, focusing on the greater-than-expected similarity of our X chromosomes, reveal that our species diverged, interbred for a time, and then diverged for good.[2] Such rustic encounters notwithstanding, all human beings currently alive appear to have descended from a single population of hunter-gatherers that lived in Africa around 50,000 BCE. These were the first members of our species to exhibit the technical and social innovations made possible by language.[3]

Genetic evidence indicates that a band of perhaps 150 of these people left Africa and gradually populated the rest of the earth. Their migration would not have been without its hardships, however, as they were not alone: *Homo neanderthalensis* laid claim to Europe and the Middle East, and *Homo erectus* occupied Asia. Both were species of archaic humans that had developed along separate evolutionary paths after one or more prior migrations out of Africa. Both possessed large brains, fashioned stone tools similar to those of *Homo sapiens,* and were well armed. And yet over the next twenty thousand years, our ancestors gradually displaced, and may have physically eradicated, all rivals.[4] Given the larger brains and sturdier build of the Neanderthals, it seems reasonable to suppose that only our species had the advantage of fully symbolic, complex speech.[5]

While there is still controversy over the biological origins of human language, as well as over its likely precursors in the communicative behavior of other animals,[6] there is no question that syntactic language lies at the root of our ability to understand the universe, to communicate ideas, to cooperate with one another in complex societies, and to build (one hopes) a sustainable, global civilization.[7] But why has language made such a difference? How has the ability to speak (and to read and write of late) given modern humans a greater purchase on the world? What, after all, has been worth communicating these last 50,000 years? I hope it will not seem philistine of me to suggest that our ability to create *fiction* has not been the driving force here. The power of language surely results from the fact that it allows mere words to substitute for direct experience and mere thoughts to simulate possible states of the world. Utterances like, "I saw some very scary guys in front of that cave yesterday," would have come in quite handy 50,000 years ago. The brain's capacity to accept such propositions as *true*—as valid guides to behavior and emotion, as predictive of future outcomes, etc.—explains the transformative power of words. There is a common term we use for this type of acceptance; we call it "belief."[8]

What Is "Belief"?

It is surprising that so little research has been done on belief, as few mental states exert so sweeping an influence over human life. While we often make a conventional distinction between "belief" and "knowledge," these categories are actually quite misleading. Knowing that George Washington was the first president of the United States and believing the statement "George Washington was the first president of the United States" amount to the same thing. When we distinguish between belief and knowledge in ordinary conversation, it is generally for the purpose of drawing attention to degrees of certainty: I'm apt to say "I know it" when I am quite certain that one of my beliefs about the world is true; when I'm less sure, I may say something like "I believe it is probably true." Most of our knowledge about the world falls between these extremes. The entire spectrum of such convictions—ranging from better-than-a-coin-toss to I-would-bet-my-life-on-it—expresses gradations of "belief."

It is reasonable to wonder, however, whether "belief" is really a single phenomenon at the level of the brain. Our growing understanding of human memory should make us cautious: over the last fifty years, the concept of "memory" has decomposed into several forms of cognition that are now known to be neurologically and evolutionarily distinct.[9] This should make us wonder whether a notion like "belief" might not also shatter into separate processes when mapped onto the brain. In fact, belief overlaps with certain types of memory, as memory can be equivalent to a belief about the past (e.g., "I had breakfast most days last week"),[10] and certain beliefs are indistinguishable from what is often called "semantic memory" (e.g., "The earth is the third planet from the sun").

There is no reason to think that any of our beliefs about the world are stored as propositions, or within discrete structures, inside the brain.[11] Merely understanding a simple proposition often requires the unconscious activation of considerable background knowledge[12] and an active process of hypothesis testing.[13] For instance, a sentence like "The team was terribly disappointed because the second stage failed to fire," while easy enough to read, cannot be understood without some general concept of a rocket launch and a team of engineers. So there is more to even basic communication than the mere decoding of words. We must expect that a similar penumbra of associations will surround specific beliefs as well.

And yet our beliefs can be represented and expressed as discrete statements. Imagine hearing any one of the following assertions from a trusted friend:

1. The CDC just announced that cell phones really do cause brain cancer.
2. My brother won $100,000 in Las Vegas over the weekend.
3. Your car is being towed.

We trade in such representations of the world all the time. The acceptance of such statements as true (or likely to be true) is the mechanism by which we acquire most of our knowledge about the world. While it would not make any sense to search for structures in the brain that correspond to specific sentences, we may be able to understand the brain states that allow us to accept such sentences as true.[14] When someone says "Your car is being towed," it is your acceptance of this statement as true that sends you racing out the door. "Belief," therefore, can be thought of as a process taking place in the present; it is the act of grasping, not the thing grasped.

The Oxford English Dictionary defines multiple senses of the term "belief":

1. The mental action, condition, or habit, of trusting to or confiding in a person or thing; trust, dependence, reliance, confidence, faith.
2. Mental acceptance of a proposition, statement, or fact as true, on the ground of authority or evidence; assent of the mind to a statement, or to the truth of a fact beyond observation, on the testimony of another, or to a fact or truth on the evidence of consciousness; the mental condition involved in this assent.
3. The thing believed; the proposition or set of propositions held true.

Definition 2 is exactly what we are after, and 1 may apply as well. These first two senses of the term are quite different from the data-centered meaning given in 3.

Consider the following claim: *Starbucks does not sell plutonium.* I suspect that most of us would be willing to wager a fair amount of money that this statement is generally true—which is to say that we *believe* it. However, before reading this statement, you are very unlikely to have considered the prospect that the world's most popular coffee chain might also trade in one of the world's most dangerous substances. Therefore, it does not seem possible for there to have been a structure in your brain that already corresponded to this belief. And yet you clearly harbored some representation of the world that *amounts* to this belief.

Many modes of information processing must lay the groundwork for us to judge the above statement as "true." Most of us know, in a variety of implicit and explicit ways, that Starbucks is not a likely proliferator of nuclear material. Several distinct capacities—episodic memory, semantic knowledge, assumptions about human behavior and economic incentives, inductive reasoning, etc.—conspire to make us accept the above proposition. To say that we *already believed* that one cannot buy plutonium at Starbucks is to merely put a name to the summation of these processes in the present moment: that is, "belief," in this case, is the disposition to accept a proposition as true (or likely to be).

This process of acceptance often does more than express our prior commitments, however. It can revise our view of the world in an instant. Imagine reading the following headline in tomorrow's *New York Times:* "Most of the World's Coffee Is Now Contaminated by Plutonium." Believing *this* statement would immediately influence your thinking on many fronts, as well as your judgment about the truth of the former proposition. Most of our beliefs have come to us in just this form: as statements that we accept on the assumption that their source is reliable, or because the sheer number of sources rules out any significant likelihood of error.

In fact, everything we know outside of our personal experience is the result of our having encountered specific linguistic propositions—*the sun is a star; Julius Caesar was a Roman emperor*; *broccoli is good for you*—and found no reason (or means) to doubt them. It is "belief" in this form, as an act of acceptance, which I have sought to better understand in my neuroscientific research.[15]

Looking for Belief in the Brain

For a physical system to be capable of complex behavior, there must be some meaningful separation between its input and output. As far as we know, this separation has been most fully achieved in the frontal lobes of the human brain. Our frontal lobes are what allow us to select among a vast range of responses to incoming information in light of our prior goals and present inferences. Such "higher-level" control of emotion and behavior is the stuff of which human personalities are made.

Clearly, the brain's capacity to believe or disbelieve statements of fact—*You left your wallet on the bar; that white powder is anthrax; your boss is in love with you*—is central to the initiation, organization, and control of our most complex behaviors.

But we are not likely to find a region of the human brain devoted solely to belief. The brain is an evolved organ, and there does not seem to be a process in nature that allows for the creation of new structures dedicated to entirely novel modes of behavior or cognition. Consequently, the brain's higher-order functions had to emerge from lower-order mechanisms. An ancient structure like the insula, for instance, helps monitor events in our gut, governing the perception of hunger and primary emotions like disgust. But it is also involved in pain perception, empathy, pride, humiliation, trust, music appreciation, and addictive behavior.[16] It may also play an important role in both belief formation and moral reasoning. Such promiscuity of function is a common feature of many regions of the brain, especially in the frontal lobes.[17]

No region of the brain evolved in a neural vacuum or in isolation from the other mutations simultaneously occurring within the genome. The human mind, therefore, is like a ship that has been built and rebuilt, plank by plank, on the open sea. Changes have been made to her sails, keel, and rudder even as the waves battered every inch of her hull. And much of our behavior and cognition, even much that now seems essential to our humanity, has not been selected for at all. There are no aspects of brain function that evolved to hold democratic elections, to run financial institutions, or to teach our children to read. We are, in every cell, the products of nature—but we have also been born again and again through culture. Much of this cultural inheritance must be realized differently in individual brains. The way in which two people think about the stock market, or recall that Christmas is a national holiday, or solve a puzzle like the Tower of Hanoi, will almost surely differ between individuals. This poses an obvious challenge when attempting to identify mental states with specific brain states.[18]

Another factor that makes the strict localization of any mental state difficult is that the human brain is characterized by massive interconnectivity: it is mostly talking to itself.[19] And the information it stores must also be more fine-grained than the concepts, symbols, objects, or states that we subjectively experience. Representation results from a pattern of activity across networks of neurons and does not generally entail stable, one-to-one mappings of things/events in the world, or concepts in the mind, to discrete structures in the brain.[20] For instance, thinking a simple thought like *Jake is married* cannot be the work of any single node in a network of neurons. It must emerge from a pattern of connections among many nodes. None of this bodes well for one who would seek a belief "center" in the human brain.

As part of my doctoral research at UCLA, I studied belief, disbelief, and uncertainty with functional magnetic resonance imaging (fMRI).[21] To do this, we had volunteers read statements from a wide variety of categories while we scanned their brains. After reading a proposition like, "California is part of the United States" or "You have brown hair," participants would judge them to be "true," "false," or "undecidable" with the click of a button. This was, to my knowledge, the first time anyone had attempted to study belief and disbelief with the tools of neuroscience. Consequently, we had no basis to form a detailed hypothesis about which regions of the brain govern these states of mind.[22] It was, nevertheless, reasonable to expect that the prefrontal cortex (PFC) would be involved, given its wider role in controlling emotion and complex behavior.[23]

The seventeenth-century philosopher Spinoza thought that merely understanding a statement entails the tacit acceptance of its being true, while disbelief requires a subsequent process of rejection.[24] Several psychological studies seem to support this conjecture.[25] Understanding a proposition may be analogous to perceiving an object in physical space: we may accept appearances as reality until they prove otherwise. The behavioral data acquired in our research support this hypothesis, as subjects judged statements to be "true" more quickly than they judged them to be "false" or "undecidable."[26]

When we compared the mental states of belief and disbelief, we found that belief was associated with greater activity in the medial prefrontal cortex (MPFC).[27] This region of the frontal lobes is involved in linking factual knowledge with relevant emotional associations,[28] in changing behavior in response to reward,[29] and in goal-based actions.[30] The MPFC is also associated with ongoing reality monitoring, and injuries here can cause people to confabulate—that is, to make patently false statements without any apparent awareness that they are not telling the truth.[31] Whatever its cause in the brain, confabulation seems to be a condition in which belief processing has run amok. The MPFC has often been associated with self-representation,[32] and one sees more activity here when subjects think about themselves than when they think about others.[33]

The greater activity we found in the MPFC for belief compared to disbelief may reflect the greater self-relevance and/or reward value of true statements. When we believe a proposition to be true, it is as though we have taken it in hand as part of our extended self: we are saying, in effect, "This is mine. I can use this. This fits my view of the world." It seems to me that such cognitive acceptance has a distinctly positive emotional valence. We actually *like* the truth, and we may, in fact, dislike falsehood.[34]

The involvement of the MPFC in belief processing suggests an anatomical link between the purely cognitive aspects of belief and emotion/reward. Even judging the truth of emotionally neutral propositions engaged regions of the brain that are strongly connected to the limbic system, which governs our positive and negative affect. In fact, mathematical belief (e.g., "2 + 6 + 8 = 16") showed a similar pattern of activity to ethical belief (e.g., "It is good to let your children know that you love them"), and these were perhaps the most dissimilar sets of stimuli used in our experiment. This suggests that the physiology of belief may be the same regardless of a proposition's content. It also suggests that the division between facts and values does not make much sense in terms of underlying brain function.[35]

Of course, we can differentiate my argument concerning the moral landscape from my fMRI work on belief. I have argued that there is no gulf between facts and values, because values reduce to a certain type of fact. This is a philosophical claim, and as such, I can make it before ever venturing into the lab. However, my research on belief suggests that the split between facts and values should look suspicious: First, belief appears to be largely mediated by the MPFC, which seems to already constitute an anatomical bridge between reasoning and value. Second, the MPFC appears to be similarly engaged, irrespective of a belief's content. This finding of content-independence challenges the fact/value distinction very directly: for if, from the point of view of the brain, believing "the sun is a star" is importantly similar to believing "cruelty is wrong," how can we say that scientific and ethical judgments have nothing in common?

And we can traverse the boundary between facts and values in other ways. As we are about to see, the norms of reasoning seem to apply equally to beliefs about facts and to beliefs about values. In both spheres, evidence of inconsistency and bias is always unflattering. Similarities of this kind suggest that there is a deep analogy, if not identity, between the two domains.

The Tides of Bias

If one wants to understand how another person thinks, it is rarely sufficient to know whether or not he believes a specific set of propositions. Two people can hold the same belief for very different reasons, and such differences generally matter. In the year 2003, it was one thing to believe that *the United States should not invade Iraq* because the ongoing war in Afghanistan was more important; it was another to believe it because you think it is an abomination for infidels to trespass on Muslim land. Knowing what a person believes on a specific subject is not identical to knowing how that person thinks.

Decades of psychological research suggest that unconscious processes influence belief formation, and not all of them assist us in our search for truth. When asked to judge the probability that an event will occur, or the likelihood that one event caused another, people are frequently misled by a variety of factors, including the unconscious influence of extraneous information. For instance, if asked to recall the last four digits of their Social Security numbers and then asked to estimate the number of doctors practicing in San Francisco, the resulting numbers will show a statistically significant relationship. Needless to say, when the order of questions is reversed, this effect disappears.[36] There have been a few efforts to put a brave face on such departures from rationality, construing them as random performance errors or as a sign that experimental subjects have misunderstood the tasks presented to them—or even as proof that research psychologists themselves have been beguiled by false norms of reasoning. But efforts to exonerate our mental limitations have generally failed. There are some things that we are just naturally bad at. And the mistakes people tend to make across a wide range of reasoning tasks are not mere errors; they are *systematic* errors that are strongly associated both within and across tasks. As one might expect, many of these errors decrease as cognitive ability increases.[37] We also know that training, using both examples and formal rules, mitigates many of these problems and can improve a person's thinking.[38]

Reasoning errors aside, we know that people often acquire their beliefs about the world for reasons that are more emotional and social than strictly cognitive. Wishful thinking, self-serving bias, in-group loyalties, and frank self-deception can lead to monstrous departures from the norms of rationality. Most beliefs are evaluated against a background of other beliefs and often in the context of an ideology that a person shares with others. Consequently, people are rarely as open to revising their views as reason would seem to dictate.

On this front, the internet has simultaneously enabled two opposing influences on belief: On the one hand, it has reduced intellectual isolation by making it more difficult for people to remain ignorant of the diversity of opinion on any given subject. But it has also allowed bad ideas to flourish—as anyone with a computer and too much time on his hands can broadcast his point of view and, often enough, find an audience. So while knowledge is increasingly open-source, ignorance is, too.

It is also true that the less competent a person is in a given domain, the more he will tend to overestimate his abilities. This often produces an ugly marriage of confidence and ignorance that is very difficult to correct for.[39] Conversely, those who are more knowledgeable about a subject tend to be acutely aware of the greater expertise of others. This creates a rather unlovely asymmetry in public discourse—one that is generally on display whenever scientists debate religious apologists. For instance, when a scientist speaks with appropriate circumspection about controversies in his field, or about the limits of his own understanding, his opponent will often make wildly unjustified assertions about just which religious doctrines can be inserted into the space provided. Thus, one often finds people with no scientific training speaking with apparent certainty about the theological implications of quantum mechanics, cosmology, or molecular biology.

This point merits a brief aside: while it is a standard rhetorical move in such debates to accuse scientists of being "arrogant," the level of humility in scientific discourse is, in fact, one of its most striking characteristics. In my experience, arrogance is about as common at a scientific conference as nudity. At any scientific meeting you will find presenter after presenter couching his or her remarks with caveats and apologies. When asked to comment on something that lies to either side of the very knife edge of their special expertise, even Nobel laureates will say things like, "Well, this isn't really my area, but I would suspect that X is . . ." or "I'm sure there a several people in this room who know more about this than I do, but as far as I know, X is . . ." The totality of scientific knowledge now *doubles every few years.* Given how much there is to know, all scientists live with the constant awareness that whenever they open their mouths in the presence of other scientists, they are guaranteed to be speaking to someone who knows more about a specific topic than they do.

Cognitive biases cannot help but influence our public discourse. Consider political conservatism: this is a fairly well-defined perspective that is characterized by a general discomfort with societal change and a ready acceptance of social inequality. As simple as political conservatism is to describe, we know that it is governed by many factors. The psychologist John Jost and colleagues analyzed data from twelve countries, acquired from 23,000 subjects, and found this attitude to be correlated with dogmatism, inflexibility, death anxiety, need for closure, and anticorrelated with openness to experience, cognitive complexity, self-esteem, and social stability.[40] Even the manipulation of a single of these variables can affect political opinions and behavior. For instance, merely reminding people of the fact of death increases their inclination to punish transgressors and to reward those who uphold cultural norms. One experiment showed that judges could be led to impose especially harsh penalties on prostitutes if they were simply prompted to think about death prior to their deliberations.[41]

And yet after reviewing the literature linking political conservatism to many obvious sources of bias, Jost and his coauthors reach the following conclusion:

> Conservative ideologies, like virtually all other belief systems, are adopted in part because they satisfy various psychological needs. To say that ideological belief systems have a strong motivational basis is not to say that they are unprincipled, unwarranted, or unresponsive to reason and evidence.[42]

This has more than a whiff of euphemism about it. Surely we can say that a belief system known to be especially beholden to dogmatism, inflexibility, death anxiety, and a need for closure will be *less* principled, *less* warranted, and *less* responsive to reason and evidence than it would otherwise be.

This is not to say that liberalism isn't also occluded by certain biases. In a recent study of moral reasoning,[43] subjects were asked to judge whether it was morally correct to sacrifice the life of one person to save one hundred, while being given subtle clues as to the races of the people involved. Conservatives proved less biased by race than liberals and, therefore, more even-handed. Liberals, as it turns out, were very eager to sacrifice a white person to save one hundred nonwhites, but not the other way around—all the while maintaining that considerations of race had not entered into their thinking. The point, of course, is that science increasingly allows us to identify aspects of our minds that cause us to deviate from norms of factual and moral reasoning—norms which, when made explicit, are generally acknowledged to be valid by all parties.

There is a sense in which all cognition can be said to be motivated: one is motivated to understand the world, to be in touch with reality, to remove doubt, etc. Alternately, one might say that motivation is an aspect of cognition itself.[44] Nevertheless, motives like wanting to find the truth, not wanting to be mistaken, etc., tend to align with epistemic goals in a way that many other commitments do not. As we have begun to see, all reasoning may be inextricable from emotion. But if a person's primary motivation in holding a belief is to hew to a positive state of mind—to mitigate feelings of anxiety, embarrassment, or guilt, for instance—this is precisely what we mean by phrases like "wishful thinking" and "self-deception." Such a person will, of necessity, be less responsive to valid chains of evidence and argument that run counter to the beliefs he is seeking to maintain. To point out non-epistemic motives in another's view of the world, therefore, is always a criticism, as it serves to cast doubt upon a person's connection to the world as it is.[45]

Mistaking Our Limits

We have long known, principally through the neurological work of Antonio Damasio and colleagues, that certain types of reasoning are inseparable from emotion.[46] To reason effectively, we must have a feeling for the truth. Our first fMRI study of belief and disbelief seemed to bear this out.[47] If believing a mathematical equation (vs. disbelieving another) and believing an ethical proposition (vs. disbelieving another) produce the same changes in neurophysiology, the boundary between scientific dispassion and judgments of value becomes difficult to establish.

However, such findings do not in the least diminish the importance of reason, nor do they blur the distinction between justified and unjustified belief. On the contrary, the inseparability of reason and emotion confirms that the validity of a belief cannot merely depend on the conviction felt by its adherents; it rests on the chains of evidence and argument that link it to reality. Feeling may be necessary to judge the truth, but it cannot be sufficient.

The neurologist Robert Burton argues that the "feeling of knowing" (i.e., the conviction that one's judgment is correct) is a primary positive emotion that often floats free of rational processes and can occasionally become wholly detached from logical or sensory evidence.[48] He infers this from neurological disorders in which subjects display pathological certainty (e.g., schizophrenia and Cotard's delusion) and pathological uncertainty (e.g., obsessive-compulsive disorder). Burton concludes that it is irrational to expect too much of human rationality. On his account, rationality is mostly aspirational in character and often little more than a façade masking pure, unprincipled feeling.

Other neuroscientists have made similar claims. Chris Frith, a pioneer in the use of functional neuroimaging, recently wrote:

> [W]here does conscious reasoning come into the picture? It is an attempt to justify the choice after it has been made. And it is, after all, the only way we have to try to explain to other people why we made a particular decision. But given our lack of access to the brain processes involved, our justification is often spurious: a post-hoc rationalization, or even a confabulation—a "story" born of the confusion between imagination and memory.[49]

I doubt Frith meant to deny that reason *ever* plays a role in decision making (though the title of his essay was "No One Really Uses Reason"). He has, however, conflated two facts about the mind: while it is true that all conscious processes, including any effort of reasoning, depend upon events of which we are not conscious, this does not mean that reasoning amounts to little more than a post hoc justification of brute sentiment. We are not aware of the neurological processes that allow us to follow the rules of algebra, but this doesn't mean that we never follow these rules or that the role they play in our mathematical calculations is generally post hoc. The fact that we are unaware of most of what goes on in our brains does not render the distinction between having good reasons for what one believes and having bad ones any less clear or consequential. Nor does it suggest that internal consistency, openness to information, self-criticism, and other cognitive virtues are less valuable than we generally assume.

There are many ways to make too much of the unconscious underpinnings of human thought. For instance, Burton observes that one's thinking on many moral issues—ranging from global warming to capital punishment—will be influenced by one's tolerance for risk. In evaluating the problem of global warming, one must weigh the risk of melting the polar ice caps; in judging the ethics of capital punishment, one must consider the risk of putting innocent people to death. However, people differ significantly with respect to risk tolerance, and these differences appear to be governed by a variety of genes—including genes for the D4 dopamine receptor and the protein stathmin (which is primarily expressed in the amygdala). Believing that there can be no optimal degree of risk aversion, Burton concludes that we can never truly reason about such ethical questions. "Reason" will simply be the name we give to our unconscious (and genetically determined) biases. But is it really true to say that every degree of risk tolerance will serve our purposes equally well as we struggle to build a global civilization? Does Burton really mean to suggest that there is no basis for distinguishing healthy from unhealthy—or even suicidal—attitudes toward risk?

As it turns out, dopamine receptor genes may play a role in religious belief as well. People who have inherited the most active form of the D4 receptor are more likely to believe in miracles and to be skeptical of science; the least active forms correlate with "rational materialism."[50] Skeptics given the drug L-dopa, which increases dopamine levels, show an increased propensity to accept mystical explanations for novel phenomena.[51] The fact that religious belief is both a cultural universal and appears to be tethered to the genome has led scientists like Burton to conclude that there is simply no getting rid of faith-based thinking.

It seems to me that Burton and Frith have misunderstood the significance of unconscious cognitive processes. On Burton's account, worldviews will remain idiosyncratic and incommensurable, and the hope that we might persuade one another through rational argument and, thereby, fuse our cognitive horizons is not only vain but symptomatic of the very unconscious processes and frank irrationality that we would presume to expunge. This leads him to conclude that any rational criticism of religious irrationality is an unseemly waste of time:

> The science-religion controversy cannot go away; it is rooted in biology . . . Scorpions sting. We talk of religion, afterlife, soul, higher powers, muses, purpose, reason, objectivity, pointlessness, and randomness. We cannot help ourselves . . . To insist that the secular and the scientific be universally adopted flies in the face of what neuroscience tells us about different personality traits generating idiosyncratic worldviews . . . Different genetics, temperaments, and experience led to contrasting worldviews. Reason isn't going to bridge this gap between believers and nonbelievers.[52]

The problem, however, is that we could have said the same about witchcraft. Historically, a preoccupation with witchcraft has been a cultural universal. And yet belief in magic is now in disrepute almost everywhere in the developed world. Is there a scientist on earth who would be tempted to argue that belief in the evil eye or in the demonic origins of epilepsy is bound to remain impervious to reason?

Lest the analogy between religion and witchcraft seem quaint, it is worth remembering that belief in magic and demonic possession is still epidemic in Africa. In Kenya elderly men and women are regularly burned alive as witches.[53] In Angola, Congo, and Nigeria the hysteria has mostly targeted children: thousands of unlucky boys and girls have been blinded, injected with battery acid, and otherwise put to torture in an effort to purge them of demons; others have been killed outright; many more have been disowned by their families and rendered homeless.[54] Needless to say, much of this lunacy has spread in the name of Christianity. The problem is especially intractable because the government officials charged with protecting these suspected witches also believe in witchcraft. As was the case in the Middle Ages, when the belief in witchcraft was omnipresent in Europe, only a truly panoramic ignorance about the physical causes of disease, crop failure, and life's other indignities allows this delusion to thrive.

What if we were to connect the fear of witches with the expression of a certain receptor subtype in the brain? Who would be tempted to say that the belief in witchcraft is, therefore, ineradicable?

As someone who has received many thousands of letters and emails from people who have ceased to believe in the God of Abraham, I know that pessimism about the power of reason is unwarranted. People can be led to notice the incongruities in their faith, the self-deception and wishful thinking of their coreligionists, and the growing conflict between the claims of scripture and the findings of modern science. Such reasoning can inspire them to question their attachment to doctrines that, in the vast majority of cases, were simply drummed into them on mother's knee. The truth is that people can transcend mere sentiment and clarify their thinking on almost any subject. Allowing competing views to collide—through open debate, a willingness to receive criticism, etc.—performs just such a function, often by exposing inconsistencies in a belief system that make its adherents profoundly uncomfortable. There are standards to guide us, even when opinions differ, and the violation of such standards generally seems consequential to everyone involved. Self-contradiction, for instance, is viewed as a problem no matter what one is talking about. And anyone who considers it a virtue is very unlikely to be taken seriously. Again, reason is not starkly opposed to feeling on this front; it entails a feeling for the truth.

Conversely, there are occasions when a true proposition just doesn't *seem* right no matter how one squints one's eyes or cocks one's head, and yet its truth can be acknowledged by anyone willing to do the necessary intellectual work. It is very difficult to grasp that tiny quantities of matter contain vast amounts of explosive energy, but the equations of physics—along with the destructive yield of our nuclear bombs—confirms that this is so. Similarly, we know that most people cannot produce or even recognize a series of digits or coin tosses that meets a statistical test for randomness. But this has not stopped us from understanding randomness mathematically—or from factoring our innate blindness to randomness into our growing understanding of cognition and economic behavior.[55]

The fact that reason must be rooted in our biology does not negate the principles of reason. Wittgenstein once observed that the logic of our language allows us to ask, "Was *that* gunfire?" but not "Was *that* a noise?"[56] This seems to be a contingent fact of neurology, rather than an absolute constraint upon logic. A synesthete, for instance, who experiences crosstalk between his primary senses (seeing sounds, tasting colors, etc.), might be able to pose the latter question without any contradiction. How the world seems to us (and what can be logically said about its seemings) depends upon facts about our brains. Our inability to say that an object is "red and green all over" is a fact about the biology of vision before it is a fact of logic. But that doesn't prevent us from seeing beyond this very contingency. As science advances, we are increasingly coming to understand the natural limits of our understanding.

Belief and Reasoning

There is a close relationship between belief and reasoning. Many of our beliefs are the product of inferences drawn from particular instances (induction) or from general principles (deduction), or both. Induction is the process by which we extrapolate from past observations to novel instances, anticipate future states of the world, and draw analogies from one domain to another.[57] Believing that you probably have a pancreas (because people generally have the same parts), or interpreting the look of disgust on your son's face to mean that he doesn't like Marmite, are examples of induction. This mode of thinking is especially important for ordinary cognition and for the practice of science, and there have been a variety of efforts to model it computationally.[58] Deduction, while less central to our lives, is an essential component of any logical argument.[59] If you believe that gold is more expensive than silver, and silver more expensive than tin, deduction reveals that you also believe gold to be more expensive than tin. Induction allows us to move beyond the facts already in hand; deduction allows us to make the implications of our current beliefs more explicit, to search for counterexamples, and to see whether our views are logically coherent. Of course, the boundaries between these (and other) forms of reasoning are not always easy to specify, and people succumb to a wide range of biases in both modes.

It is worth reflecting on what a reasoning bias actually is: a bias is not merely a source of error; it is a *reliable pattern* of error. Every bias, therefore, reveals something about the structure of the human mind. And diagnosing a pattern of errors as a "bias" can only occur with reference to specific norms—and norms can sometimes be in conflict. The norms of logic, for instance, don't always correspond to the norms of practical reasoning. An argument can be logically valid, but unsound in that it contains a false premise and, therefore, leads to a false conclusion (e.g., Scientists are smart; smart people do not make mistakes; therefore, scientists do not make mistakes).[60] Much research on deductive reasoning suggests that people have a "bias" for sound conclusions and will judge a valid argument to be invalid if its conclusion lacks credibility. It's not clear that this "belief bias" should be considered a symptom of native irrationality. Rather, it seems an instance in which the norms of abstract logic and practical reason may simply be in conflict.

Neuroimaging studies have been performed on various types of human reasoning.[61] As we have seen, however, accepting the fruits of such reasoning (i.e., belief) seems to be an independent process. While this is suggested by my own neuroimaging research, it also follows directly from the fact that reasoning accounts only for a subset of our beliefs about the world. Consider the following statements:

1. All known soil samples contain bacteria; so the soil in my garden probably contains bacteria as well (induction).
2. Dan is a philosopher, all philosophers have opinions about Nietzsche; therefore, Dan has an opinion about Nietzsche (deduction).
3. Mexico shares a border with the United States.
4. You are reading at this moment.

Each of these statements must be evaluated by different channels of neural processing (and only the first two require reasoning). And yet each has the same cognitive valence: being true, each inspires belief (or being believed, each is deemed "true"). Such cognitive acceptance allows any apparent truth to take its place in the economy of our thoughts and actions, at which time it becomes as potent as its propositional content demands.

A World Without Lying?

Knowing what a person believes is equivalent to knowing whether or not he is telling the truth. Consequently, any external means of determining which propositions a subject believes would constitute a de facto "lie detector." Neuroimaging research on belief and disbelief may one day enable researchers to put this equivalence to use in the study of deception.[62] It is possible that this new approach could circumvent many of the impediments that have hindered the study of deception in the past.

When evaluating the social cost of deception, we need to consider all of the misdeeds—premeditated murders, terrorist atrocities, genocides, Ponzi schemes, etc.—that must be nurtured and shored up, at every turn, by lies. Viewed in this wider context, deception commends itself, perhaps even above violence, as the principal enemy of human cooperation. Imagine how our world would change if, when the truth really mattered, it became impossible to lie. What would international relations be like if every time a person shaded the truth on the floor of the United Nations an alarm went off throughout the building?

The forensic use of DNA evidence has already made the act of denying one's culpability for certain actions comically ineffectual. Recall how Bill Clinton's cantatas of indignation were abruptly silenced the moment he learned that a semen-stained dress was en route to the lab. The mere threat of a DNA analysis produced what no grand jury ever could—instantaneous communication with the great man's conscience, which appeared to be located in another galaxy. We can be sure that a dependable method of lie detection would produce similar transformations, on far more consequential subjects.

The development of mind-reading technology is just beginning—but reliable lie detection will be much easier to achieve than accurate mind reading. Whether or not we ever crack the neural code, enabling us to download a person's private thoughts, memories, and perceptions without distortion, we will almost surely be able to determine, to a moral certainty, whether a person is representing his thoughts, memories, and perceptions honestly in conversation. The development of a reliable lie detector would only require a very modest advance over what is currently possible through neuroimaging.

Traditional methods for detecting deception through polygraphy never achieved widespread acceptance,[63] as they measure the peripheral signs of emotional arousal rather than the neural activity associated with deception itself. In 2002, in a 245-page report, the National Research Council (an arm of the National Academy of Sciences) dismissed the entire body of research underlying polygraphy as "weak" and "lacking in scientific rigor."[64] More modern approaches to lie detection, using thermal imaging of the eyes,[65] suffer a similar lack of specificity. Techniques that employ electrical signals at the scalp to detect "guilty knowledge" have limited application, and it is unclear how one can use these methods to differentiate guilty knowledge from other forms of knowledge in any case.[66]

Methodological problems notwithstanding, it is difficult to exaggerate how fully our world would change if lie detectors ever became reliable, affordable, and unobtrusive. Rather than spirit criminal defendants and hedge fund managers off to the lab for a disconcerting hour of brain scanning, there may come a time when every courtroom or boardroom will have the requisite technology discreetly concealed behind its wood paneling. Thereafter, civilized men and women might share a common presumption: that wherever important conversations are held, the truthfulness of all participants will be monitored. Well-intentioned people would happily pass between zones of obligatory candor, and these transitions will cease to be remarkable. Just as we've come to expect that certain public spaces will be free of nudity, sex, loud swearing, and cigarette smoke—and now think nothing of the behavioral constraints imposed upon us whenever we leave the privacy of our homes—we may come to expect that certain places and occasions will require scrupulous truth telling. Many of us might no more feel deprived of the freedom to lie during a job interview or at a press conference than we currently feel deprived of the freedom to remove our pants in the supermarket. Whether or not the technology works as well as we hope, the belief that it generally does work would change our culture profoundly.

In a legal context, some scholars have already begun to worry that reliable lie detection will constitute an infringement of a person's Fifth Amendment privilege against self-incrimination.[67] However, the Fifth Amendment has already succumbed to advances in technology. The Supreme Court has ruled that defendants can be forced to provide samples of their blood, saliva, and other physical evidence that may incriminate them. Will neuroimaging data be added to this list, or will it be considered a form of forced testimony? Diaries, emails, and other records of a person's thoughts are already freely admissible as evidence. It is not at all clear that there is a distinction between these diverse sources of information that should be ethically or legally relevant to us.

In fact, the prohibition against compelled testimony itself appears to be a relic of a more superstitious age. It was once widely believed that lying under oath would damn a person's soul for eternity, and it was thought that no one, not even a murderer, should be placed between the rock of Justice and so hard a place as hell. But I doubt whether even many fundamentalist Christians currently imagine that an oath sworn on a courtroom Bible has such cosmic significance.

Of course, no technology is ever perfect. Once we have a proper lie detector in hand, well-intentioned people will begin to suffer its propensity for positive and negative error. This will raise ethical and legal concerns. It is inevitable, however, that we will deem some rate of error to be acceptable. If you doubt this, remember that we currently lock people away in prison for decades—or kill them—all the while knowing that some percentage of the condemned must be innocent, while some percentage of those returned to our streets will be dangerous psychopaths guaranteed to reoffend. We are currently living with a system in which the occasional unlucky person gets falsely convicted of murder, suffers for years in prison in the company of terrifying predators, only to be finally executed by the state. Consider the tragic case of Cameron Todd Willingham, who was convicted of setting fire to the family home and thereby murdering his three children. While protesting his innocence, Willingham served over a decade on death row and was finally executed. It now seems that he was almost surely innocent—the victim of a chance electrical fire, forensic pseudoscience, and of a justice system that has no reliable means of determining when people are telling the truth.[68]

We have no choice but to rely upon our criminal justice system, despite the fact that judges and juries are very poorly calibrated truth detectors, prone to both type I (false positive) and type II (false negative) errors. Anything that can improve the performance of this antiquated system, even slightly, will raise the quotient of justice in our world.[69]

Do We Have Freedom of Belief?

While belief might prove difficult to pinpoint in the brain, many of its mental properties are plain to see. For instance, people do not knowingly believe propositions for bad reasons. If you doubt this, imagine hearing the following account of a failed New Year's resolution:

> This year, I vowed to be more rational, but by the end of January, I found that I had fallen back into my old ways, believing things for bad reasons. Currently, I believe that robbing others is a harmless activity, that my dead brother will return to life, and that I am destined to marry Angelina Jolie, just because these beliefs make me feel good.

This is not how our minds work. A belief—to be actually believed—entails the corollary belief that we have accepted it *because* it seems to be true. To really believe a proposition—whether about facts or values—we must also believe that we are in touch with reality in such a way that if it were *not* true, one would not believe it. We must believe, therefore, that we are not flagrantly in error, deluded, insane, self-deceived, etc.

While the preceding sentences do not suffice as a full account of epistemology, they go a long way toward uniting science and common sense, as well as reconciling their frequent disagreements. There can be no doubt that there is an important difference between a belief that is motivated by an unconscious emotional bias (or other nonepistemic commitments) and a belief that is comparatively free of such bias.

And yet many secularists and academics imagine that people of faith knowingly believe things for reasons that have nothing to do with their perception of the truth. A written debate I had with Philip Ball—who is a scientist, a science journalist, and an editor at *Nature*—brought this issue into focus. Ball thought it reasonable for a person to believe a proposition just because it makes him "feel better," and he seemed to think that people are perfectly free to acquire beliefs in this way. People often do this unconsciously, of course, and such motivated reasoning has been discussed above. But Ball seemed to think that beliefs can be consciously adopted simply because a person feels better while under their spell. Let's see how this might work. Imagine someone making the following statement of religious conviction:

> I believe Jesus was born of a virgin, was resurrected, and now answers prayers because believing these things makes me feel better. By adopting this faith, I am merely exercising my freedom to believe in propositions that make me feel good.

How would such a person respond to information that contradicted his cherished belief? Given that his belief is based purely on how it makes him feel, and not on evidence or argument, he shouldn't care about any new evidence or argument that might come his way. In fact, the only thing that should change his view of Jesus is a change in how the above propositions make him *feel*. Imagine our believer undergoing the following epiphany:

> For the last few months, I've found that my belief in the divinity of Jesus no longer makes me feel good. The truth is, I just met a Muslim woman who I greatly admire, and I want to ask her out

> on a date. As Muslims believe Jesus was *not* divine, I am worried that my belief in the divinity of Jesus could hinder my chances with her. As I do not like feeling this way, and very much want to go out with this woman, I now believe that Jesus was *not* divine.

Has a person like this ever existed? I highly doubt it. Why do these thoughts not make any sense? Because beliefs are *intrinsically* epistemic: they purport to represent the world as it is. In this case, our man is making specific claims about the historical Jesus, about the manner of his birth and death, and about his special connection to the Creator of the Universe. And yet while claiming to represent the world in this way, it is perfectly clear that he is making no effort to stay in touch with the features of the world that should inform his belief. He is only concerned about how he feels. Given this disparity, it should be clear that his beliefs are not based on any foundation that would (or should) justify them to others, or even to himself.

Of course, people do often believe things in part because these beliefs make them feel better. But they do not do this in the full light of consciousness. Self-deception, emotional bias, and muddled thinking are facts of human cognition. And it is a common practice to act *as if* a proposition were true, in the spirit of: "I'm going to act on X because I like what it does for me and, who knows, X might be true." But these phenomena are not at all the same as *knowingly* believing a proposition simply because one wants it to be true.

Strangely, people often view such claims about the constraints of rationality as a sign of "intolerance." Consider the following from Ball:

> I do wonder what [Sam Harris] is implying here. It is hard to see it as anything other than an injunction that "you should not be free to choose what you believe." I guess that if all Sam means is that we should not leave people so ill-informed that they have no reasonable basis on which to make those decisions, then fair enough. But it does seem to go further—to say that "you should not be permitted to choose what you believe, simply because it makes you feel better." Doesn't this sound a little like a Marxist

> denouncement of "false consciousness," with the implication that it needs to be corrected forthwith? I think (I hope?) we can at least agree that there are different categories of belief—that to believe one's children are the loveliest in the world because that makes you feel better is a permissible (even laudable) thing. But I slightly shudder at the notion, hinted here, that a well-informed person should not be allowed to choose their belief freely . . . surely we cannot let ourselves become proscriptive to this degree?[70]

What cognitive freedom is Ball talking about? I happen to believe that George Washington was the first president of the United States. Have I, on Ball's terms, chosen this belief "freely"? No. Am I free to believe otherwise? Of course not. I am a slave to the evidence. I live under the lash of historical opinion. While I may *want* to believe otherwise, I simply cannot overlook the incessant pairing of the name "George Washington" with the phrase "first president of the United States" in any discussion of American history. If I wanted to be thought an idiot, I could *profess* some other belief, but I would be lying. Likewise, if the evidence were to suddenly change—if, for instance, compelling evidence of a great hoax emerged and historians reconsidered Washington's biography, I would be helplessly stripped of my belief—again, through no choice of my own. Choosing beliefs freely is not what rational minds do.

This does not mean, of course, that we have no mental freedom whatsoever. We can choose to focus on certain facts to the exclusion of others, to emphasize the good rather than the bad, etc. And such choices have consequences for how we view the world. One can, for instance, view Kim Jong-il as an evil dictator; one can also view him as a man who was once the child of a dangerous psychopath. Both statements are, to a first approximation, true. (Obviously, when I speak about "freedom" and "choices" of this sort, I am not endorsing a metaphysical notion of "free will.")

As to whether there are "different categories of belief": perhaps, but not in the way that Ball suggests. I happen to have a young daughter who does strike me as the "loveliest in the world." But is this an accurate account of what I believe? Do I, in other words, believe that my daughter is *really* the loveliest girl in the world? If I learned that another father thought his daughter the loveliest in the world, would I insist that he was mistaken? Of course not. Ball has mischaracterized what a proud (and sane and intellectually honest) father actually believes. Here is what I believe: I believe that I have a special attachment to my daughter that largely determines my view of her (which is as it should be). I fully expect other fathers to have a similar bias toward their own daughters. Therefore, I do not believe that my daughter is the loveliest girl in the world in any objective sense. Ball is simply describing what it's like to love one's daughter more than other girls; he is not describing belief as a representation of the world. What I really believe is that my daughter is the loveliest girl in the world *for me.*

One thing that both factual and moral beliefs generally share is the presumption that we have not been misled by extraneous information.[71] Situational variables, like the order in which unrelated facts are presented, or whether identical outcomes are described in terms of gains or losses, should not influence the decision process. Of course, the fact that such manipulations can *strongly* influence our judgment has given rise to some of the most interesting work in psychology. However, a person's vulnerability to such manipulations is never considered a cognitive virtue; rather, it is a source of inconsistency that cries out for remedy.

Consider one of the more famous cases from the experimental literature, The Asian Disease Problem:[72]

> Imagine that the United States is preparing for the outbreak of an unusual Asian disease, which is expected to kill 600 people. Two alternative programs to combat the disease have been proposed. Assume that the exact scientific estimates of the consequences of the programs are as follows:
>
> If Program A is adopted, 200 people will be saved.
> If Program B is adopted, there is a one-third probability that 600

people will be saved and a two-thirds probability that no people will be saved.

Which one of the two programs would you favor?

In this version of the problem, a significant majority of people favor Program A. The problem, however, can be restated this way:

If Program A is adopted, 400 people will die.
If Program B is adopted, there is a one-third probability that nobody will die and a two-thirds probability that 600 people will die.

Which one of the two programs would you favor?

Put this way, a majority of respondents will now favor Program B. And yet there is no material or moral difference between these two scenarios, because their outcomes are the same. What this shows is that people tend to be risk-averse when considering potential gains and risk seeking when considering potential losses, so describing the same event in terms of gains and losses evokes different responses. Another way of stating this is that people tend to overvalue certainty: finding the certainty of saving life inordinately attractive and the certainty of losing life inordinately painful. When presented with the Asian Disease Problem in both forms, however, people agree that each scenario merits the same response. Invariance of reasoning, both logical and moral, is a norm to which we all aspire. And when we catch others departing from this norm, whatever the other merits of their thinking, the incoherency of their position suddenly becomes its most impressive characteristic.

Of course, there are many other ways in which we can be misled by context. Few studies illustrate this more powerfully than one conducted by the psychologist David L. Rosenhan,[73] in which he and seven confederates had themselves committed to psychiatric hospitals in five different states in an effort to determine whether mental health professionals could detect the presence of the sane among the mentally ill. In order to get committed, each researcher complained of hearing a voice repeating the words "empty," "hollow," and "thud." Beyond that, each behaved perfectly normally. Upon winning admission to the psychiatric ward, the pseudopatients stopped complaining of their symptoms and immediately sought to convince the doctors, nurses, and staff that they felt fine and were fit to be released. This proved surprisingly difficult. While these genuinely sane patients wanted to leave the hospital, repeatedly declared that they experienced no symptoms, and became "paragons of cooperation," their average length of hospitalization was nineteen days (ranging from seven to fifty-two days), during which they were bombarded with an astounding range of powerful drugs (which they discreetly deposited in the toilet). None were pronounced healthy. Each was ultimately discharged with a diagnosis of schizophrenia "in remission" (with the exception of one who received a diagnosis of bipolar disorder). Interestingly, while the doctors, nurses, and staff were apparently blind to the presence of normal people on the ward, actual mental patients frequently remarked on the obvious sanity of the researchers, saying things like "You're not crazy. You're a journalist."

In a brilliant response to the skeptics at one hospital who had heard of this research before it was published, Rosenhan announced that he would send a few confederates their way and challenged them to spot the coming pseudopatients. The hospital kept vigil, while Rosenhan, in fact, sent no one. This did not stop the hospital from "detecting" a steady stream of pseudopatients. Over a period of a few months fully 10 percent of their new patients were deemed to be shamming by both a psychiatrist and a member of the staff. While we have all grown familiar with phenomena of this sort, it is startling to see the principle so clearly demonstrated: expectation can be, if not everything, *almost* everything. Rosenhan concluded his paper with this damning summary: "It is clear that we cannot distinguish the sane from the insane in psychiatric hospitals."

There is no question that human beings regularly fail to achieve the norms of rationality. But we do not merely fail—we fail reliably. We can, in other words, use reason to understand, quantify, and predict our violations of its norms. This has moral implications. We know, for instance, that the choice to undergo a risky medical procedure will be heavily influenced by whether its possible outcomes are framed in terms of survival rates or mortality rates. We know, in fact, that this framing effect is no less pronounced among doctors than among patients.[74] Given this knowledge, physicians have a moral obligation to handle medical statistics in ways that minimize unconscious bias. Otherwise, they cannot help but inadvertently manipulate both their patients and one another, guaranteeing that some of the most important decisions in life will be unprincipled.[75]

Admittedly, it is difficult to know how we should treat all of the variables that influence our judgment about ethical norms. If I were asked, for instance, whether I would sanction the murder of an innocent person if it would guarantee a cure for cancer, I would find it very difficult to say "yes," despite the obvious consequentialist argument in favor of such an action. If I were asked to impose a one in a billion risk of death on everyone for this purpose, however, I would not hesitate. The latter course would be expected to kill six or seven people, and yet it still strikes me as obviously ethical. In fact, such a diffusion of risk aptly describes how medical research is currently conducted. And we routinely impose far greater risks than this on friends and strangers whenever we get behind the wheel of our cars. If my next drive down the highway were guaranteed to deliver a cure for cancer, I would consider it the most ethically important act of my life. No doubt the role that probability is playing here could be experimentally calibrated. We could ask subjects whether they would impose a 50 percent chance of death upon two innocent people, a 10 percent chance on ten innocent people, etc. How we should view the role that probability plays in our moral judgments is not clear, however. It seems difficult to imagine ever fully escaping such framing effects.

Science has long been in the values business. Despite a widespread belief to the contrary, scientific validity is not the result of scientists abstaining from making value judgments; rather, scientific validity is the result of scientists making their best effort to *value* principles of reasoning that link their beliefs to reality, through reliable chains of evidence and argument. This is how norms of rational thought are made effective.

To say that judgments of truth and goodness both invoke specific norms seems another way of saying that they are both matters of cognition, as opposed to mere sentiment. That is why one cannot defend one's factual or moral position by reference to one's preferences. One cannot say that *water is* H_2O or that *lying is wrong* simply because one wants to think this way. To defend such propositions, one must invoke a deeper principle. To believe that X is true or that Y is ethical is also to believe others should share these beliefs under similar circumstances.

The answer to the question "What should I believe, and why should I believe it?" is generally a scientific one. Believe a proposition because it is well supported by theory and evidence; believe it because it has been experimentally verified; believe it because a generation of smart people have tried their best to falsify it and failed; believe it because it is *true* (or seems so). This is a norm of cognition as well as the core of any scientific mission statement. As far as our understanding of the world is concerned—*there are no facts without values.*

Chapter 4

RELIGION

Since the nineteenth century, it has been widely assumed that the spread of industrialized society would spell the end of religion. Marx,[1] Freud,[2] and Weber[3]—along with innumerable anthropologists, sociologists, historians, and psychologists influenced by their work—expected religious belief to wither in the light of modernity. It has not come to pass. Religion remains one of the most important aspects of human life in the twenty-first century. While most developed societies have grown predominantly secular,[4] with the curious exception of the United States, orthodox religion is in florid bloom throughout the developing world. In fact, humanity seems to be growing proportionally more religious, as prosperous, nonreligious people have the fewest babies.[5] When one considers the rise of Islamism throughout the Muslim world, the explosive spread of Pentecostalism throughout Africa, and the anomalous piety of the United States, it becomes clear that religion will have geopolitical consequences for a long time to come.

Despite the explicit separation of church and state provided for by the U.S. Constitution, the level of religious belief in the United States (and the concomitant significance of religion in American life and political discourse) rivals that of many theocracies. The reason for this is unclear. While it has been widely argued that religious pluralism and competition have caused religion to flourish in the United States, with state-church monopolies leading to its decline in Western Europe,[6] the support for this "religious market theory" now appears weak. It seems, rather, that religiosity is strongly coupled to perceptions of societal insecurity. Within a rich nation like the United States, high levels of socioeconomic inequality may dictate levels of religiosity generally associated with less developed (and less secure) societies. In addition to being the most religious of developed nations, the United States also has the greatest economic inequality.[7] The poor tend to be more religious than the rich, both within and between nations.[8]

Fifty-seven percent of Americans think that one must believe in God to have good values and to be moral,[9] and 69 percent want a president who is guided by "strong religious beliefs."[10] Such views are unsurprising, given that even secular scientists regularly acknowledge religion to be the most common source of meaning and morality. It is true that most religions offer a prescribed response to specific moral questions—the Catholic Church forbids abortion, for instance. But research on people's responses to unfamiliar moral dilemmas suggests that religion has no effect on moral judgments that involve weighing harms against benefits (e.g., lives lost vs. lives saved).[11]

And on almost every measure of societal health, the least religious countries are better off than the most religious. Countries like Denmark, Sweden, Norway, and the Netherlands—which are the most atheistic societies on earth—consistently rate better than religious nations on measures like life expectancy, infant mortality, crime, literacy, GDP, child welfare, economic equality, economic competitiveness, gender equality, health care, investments in education, rates of university enrollment, internet access, environmental protection, lack of corruption, political stability, and charity to poorer nations, etc.[12] The independent researcher Gregory Paul has cast further light on this terrain by creating two scales—the Successful Societies Scale and Popular Religiosity Versus Secularism Scale—which offer greater support for a link between religious conviction and societal insecurity.[13] And there is another finding which may be relevant to this variable of societal insecurity: religious commitment in the United States is highly correlated with racism.[14]

While the mere correlation between societal dysfunction and religious belief does not tell us what the connection is between them, these data should abolish the ever-present claim that religion is the most important guarantor of societal health. They also prove, conclusively, that a high level of unbelief need not lead to the fall of civilization.[15]

Whether religion contributes to societal dysfunction, it seems clear that as societies become more prosperous, stable, and democratic, they tend to become more secular. Even in the United States, the trend toward secularism is visible. As Paul points out, this suggests that, contrary to the opinions of many anthropologists and psychologists, religious commitment "is superficial enough to be readily abandoned when conditions improve to the required degree."[16]

Religion and Evolution

The evolutionary origins of religion remain obscure. The earliest signs of human burial practices date to 95,000 years ago, and many take these as evidence of the emergence of religious belief.[17] Some researchers consider the connection between religion and evolution to be straightforward insofar as religious doctrines tend to view sexual conduct as morally problematic and attempt to regulate it, both to encourage fertility and to protect against sexual infidelity. Clearly, it is in the genetic interests of every man that he not spend his life rearing another man's children, and it is in the genetic interests of every woman that her mate not squander his resources on other women and their offspring. The fact that the world's religions generally codify these interests, often prescribing harsh penalties for their transgression, forms the basis for one of their more persistent claims to social utility. It is, therefore, tempting to trace a line between religious doctrines regarding marriage and sexuality to evolutionary fitness.[18] Even here, however, the link to evolution appears less than straightforward: as evolution should actually favor indiscriminate heterosexual activity on the part of men, as long as these scoundrels can avoid squandering their resources in ways that imperil the reproductive success of their offspring.[19]

Human beings may be genetically predisposed to superstition: for natural selection should favor rampant belief formation as long as the benefits of the occasional, correct belief are great enough.[20] The manufacture of new religious doctrines and identities, resulting in group conformity and xenophobia, may have offered some protection against infectious illness: for to the degree that religion divides people, it would inhibit the spread of novel pathogens.[21] However, the question of whether religion (or anything else) might have given groups of human beings an evolutionary advantage (so-called "group selection") has been widely debated.[22] And even if tribes have occasionally been the vehicles of natural selection, and religion proved adaptive, it would remain an open question whether religion increases human fitness today. As already mentioned, there are a wide variety of genetically entrenched human traits (e.g., out-group aggression, infidelity, superstition, etc.) that, while probably adaptive at some point in our past, may have been less than optimal even in the Pleistocene. In a world that is growing ever more crowded and complex, many of these biologically selected traits may yet imperil us.

Clearly, religion cannot be reduced to a mere concatenation of religious beliefs. Every religion consists of rites, rituals, prayers, social institutions, holidays, etc., and these serve a wide variety of purposes, conscious and otherwise.[23] However, religious *belief*—that is, the acceptance of specific historical and metaphysical propositions as being true—is generally what renders these enterprises relevant, or even comprehensible. I share with anthropologist Rodney Stark the view that belief precedes ritual and that a practice like prayer is usually thought to be a genuine act of communication with a God (or gods).[24] Religious adherents generally believe that they possess knowledge of sacred truths, and every faith provides a framework for interpreting experience so as to lend further credence to its doctrine.[25]

There seems little question that most religious practices are the direct consequence of what people believe to be true about both external and internal reality. Indeed, most religious practices become intelligible only in light of these underlying beliefs. The fact that many people have begun to doubt specific religious doctrines in the meantime, while still mouthing the liturgy and aping the rituals, is beside the point. What faith is best exemplified by those who are in the process of losing it? While there may be many Catholics, for instance, who value the ritual of the Mass without believing that the bread and wine are actually transformed into the body and blood of Jesus Christ, the doctrine of Transubstantiation remains the most plausible origin of this ritual. And the primacy of the Mass within the Church hinges on the fact that many Catholics still consider the underlying doctrine to be true—which is a direct consequence of the fact that the Church still promulgates and defends it. The following passage, taken from *The Profession of Faith of the Roman Catholic Church,* represents the relevant case, and illustrates the kind of assertions about reality that lie at the heart of most religions:

> I likewise profess that in the Mass a true, proper, and propitiatory sacrifice is offered to God on behalf of the living and the dead, and that the Body and the Blood, together with the soul and the divinity, of our Lord Jesus Christ is truly, really, and substantially present in the most holy sacrament of the Eucharist, and there is a change of the whole substance of the bread into the Body, and of the whole substance of the wine into Blood; and this change the Catholic Mass calls transubstantiation. I also profess that the whole and entire Christ and a true sacrament is received under each separate species.

There is, of course, a distinction to be made between mere profession of such beliefs and actual belief[26]—a distinction that, while important, makes sense only in a world in which some people actually believe what they say they believe. There seems little reason to doubt that a significant percentage of human beings, likely a majority, falls into this latter category with respect to one or another religious creed.

What is surprising, from a scientific point of view, is that 42 percent of Americans believe that life has existed in its present form since the beginning of the world, and another 21 percent believe that while life may have evolved, its evolution has been guided by the hand of God (only 26 percent believe in evolution through natural selection).[27]

Seventy-eight percent of Americans believe that the Bible is the word of God (either literal or "inspired"); and 79 percent of Christians believe that Jesus Christ will physically return to earth at some point in the future.[28]

How is it possible that so many millions of people believe these things? Clearly, the taboo around criticizing religious beliefs must contribute to their survival. But, as the anthropologist Pascal Boyer points out, the failure of reality testing does not explain the specific character of religious beliefs:

> People have stories about vanishing islands and talking cats, but they usually do not insert them in their religious beliefs. In contrast, people produce concepts of ghosts and person-like gods and make use of these concepts when they think about a whole variety of social questions (what is moral behavior, what to do with dead people, how misfortune occurs, why perform rituals, etc.). This is much more *precise* than just relaxing the usual principles of sound reasoning.[29]

According to Boyer, religious concepts must arise from mental categories that predate religion—and these underlying structures determine the stereotypical form that religious beliefs and practices take. These categories of thought relate to things like living beings, social exchange, moral infractions, natural hazards, and ways of understanding human misfortune. On Boyer's account, people do not accept incredible religious doctrines because they have relaxed their standards of rationality; they relax their standards of rationality because certain doctrines fit their "inference machinery" in such a way as to seem credible. And what most religious propositions may lack in plausibility they make up for by being memorable, emotionally salient, and socially consequential. All of these properties are a product of the underlying structure of human cognition, and most of this architecture is not consciously accessible. Boyer argues, therefore, that explicit theologies and consciously held dogmas are not a reliable indicator of the real contents or causes of a person's religious beliefs.

Boyer may be correct in his assertion that we have cognitive templates for religious ideas that run deeper than culture (in the same way that we appear to have deep, abstract concepts like "animal" and "tool"). The psychologist Justin Barrett makes a similar claim, likening religion to language acquisition: we come into this world cognitively prepared for language; our culture and upbringing merely dictate which languages we will be exposed to.[30] We may also be what the psychologist Paul Bloom has called "common sense dualists"—that is, we may be naturally inclined to see the mind as distinct from the body and, therefore, we tend to intuit the existence of disembodied minds at work in the world.[31] This propensity could lead us to presume ongoing relationships with dead friends and relatives, to anticipate our own survival of death, and generally to conceive of people as having immaterial souls. Similarly, several experiments suggest that children are predisposed to assume both design and intention behind natural events—leaving many psychologists and anthropologists to believe that children, left entirely to their own devices, would invent some conception of God.[32] The psychologist Margaret Evans has found that children between the ages of eight and ten, whatever their upbringing, are consistently more inclined to give a Creationist account of the natural world than their parents are.[33]

The psychologist Bruce Hood likens our susceptibility to religious ideas to the fact that people tend to develop phobias for evolutionarily relevant threats (like snakes and spiders) rather than for things that are far more likely to kill them (like automobiles and electrical sockets).[34] And because our minds have evolved to detect patterns in the world, we often detect patterns that aren't actually there—ranging from faces in the clouds to a divine hand in the workings of Nature. Hood posits an additional cognitive schema that he calls "supersense"—a tendency to infer hidden forces in the world, working for good or for ill. On his account, supersense generates beliefs in the supernatural (religious and otherwise) all on its own, and such beliefs are thereafter modulated, rather than instilled, by culture.

While religious affiliation is strictly a matter of cultural inheritance, religious attitudes (e.g., social conservatism) and behaviors (e.g., church attendance) seem to be moderately influenced by genetic factors.[35] The relevance of the brain's dopaminergic systems to religious experience, belief, and behavior is suggested by several lines of evidence, including the fact that several clinical conditions involving the neurotransmitter dopamine—mania, obsessive-compulsive disorder (OCD), and schizophrenia—are regularly associated with hyperreligiosity.[36] Serotonin has also been implicated, as drugs known to modulate it—like LSD, psilocybin, mescaline, N,N-dimethyltryptamine ("DMT"), and 3,4-methylenedioxymethamphetamine ("ecstasy")—seem to be especially potent drivers of religious/spiritual experience.[37] Links have also been drawn between religious experience and temporal lobe epilepsy.[38]

However predisposed the human mind may be to harboring religious beliefs, it remains a fact that each new generation receives a religious worldview, at least in part, in the form of linguistic propositions—far more so in some societies than in others. Whatever the evolutionary underpinnings of religion, it seems extraordinarily unlikely that there is a genetic explanation for the fact that the French, Swedes, and Japanese tend not to believe in God while Americans, Saudis, and Somalis do. Clearly, religion is largely a matter of what people teach their children to believe about the nature of reality.

Is Religious Belief Special?

While religious faith remains one of the most significant features of human life, little has been known about its relationship to ordinary belief at the level of the brain. Nor has it been clear whether religious believers and nonbelievers differ in how they evaluate statements of fact. Several neuroimaging and EEG studies have been done on religious practice and experience—primarily focusing on meditation[39] and prayer.[40] But the purpose of this research has been to evoke spiritual/contemplative experiences in religious subjects and to compare these to more conventional states of consciousness. None of these studies was designed to isolate belief itself.

Working in Mark Cohen's cognitive neuroscience lab at UCLA, I published the first neuroimaging study of belief as a general mode of cognition[41] (discussed in the previous chapter). While another group at the National Institutes of Health later looked specifically at religious belief,[42] no research had compared these two forms of belief directly. In a subsequent study, Jonas T. Kaplan and I used fMRI to measure signal changes in the brains of both Christians and nonbelievers as they evaluated the truth and falsity of religious and nonreligious propositions.[43] For each trial, subjects were presented with either a religious statement (e.g., "Jesus Christ really performed the miracles attributed to him in the Bible") or a nonreligious statement (e.g., "Alexander the Great was a very famous military leader"), and they pressed a button to indicate whether the statement was true or false.

For both groups, and in both categories of stimuli, our results were largely consistent with our earlier findings. Believing a statement to be true was associated with greater activity in the medial prefrontal cortex (MPFC), a region important for self-representation,[44] emotional associations,[45] reward,[46] and goal-driven behavior.[47] This area showed greater activity whether subjects believed statements about God and the Virgin Birth or statements about ordinary facts.[48]

Our study was designed to elicit the same responses from the two groups on nonreligious stimuli (e.g., "Eagles really exist") and opposite responses on religious stimuli (e.g., "Angels really exist"). The fact that we obtained essentially the same result for belief in both devout Christians and nonbelievers, on both categories of content, argues strongly that the difference between belief and disbelief is the same, regardless of what is being thought about.[49]

While the comparison between belief and disbelief produced similar activity for both categories of questions, the comparison of all religious thinking to all nonreligious thinking yielded a wide range of differences throughout the brain. Religious thinking was associated with greater signal in the anterior insula and the ventral striatum. The anterior insula has been linked to pain perception,[50] to the perception of pain in others,[51] and to negative feelings like disgust.[52] The ventral striatum has been frequently linked to reward.[53] It would not be surprising if religious statements provoked more positive and negative emotion in both groups of subjects.

It also seems that both Christians and nonbelievers were probably less certain of their religious beliefs. In our previous study of belief, in which a third of our stimuli were designed to provoke uncertainty, we found greater signal in the anterior cingulate cortex (ACC) when subjects could not assess the truth-value of a proposition. Here we found that religious thinking (when compared with nonreligious thinking) elicited this same pattern in both groups. Both groups also took considerably longer to respond to religious stimuli, despite the fact that these statements were no more complex than those in the other category. Perhaps both atheists and religious believers are generally less sure about the truth and falsity of religious statements.[54]

Despite vast differences in the underlying processing responsible for religious and nonreligious modes of thought, the distinction between believing and disbelieving a proposition appears to transcend content. Our research suggests that these opposing states of mind can be detected by current techniques of neuroimaging and are intimately tied to networks involved in self-representation and reward. These findings may have many areas of application—ranging from the neuropsychology of religion, to the use of "belief detection" as a surrogate for "lie detection," to understanding how the practice of science itself, and truth claims generally, emerge from the biology of the human brain. And again, results of this kind further suggest that a sharp boundary between facts and values does not exist as a matter of human cognition.

Does Religion Matter?

While religious belief may be nothing more than ordinary belief applied to religious content, such beliefs are clearly special in so far as they are deemed special by their adherents. They also appear especially resistant to change. This is often attributed to the fact that such beliefs treat matters aloof from the five senses, and thus are not usually susceptible to disproof. But this cannot be the whole story. Many religious groups, ranging from Christian sects to flying saucer cults, have anchored their worldviews to specific, testable predictions. For instance, such groups occasionally claim that a great cataclysm will befall the earth on a specific date in the near future. Inevitably, enthusiasts of these prophecies also believe that once the earth starts to shake or the floodwaters begin to rise, they will be spirited away to safety by otherworldly powers. Such people often sell their homes and other possessions, abandon their jobs, and renounce the company of skeptical friends and family—all in apparent certainty that the end of the world is at hand. When the date arrives, and with it the absolute refutation of a cherished doctrine, many members of these groups rationalize the failure of prophecy with remarkable agility.[55] In fact, such crises of faith are often attended by increased proselytizing and the manufacture of fresh prophecy—which provides the next target for zealotry and, alas, subsequent collisions with empirical reality. Phenomena of this sort have led many people to conclude that religious faith must be distinct from ordinary belief.

On the other hand, one often encounters bewildering denials of the power of religious belief, especially from scientists who are not themselves religious. For instance, the anthropologist Scott Atran alleges that "core religious beliefs are literally senseless and lacking in truth conditions"[56] and, therefore, cannot actually influence a person's behavior. According to Atran, Muslim suicide bombing has absolutely nothing to do with Islamic ideas about martyrdom and jihad; rather, it is the product of bonding among "fictive kin." Atran has publicly stated that the greatest predictor of whether a Muslim will move from merely supporting jihad to actually perpetrating an act of suicidal violence "has nothing to do with religion, it has to do with whether you belong to a soccer club."[57]

Atran's analysis of the causes of Muslim violence is relentlessly oblivious to what jihadists themselves say about their own motives.[58] He even ignores the role of religious belief in inspiring Muslim terrorism when it bursts into view in his own research. Here is a passage from one of his papers in which he summarizes his interviews with jihadists:

> All were asked questions of the sort, 'So what if your family were to be killed in retaliation for your action?' or 'What if your father were dying and your mother found out your plans for a martyrdom attack and asked you to delay until the family could get back

> on its feet?' To a person they answered along lines that there is duty to family but duty to God cannot be postponed. 'And what if your action resulted in no one's death but your own?' The typical response is, 'God will love you just the same.' For example, when these questions were posed to the alleged Emir of Jemaah Islamiyah, Abu Bakr Ba'asyir, in Jakarta's Cipinang prison in August 2005, he responded that martyrdom for the sake of jihad is the ultimate fardh 'ain, an inescapable individual obligation that trumps all others, including four of the five pillars of Islam (only profession of faith equals jihad). What matters for him as for most would-be martyrs and their sponsors I have interviewed is the martyr's intention and commitment to God, so that blowing up only oneself has the same value and reward as killing however many of the enemy.[59]

What may appear to the untutored eye as patent declarations of religious conviction are, on Atran's account, merely "sacred values" and "moral obligations" shared among kin and confederates; they have no propositional content. Atran's bizarre interpretation of his own data ignores the widespread Muslim belief that martyrs go straight to Paradise and secure a place for their nearest and dearest there. In light of such religious ideas, solidarity within a community takes on another dimension. And phrases like "God will love you just the same" have a meaning worth unpacking. First, it is pretty clear that Atran's subjects believe that God exists. What is God's love good for? It is good for escaping the fires of hell and reaping an eternity of happiness after death. To say that the behavior of Muslim jihadists has nothing to do with their religious beliefs is like saying that honor killings have nothing to do with what their perpetrators believe about women, sexuality, and male honor.

Beliefs have consequences. In Tanzania, there is a growing criminal trade in the body parts of albino human beings—as it is widely imagined that albino flesh has magical properties. Fishermen even weave the hair of albinos into their nets with the expectation of catching more fish.[60] I would not be in the least surprised if an anthropologist like Atran refused to accept this macabre irrationality at face value and sought a "deeper" explanation that had nothing to do with the belief in the magical power of albino body parts. Many social scientists have a perverse inability to accept that people often believe exactly what they say they believe. In fact, the belief in the curative powers of human flesh is widespread in Africa, and it used to be common in the West. It is said that "mummy paint" (a salve made from ground mummy parts) was applied to Lincoln's wounds as he lay dying outside Ford's Theatre. As late as 1908 the Merck medical catalog sold "genuine Egyptian mummy" to treat epilepsy, abscesses, fractures and the like.[61] How can we explain this behavior apart from the content of people's beliefs? We need not try. Especially when, given the clarity with which they articulate their core beliefs, there is no mystery whatsoever as to why certain people behave as they do.

The Diagnostic and Statistical Manual of Mental Disorders (DSM-IV), published by the American Psychiatric Association, is the most widely used reference work for clinicians in the field of mental health. It defines "delusion" as a "false belief based on incorrect inference about external reality that is firmly sustained despite what almost everyone else believes and despite what constitutes incontrovertible and obvious proof or evidence to the contrary." Lest we think that certain religious beliefs might fall under the shadow of this definition, the authors exonerate religious doctrines, in principle, in the next sentence: "The belief is not one ordinarily accepted by other members of the person's culture or subculture (e.g., it is not an article of religious faith)" (p. 765). As others have observed, there are several problems with this definition.[62] As any clinician can attest, delusional patients often suffer from *religious* delusions. And the criterion that a belief be widely shared suggests that a belief can be delusional in one context and normative in another, even if the reasons for believing it are held constant. Does a lone psychotic become sane merely by attracting a crowd of devotees? If we are measuring sanity in terms of sheer numbers of subscribers, then atheists and agnostics in the United States must be delusional: a diagnosis which would impugn 93 percent of the members of the National Academy of Sciences.[63] There are, in fact, more people in the United States who cannot read than who doubt the existence of Yahweh.[64] In twenty-first-century America, disbelief in the God of Abraham is about as fringe a phenomenon as can be named. But so is a commitment to the basic principles of scientific thinking—not to mention a detailed understanding of genetics, special relativity, or Bayesian statistics.

The boundary between mental illness and respectable religious belief can be difficult to discern. This was made especially vivid in a recent court case involving a small group of very committed Christians accused of murdering an eighteen-month-old infant.[65] The trouble began when the boy ceased to say "Amen" before meals. Believing that he had developed "a spirit of rebellion," the group, which included the boy's mother, deprived him of food and water until he died. Upon being indicted, the mother accepted an unusual plea agreement: she vowed to cooperate in the prosecution of her codefendants under the condition that all charges be dropped if her son were resurrected. The prosecutor accepted this plea provided that that resurrection was "Jesus-like" and did not include reincarnation as another person or animal. Despite the fact that this band of lunatics carried the boy's corpse around in a green suitcase for over a year, awaiting his reanimation, there is no reason to believe that any of them suffer from a mental illness. It is obvious, however, that they suffer from religion.

The Clash Between Faith and Reason

Introspection offers no clue that our experience of the world around us, and of ourselves within it, depends upon voltage changes and chemical interactions taking place inside our heads. And yet a century and a half of brain science declares it to be so. What will it mean to finally understand the most prized, lamented, and intimate features of our subjectivity in terms of neural circuits and information processing?

With respect to our current scientific understanding of the mind, the major religions remain wedded to doctrines that are growing less plausible by the day. While the ultimate relationship between consciousness and matter has not been settled, any naïve conception of a soul can now be jettisoned on account of the mind's obvious dependency upon the brain. The idea that there might be an immortal soul capable of reasoning, feeling love, remembering life events, etc., all the while being metaphysically independent of the brain, seems untenable given that damage to the relevant neural circuits obliterates these capacities in a living person. Does the soul of a person suffering from total *aphasia* (loss of language ability) still speak and think fluently? This is rather like asking whether the soul of a diabetic produces abundant insulin. The specific character of the mind's dependency on the brain also suggests that there cannot be a unified self at work in each of us. There are simply too many separable components to the human mind—each susceptible to independent disruption—for there to be a single entity to stand as rider to the horse.[66]

The soul doctrine suffers further upheaval in light of the fatal resemblance of the human brain to the brains of other animals. The obvious continuity of our mental powers with those of ostensibly soulless primates raises special difficulties. If the joint ancestors of chimpanzees and human beings did not have souls, when did we acquire ours?[67] Many of the world's major religions ignore these awkward facts and simply assert that human beings possess a unique form of subjectivity that has no connection to the inner lives of other animals. The soul is the preeminent keepsake here, but the claim of human uniqueness generally extends to the moral sense as well: animals are thought to possess nothing like it. Our moral intuitions must, therefore, be the work of God. Given the pervasiveness of this claim, intellectually honest scientists cannot help but fall into overt conflict with religion regarding the origins of morality.

Nevertheless, it is widely imagined that there is no conflict, in principle, between science and religion because many scientists are themselves "religious," and some even believe in the God of Abraham and in the truth of ancient miracles. Even religious extremists value *some* of the products of science—antibiotics, computers, bombs, etc.—and these seeds of inquisitiveness, we are told, can be patiently nurtured in a way that offers no insult to religious faith.

This prayer of reconciliation goes by many names and now has many advocates. But it is based on a fallacy. The fact that some scientists do not detect any problem with religious faith merely proves that a juxtaposition of good ideas and bad ones is possible. Is there a conflict between marriage and infidelity? The two regularly coincide. The fact that intellectual honesty can be confined to a ghetto—in a single brain, in an institution, or in a culture—does not mean that there isn't a perfect contradiction between reason and faith, or between the worldview of science taken as a whole and those advanced by the world's "great," and greatly discrepant, religions.

What *can* be shown by example is how poorly religious scientists manage to reconcile reason and faith when they actually attempt to do so. Few such efforts have received more public attention than the work of Francis Collins. Collins is currently the director of the National Institutes of Health, having been appointed to the post by President Obama. One must admit that his credentials were impeccable: he is a physical chemist, a medical geneticist, and the former head of the Human Genome Project. He is also, by his own account, living proof that there can be no conflict between science and religion. I will discuss Collins's views at some length, because he is widely considered the most impressive example of "sophisticated" faith in action.

In 2006, Collins published a bestselling book, *The Language of God*,[68] in which he claimed to demonstrate "a consistent and profoundly satisfying harmony" between twenty-first-century science and Evangelical Christianity. *The Language of God* is a genuinely astonishing book. To read it is to witness nothing less than an intellectual suicide. It is, however, a suicide that has gone almost entirely unacknowledged: The body yielded to the rope; the neck snapped; the breath subsided; and the corpse dangles in ghastly discomposure even now—and yet polite people everywhere continue to celebrate the great man's health.

Collins is regularly praised by his fellow scientists for what he is not: he is not a "young earth creationist," nor is he a proponent of "intelligent design." Given the state of the evidence for evolution, these are both very good things for a scientist not to be. But as director of the NIH, Collins now has more responsibility for biomedical and health-related research than any person on earth, controlling an annual budget of more than $30 billion. He is also one of the foremost representatives of science in the United States. We need not congratulate him for believing in evolution.

Here is how Collins, as a scientist and educator, summarizes his understanding of the universe for the general public (what follows are a series of slides, presented in order, from a lecture Collins gave at the University of California, Berkeley, in 2008):

Slide 1

Almighty God, who is not limited in space or time, created a universe 13.7 billion years ago with its parameters precisely tuned to allow the development of complexity over long periods of time.

Slide 2

God's plan included the mechanism of evolution to create the marvelous diversity of living things on our planet. Most especially, that creative plan included human beings.

Slide 3

After evolution had prepared a sufficiently advanced "house" (the human brain), God gifted humanity with the knowledge of good and evil (the Moral Law), with free will, and with an immortal soul.

Slide 4

We humans use our free will to break the moral law, leading to our estrangement from God. For Christians, Jesus is the solution to that estrangement.

Slide 5

If the Moral Law is just a side effect of evolution, then there is no such thing as good or evil. It's all an illusion. We've been hoodwinked. Are any of us, especially the strong atheists, really prepared to live our lives within that worldview?

Is it really so difficult to perceive a conflict between Collin's science and his religion? Just imagine how scientific it would seem to most Americans if Collins, as a devout Hindu, informed his audience that Lord Brahma had created the universe and now sleeps; Lord Vishnu sustains it and tinkers with our DNA (in a way that respects the law of karma and rebirth); and Lord Shiva will eventually destroy it in a great conflagration.[69] Is there any chance that Collins would be running the NIH if he were an outspoken polytheist?

Early in his career as a physician, Collins attempted to fill the God-shaped hole in his life by studying the world's major religions. He admits, however, that he did not get very far with this research before seeking the tender mercies of "a Methodist minister who lived down the street." In fact, Collins's ignorance of world religion appears prodigious. For instance, he regularly repeats the Christian canard about Jesus being the only person in human history who ever claimed to be God (as though this would render the opinions of an uneducated carpenter of the first century especially credible). Collins seems oblivious to the fact that saints, yogis, charlatans, and schizophrenics by the thousands claim to be God at this very instant. And it has always been thus. Forty years ago, a very unprepossessing Charles Manson convinced a band of misfits in the San Fernando Valley that he was both God *and* Jesus. Should we, therefore, consult Manson on questions of cosmology? He still walks among us—or at least sits—in Corcoran State Prison. The fact that Collins, as both a scientist and as an influential apologist for religion, repeatedly emphasizes the silly fiction of Jesus' singular self-appraisal is one of many embarrassing signs that he has lived too long in the echo chamber of Evangelical Christianity.

But the pilgrim continues his progress: next, we learn that Collins's uncertainty about the identity of God could not survive a collision with C. S. Lewis. The following passage from Lewis proved decisive:

> I am trying here to prevent anyone saying the really foolish thing that people often say about Him: "I'm ready to accept Jesus as a

> great moral teacher, but I don't accept His claim to be God." That is one thing we must not say. A man who was merely a man and said the sort of things Jesus said would not be a great moral teacher. He would either be a lunatic—on a level with the man who says He is a poached egg—or else He would be the Devil of Hell. You must make your choice. Either this man was, and is, the Son of God: or else a madman or something worse. You can shut Him up for a fool, you can spit at Him and kill Him as a demon; or you can fall at His feet and call him Lord and God. But let us not come with any patronizing nonsense about His being a great human teacher. He has not left that open to us. He did not intend to.

Collins provides this pabulum for our contemplation and then describes how it irrevocably altered his view of the universe:

> Lewis was right. I had to make a choice. A full year had passed since I decided to believe in some sort of God, and now I was being called to account. On a beautiful fall day, as I was hiking in the Cascade Mountains during my first trip west of the Mississippi, the majesty and beauty of God's creation overwhelmed my resistance. As I rounded a corner and saw a beautiful and unexpected frozen waterfall, hundreds of feet high, I knew the search was over. The next morning, I knelt in the dewy grass as the sun rose and surrendered to Jesus Christ.[70]

This is self-deception at full gallop. It is simply astounding that this passage was written by a scientist with the intent of demonstrating the compatibility of faith and reason. And if we thought Collins's reasoning could grow no more labile, he has since divulged that the waterfall was frozen into *three* streams, which put him in mind of the Holy Trinity.[71]

It should go without saying that if a frozen waterfall can confirm the specific tenets of Christianity, anything can confirm anything. But this truth was not obvious to Collins as he "knelt in the dewy grass," and it is not obvious to him now. Nor was it obvious to the editors of *Nature*, which is the most important scientific publication in any language. The journal praised Collins for engaging "with people of faith to explore how science—both in its mode of thought and its results—is consistent with their religious beliefs."[72] According to *Nature,* Collins was engaged in the "moving" and "laudable" exercise of building "a bridge across the social and intellectual divide that exists between most of U.S. academia and the so-called heartlands." And here is Collins, hard at work on that bridge:

> As believers, you are right to hold fast to the concept of God as Creator; you are right to hold fast to the truths of the Bible; you are right to hold fast to the conclusion that science offers no answers to the most pressing questions of human existence; and you are right to hold fast to the certainty that the claims of atheistic materialism must be steadfastly resisted.[73]

> God, who is not limited to space and time, created the universe and established natural laws that govern it. Seeking to populate this otherwise sterile universe with living creatures, God chose the elegant mechanism of evolution to create microbes, plants, and animals of all sorts. Most remarkably, God intentionally chose the same mechanism to give rise to special creatures who would have intelligence, a knowledge of right and wrong, free will, and a desire to seek fellowship with Him. He also knew these creatures would ultimately choose to disobey the Moral Law.[74]

Imagine: the year is 2006; half of the American population believes that the universe is 6,000 years old; our president has just used his first veto to block federal funding for the world's most promising medical research on religious grounds; and one of the foremost scientists in the land has this to say, straight from the heart (if not the brain).

Of course, once the eyes of faith have opened, confirmation can be found everywhere. Here Collins considers whether to accept the directorship of the Human Genome Project:

> I spent a long afternoon praying in a little chapel, seeking guidance about this decision. I did not "hear" God speak—in fact,

> I've never had that experience. But during those hours, ending in an evensong service that I had not expected, a peace settled over me. A few days later, I accepted the offer.[75]

One hopes to see, but does not find, the phrase "Dear Diary" framing these solemn excursions from honest reasoning. Again we find a peculiar emphasis on the most unremarkable violations of expectation: just as Collins had not expected to see a frozen waterfall, he had not expected an evensong service. How unlikely would it be to encounter an evensong service (generally celebrated just before sunset) while spending "a long afternoon praying in a little chapel"? And what of Collins's feeling of "peace"? We are clearly meant to view it as some indication, however slight, of the veracity of his religious beliefs. Elsewhere in his book Collins states, correctly, that "monotheism and polytheism cannot both be right." But doesn't he think that at some point in the last thousand years a Hindu or two has prayed in a temple, perhaps to the elephant-headed god Ganesh, and experienced similar feelings of peace? What might he, as a scientist, make of this fact?

I should say at this point that I see nothing irrational about seeking the states of mind that lie at the core of many of the world's religions. Compassion, awe, devotion, and feelings of oneness are surely among the most valuable experiences a person can have. What is irrational, and irresponsible in a scientist and educator, is to make unjustified and unjustifiable claims about the structure of the universe, about the divine origin of certain books, and about the future of humanity on the basis of such experiences. And by the standards of even ordinary contemplative experience, the phenomena that Collins puts forward in support of his religious beliefs scarcely merit discussion. A beautiful waterfall? An unexpected church service? A feeling of peace? The fact that these are the most salient landmarks on Collins's journey out of bondage may be the most troubling detail in this positive sea of troubles.

Collins argues that science makes belief in God "intensely plausible"—the Big Bang, the fine-tuning of Nature's constants, the emergence of complex life, the effectiveness of mathematics,[76] all suggest to him that a "loving, logical, and consistent" God exists. But when challenged with alternate (and far more plausible) accounts of these phenomena—or with evidence that suggests that God might be unloving, illogical, inconsistent, or, indeed, absent—Collins declares that God stands outside of Nature, and thus science cannot address the question of His existence at all. Similarly, Collins insists that our moral intuitions attest to God's existence, to His perfectly moral character, and to His desire to have fellowship with every member of our species; but when our moral intuitions recoil at the casual destruction of innocent children by tidal wave or earthquake, Collins assures us that our time-bound notions of good and evil cannot be trusted and that God's will is a perfect mystery.[77] As is often the case with religious apology, it is a case of heads, faith wins; tails, reason loses.

Like most Christians, Collins believes in a suite of canonical miracles, including the virgin birth and literal resurrection of Jesus Christ. He cites N. T. Wright[78] and John Polkinghorne[79] as the best authorities on these matters, and when pressed on points of theology, he recommends that people consult their books for further illumination. To give readers a taste of this literature, here is Polkinghorne describing the physics of the coming resurrection of the dead:

> If we regard human beings as psychosomatic unities, as I believe both the Bible and contemporary experience of the intimate connection between mind and brain encourage us to do, then the soul will have to be understood in an Aristotelian sense as the "form," or information-bearing pattern, of the body. Though this pattern is dissolved at death it seems perfectly rational to believe that it will be remembered by God and reconstituted in a divine act of resurrection. The "matter" of the world to come, which will be the carrier of the reembodiment, will be the transformed matter of the present universe, itself redeemed by God beyond *its* cosmic death. The resurrected universe is not a second attempt by the Creator to produce a world *ex nihilo* but it is the transmutation of the present world in an act of new creation *ex vetere*. God

> will then truly be "all in all" (1 Cor. 15:28) in a totally sacramental universe whose divine infused "matter" will be delivered from the transience and decay inherent in the present physical process. Such mysterious and exciting beliefs depend for their motivation not only on the faithfulness of God, but also on Christ's resurrection, understood as the seminal event from which the new creation grows, and indeed also on the detail of the empty tomb, with its implication that the Lord's risen and glorified body is the transmutation of his dead body, just as the world to come will be the transformation of this present mortal world.[80]

These beliefs are, indeed, "mysterious and exciting." As it happens, Polkinghorne is also a scientist. The problem, however, is that it is impossible to differentiate his writing on religion—which now fills an entire shelf of books—from an extraordinarily patient Sokal-style hoax.[81] If one intended to embarrass the religious establishment with carefully constructed nonsense, this is exactly the sort of pseudoscience, pseudoscholarship, and pseudoreasoning one would employ. Unfortunately, I see no reason to doubt Polkinghorne's sincerity. Neither, it would seem, does Francis Collins.

Even for a scientist of Collins's stature, who has struggled to reconcile his belief in the divinity of Jesus with modern science, it all boils down to the "empty tomb." Collins freely admits that if all his scientific arguments for the plausibility of God were proven to be in error, his faith would be undiminished, as it is founded upon the belief, shared by all serious Christians, that the Gospel account of the miracles of Jesus is true. The problem, however, is that miracle stories are as common as house dust, even in the twenty-first century. For instance, all of Jesus' otherworldly powers have been attributed to the South Indian guru Sathya Sai Baba by vast numbers of living eyewitnesses. Sai Baba even claims to have been born of a virgin. This is actually not an uncommon claim in the history of religion, or in history generally. Even worldly men like Genghis Khan and Alexander were once thought to have been born of virgins (parthenogenesis apparently offers no guarantee that a man will turn the other cheek). Thus, Collins's faith is predicated on the claim that miracle stories of the sort that today surround a person like Sathya Sai Baba—and do not even merit an hour on cable television—somehow become especially credible when set in the prescientific religious context of the first-century Roman Empire, decades *after* their supposed occurrence, as evidenced by discrepant and fragmentary copies of copies of copies of ancient Greek manuscripts.[82] It is on this basis that the current head of the NIH recommends that we believe the following propositions:

1. Jesus Christ, a carpenter by trade, was born of a virgin, ritually murdered as a scapegoat for the collective sins of his species, and then resurrected from death after an interval of three days.
2. He promptly ascended, bodily, to "heaven"—where, for two millennia, he has eavesdropped upon (and, on occasion, even answered) the simultaneous prayers of billions of beleaguered human beings.
3. Not content to maintain this numinous arrangement indefinitely, this invisible carpenter will one day return to earth to judge humanity for its sexual indiscretions and skeptical doubts, at which time he will grant immortality to anyone who has had the good fortune to be convinced, on Mother's knee, that this baffling litany of miracles is the most important series of truths ever revealed about the cosmos.
4. Every other member of our species, past and present, from Cleopatra to Einstein, no matter what his or her terrestrial accomplishments, will be consigned to a far less desirable fate, best left unspecified.
5. In the meantime, God/Jesus may or may not intervene in our world, as He pleases, curing the occasional end-stage cancer (or not), answering an especially earnest prayer for guidance (or not), consoling the bereaved (or not), through His perfectly wise and loving agency.

Just how many scientific laws would be violated by this scheme? One is tempted to say "all of them." And yet, judging from the way that journals like *Nature* have treated Collins, one can only conclude that there is nothing in the scientific worldview, or in the intellectual rigor and self-criticism that gave rise to it, that casts these convictions in an unfavorable light.

Prior to his appointment as head of the NIH, Collins started an organization called the BioLogos Foundation, whose purpose (in the words of its mission statement) is to communicate "the compatibility of the Christian faith with scientific discoveries about the origins of the universe and life." BioLogos is funded by the Templeton Foundation, an organization that claims to seek answers to "life's biggest questions," but appears primarily dedicated to erasing the boundary between religion and science. Because of its astonishing wealth, Templeton seems able to purchase the complicity of otherwise secular academics as it seeks to rebrand religious faith as a legitimate arm of science. True to form, *Nature* has adopted an embarrassingly supine posture with respect to Templeton as well.[83]

Would Collins have received the same treatment in *Nature* if he had argued for the compatibility between science and witchcraft, astrology, or Tarot cards? On the contrary, he would have been met by an inferno of criticism. As a point of comparison, we should recall that the biochemist Rupert Sheldrake had his academic career neatly decapitated by a single *Nature* editorial.[84] In his book *A New Science of Life*, Sheldrake advanced a theory of "morphic resonance," in an attempt to account for how living systems and other patterns in nature develop.[85] Needless to say, the theory stands a very good chance of being utterly wrong. But there is not a single sentence in Sheldrake's book to rival the intellectual dishonesty that Collins achieves on nearly every page of *The Language of God*.[86] What accounts for the double standard? Clearly, it remains taboo to criticize mainstream religion (which, in the West, means Christianity, Judaism, and Islam).

According to Collins, the moral law applies exclusively to human beings:

> Though other animals may at times appear to show glimmerings of a moral sense, they are certainly not widespread, and in many

> instances other species' behavior seems to be in dramatic contrast to any sense of universal rightness.[87]

One wonders if the author has ever read a newspaper. The behavior of humans offers no such "dramatic contrast"? How badly must human beings behave to put this "sense of universal rightness" in doubt? While no other species can match us for altruism, none can match us for sadistic cruelty either. And just how widespread must "glimmerings" of morality be among other animals before Collins—who, after all, knows a thing or two about genes—begins to wonder whether our moral sense has evolutionary precursors? What if mice show greater distress at the suffering of familiar mice than unfamiliar ones? (They do.[88]) What if monkeys will starve themselves to prevent their cage mates from receiving painful shocks? (They will.[89]) What if chimps have a demonstrable sense of fairness when receiving food rewards? (They have.[90]) What if dogs do too? (Ditto.[91]) Wouldn't these be precisely the sorts of findings one would expect if our morality were the product of evolution?

Collins's case for the supernatural origin of morality rests on the further assertion that there can be no evolutionary explanation for genuine altruism. Because self-sacrifice cannot increase the likelihood that an individual creature will survive and reproduce, truly self-sacrificing behavior stands as a primordial rejoinder to any biological account of morality. In Collins's view, therefore, the mere existence of altruism offers compelling evidence of a personal God. A moment's thought reveals, however, that if we were to accept this neutered biology, almost everything about us would be bathed in the warm glow of religious mystery. Smoking cigarettes isn't a healthy habit and is unlikely to offer an adaptive advantage—and there were no cigarettes in the Paleolithic—but this habit is very widespread and compelling. Is God, by any chance, a tobacco farmer? Collins can't seem to see that human morality and selfless love may arise from more basic biological and psychological traits, which were themselves products of evolution. It is hard to interpret this oversight in light of his scientific training. If one didn't know better, one might be tempted to conclude that religious dogmatism presents an obstacle to scientific reasoning.

There are, of course, ethical implications to believing that human beings are the only species made in God's image and vouchsafed with "immortal souls." Concern about souls is a very poor guide to ethical behavior—that is, to actually mitigating the suffering of conscious creatures like ourselves. The belief that the soul enters the zygote at (or very near) the moment of conception leads to spurious worries about the fate of undifferentiated cells in Petri dishes and, therefore, to profound qualms over embryonic stem cell research. Rather often, a belief in souls leaves people indifferent to the suffering of creatures thought not to possess them. There are many species of animals that can suffer in ways that three-day-old human embryos cannot. The use of apes in medical research, the exposure of whales and dolphins to military sonar[92]—these are real ethical dilemmas, with real suffering at issue. Concern over human embryos smaller than the period at the end of this sentence—when, for years they have constituted one of the most promising contexts for medical research—is one of the many delusional products of religion that has led to an ethical blind alley, and to terrible failures of compassion. While Collins appears to support embryonic stem-cell research, he does so after much (literal) soul searching and under considerable theological duress. Everything he has said and written about the subject needlessly complicates an ethical question that is—if one is actually concerned about human and animal well-being—utterly straightforward.

The ethics of embryonic stem-cell research, which currently entails the destruction of human embryos, can be judged only by considering what embryos at the 150-cell-stage actually are. We must contemplate their destruction in light of how we treat organisms at similar and greater stages of complexity, as well as how we treat human beings at later stages of development. For instance, there are a variety of conditions that can occur during gestation, the remedy for which entails the destruction of far more developed embryos—and yet these interventions offer far less potential benefit to society. Curiously, no one objects to such procedures. A child can be born with his underdeveloped yet living twin lodged inside him—a condition known as *fetus in fetu*. Occasionally this condition isn't discovered until years after birth, when the first child complains about having something moving around inside his body. This second child is then removed like a tumor and destroyed.[93] As God seems to love diversity, there are countless permutations of this condition, and twins can fuse in almost any way imaginable. The second twin can also be a disorganized mass called a *teratoma*. Needless to say, any parasitic twin, however disorganized, will be a far more developed entity than an embryo at the 150-cell stage. Even the intentional sacrifice of one conjoined ("Siamese") twin to save the other has occurred in the United States, with shared organs being given to the survivor. In fact, there have been cases where unshared organs have been transferred from the twin that is to be sacrificed.[94]

Some have argued that the "viability" of an organism is the primary issue here: for without some extraordinary intervention such twins cannot survive. But many fully developed human beings answer to this condition of utter dependency at some point in their lives (e.g., a kidney patient on dialysis). And embryos themselves are not viable unless placed in the proper conditions. Indeed, embryos could be engineered to not be viable past a certain age even if implanted in a womb. Would this obviate the ethical concerns of those who oppose embryonic stem-cell research?

At the time of this writing, the Obama administration still has not removed the most important impediments to embryonic stem-cell research. Currently, federal funding is only allowed for work on stem cells that have been derived from surplus embryos at fertility clinics. This delicacy is a clear concession to the religious convictions of the American electorate. While Collins seems willing to go further and support research on embryos created through somatic-cell nuclear transfer (SCNT), he is very far from being a voice of ethical clarity in this debate. For instance, he considers embryos created through SCNT to be distinct from those formed through the union of sperm and egg because the former are "not part of God's plan to create a human individual" while "the latter is very much part of God's plan, carried out through the millennia by our own species and many others."[95] What is to be gained in a serious discussion of bioethics by talking about "God's plan"? If such embryos were brought to term and became sentient and suffering human beings, would it be ethical to kill these people and harvest their organs because they had been conceived apart from "God's plan"? While Collins's stewardship of the NIH seems unlikely to impede our mincing progress on embryonic stem-cell research, his appointment is one of President Obama's efforts to split the difference between real science and real ethics on the one hand and religious superstition and taboo on the other.

Collins has written that "science offers no answers to the most pressing questions of human existence" and that "the claims of atheistic materialism must be steadfastly resisted." One can only hope that these convictions will not affect his judgment at the NIH. As I have argued throughout this book, understanding human well-being at the level of the brain might very well offer some answers to the most pressing questions of human existence—questions like, *Why do we suffer? How can we achieve the deepest forms of happiness?* Or, indeed, *Is it possible to love one's neighbor as oneself?* And wouldn't any effort to explain human nature without reference to a soul, and to explain morality without reference to God, constitute "atheistic materialism"? Is it really wise to entrust the future of biomedical research in the United States to a man who believes that understanding ourselves through science is impossible, while our resurrection from death is inevitable?

When I criticized President Obama's appointment of Collins in *The New York Times,* many readers considered it an overt expression of "intolerance."[96] For instance, the biologist Kenneth Miller claimed in a letter to the editor that my view was purely the product of my own "deeply held prejudices against religion" and that I opposed Collins merely because "he is a Christian."[97] Writing in *The Guardian,* Andrew Brown called my criticism of Collins a "fantastically illiberal and embryonically totalitarian position that goes against every possible notion of human rights and even the American constitution." Miller and Brown clearly feel that unjustified beliefs and disordered thinking should not be challenged as long as they are associated with a mainstream religion—and that to do so is synonymous with bigotry. They are not alone.

There is now a large and growing literature—spanning dozens of books and hundreds of articles—attacking Richard Dawkins, Daniel Dennett, Christopher Hitchens, and me (the so-called New Atheists) for our alleged incivility, bias, and ignorance of how "sophisticated" believers practice their faith. It is often said that we caricature religion, taking its most extreme forms to represent the whole. We do no such thing. We simply do what a paragon of sophisticated faith like Francis Collins does: we take the specific claims of religion seriously.

Many of our secular critics worry that if we oblige people to choose between reason and faith, they will choose faith and cease to support scientific research; if, on the other hand, we ceaselessly reiterate that there is no conflict between religion and science, we might cajole great multitudes into accepting the truth of evolution (as though this were an end in itself). Here is a version of this charge that, I fear, most people would accept, taken from journalist Chris Mooney and marine biologist Sheril Kirshenbaum's book *Unscientific America*:

> If the goal is to create an America more friendly toward science and reason, the combativeness of the New Atheists is strongly counterproductive. If anything, they work in ironic combination with their dire enemies, the anti-science conservative Christians who populate the creation science and intelligent design movements, to ensure we'll continue to be polarized over subjects like the teaching of evolution when we don't have to be. America is a very religious nation, and if forced to choose between faith and science, vast numbers of Americans will select the former. The New Atheists err in insisting that such a choice needs to be made. Atheism is not the logically inevitable outcome of scientific reasoning, any more than intelligent design is a necessary corollary of religious faith. A great many scientists believe in God with no sense of internal contradiction, just as many religious believers accept evolution as the correct theory to explain the development, diversity, and inter-relatedness of life on Earth. The New Atheists, like the fundamentalists they so despise, are setting up a false dichotomy that can only damage the cause of scientific

> literacy for generations to come. It threatens to leave science itself caught in the middle between extremes, unable to find cover in a destructive, seemingly unending, culture war.[98]

The first thing to observe is that Mooney and Kirshenbaum are confused about the nature of the problem. The goal is not to get more Americans to merely accept the truth of evolution (or any other scientific theory); the goal is to get them to value the principles of reasoning and educated discourse that now make a belief in evolution obligatory. Doubt about evolution is merely a symptom of an underlying condition; the condition is faith itself—conviction without sufficient reason, hope mistaken for knowledge, bad ideas protected from good ones, good ideas obscured by bad ones, wishful thinking elevated to a principle of salvation, etc. Mooney and Kirshenbaum seem to imagine that we can get people to value intellectual honesty by lying to them.

While it is invariably advertised as an expression of "respect" for people of faith, the accommodationism that Mooney and Kirshenbaum recommend is nothing more than naked condescension, motivated by fear. They assure us that people will choose religion over science, *no matter how good a case is made against religion.* In certain contexts, this fear is probably warranted. I wouldn't be eager to spell out the irrationality of Islam while standing in the Great Mosque in Mecca. But let's be honest about how Mooney and Kirshenbaum view public discourse in the United States: *Watch what you say, or the Christian mob will burn down the Library of Alexandria all over again.* By comparison, the "combativeness" of the "New Atheists" seems quite collegial. We are merely guilty of assuming that our fellow *Homo sapiens* possess the requisite intelligence and emotional maturity to respond to rational argument, satire, and ridicule on the subject of religion—just as they respond to these discursive pressures on all other subjects. Of course, we could be wrong. But let's admit which side in this debate currently views our neighbors as dangerous children and which views them as adults who might prefer not to be completely mistaken about the nature of reality.

Finally, we come to the kernel of confusion that has been the subject of this section—the irrelevant claim that "a great many scientists believe in God with no sense of internal contradiction."[99] The fact that certain people can reason poorly with a clear conscience—or can do so while *saying* that they have a clear conscience—proves absolutely nothing about the compatibility of religious and scientific ideas, goals, or ways of thinking. It is possible to be wrong and to not know it (we call this "ignorance"). It is possible to be wrong and to know it, but to be reluctant to incur the social cost of admitting this publicly (we call this "hypocrisy"). And it may also be possible to be wrong, to dimly glimpse this fact, but to allow the fear of being wrong to increase one's commitment to one's erroneous beliefs (we call this "self-deception"). It seems clear that these frames of mind do an unusual amount of work in the service of religion.

There is an epidemic of scientific ignorance in the United States. This isn't surprising, as very few scientific truths are self-evident and many are deeply counterintuitive. It is by no means obvious that empty space has structure or that we share a common ancestor with both the housefly and the banana. It can be difficult to think like a scientist (even, we have begun to see, when one is a scientist). But it would seem that few things make thinking like a scientist more difficult than an attachment to religion.

Chapter 5

THE FUTURE OF HAPPINESS

No one has ever mistaken me for an optimist. And yet when I consider one of the more pristine sources of pessimism—the moral development of our species—I find reasons for hope. Despite our perennial bad behavior, our moral progress seems to me unmistakable. Our powers of empathy are clearly growing. Today, we are surely more likely to act for the benefit of humanity as a whole than at any point in the past.

Of course, the twentieth century delivered some unprecedented horrors. But those of us who live in the developed world are becoming increasingly disturbed by our capacity to do one another harm. We are less tolerant of "collateral damage" in times of war—undoubtedly because we now see images of it—and we are less comfortable with ideologies that demonize whole populations, justifying their abuse or outright destruction.

Consider the degree to which racism in the United States has diminished in the last hundred years. Racism is still a problem, of course. But the evidence of change is undeniable. Most readers will have seen photos of lynchings from the first half of the twentieth century, in which whole towns turned out, as though for a carnival, simply to enjoy the sight of some young man or woman being tortured to death and strung up on a tree or lamppost for all to see. These pictures often reveal bankers, lawyers, doctors, teachers, church elders, newspaper editors, policemen, even the occasional senator and congressman, smiling in their Sunday best, having consciously posed for a postcard photo under a dangling, lacerated, and often partially cremated person. Such images are shocking enough. But realize that these genteel people often took souvenirs of the body—teeth, ears, fingers, kneecaps, genitalia, and internal organs—home to show their friends and family. Sometimes, they even displayed these ghoulish trophies in their places of business.[1]

Consider the following response to boxer Jack Johnson's successful title defense against Jim Jeffries, the so-called "Great White Hope":

A Word to the Black Man:

Do not point your nose too high
Do not swell your chest too much
Do not boast too loudly
Do not be puffed up
Let not your ambition be inordinate
Or take a wrong direction
Remember you have done nothing at all
You are just the same member of society you were last week
You are on no higher plane
Deserve no new consideration
And will get none
No man will think a bit higher of you
Because your complexion is the same
Of that of the victor at Reno[2]

A modern reader can only assume that this dollop of racist hatred appeared on a leaflet printed by the Ku Klux Klan. On the contrary, this was the measured opinion of the editors at the *Los Angeles Times* exactly a century ago. Is it conceivable that our mainstream media will ever again give voice to such racism? I think it far more likely that we will proceed along our current path: racism will continue to lose its subscribers; the history of slavery in the United States will become even more flabbergasting to contemplate; and future generations will marvel at the the ways that we, too, failed in our commitment to the common good. We will embarrass our descendants, just as our ancestors embarrass us. This is moral progress.

I am bolstered in this expectation by my view of the moral landscape: the belief that morality is a genuine sphere of human inquiry, and not a mere product of culture, suggests that progress is possible. If moral truths transcend the contingencies of culture, human beings should eventually converge in their moral judgments. I am painfully aware, however, that we are living at a time when Muslims riot by the hundreds of thousands over cartoons, Catholics oppose condom use in villages decimated by AIDS, and one of the few "moral" judgments guaranteed to unite the better part of humanity is that homosexuality is an abomination. And yet I can detect moral progress even while believing that most people are profoundly confused about good and evil. I may be a greater optimist than I thought.

Science and Philosophy

Throughout this book, I have argued that the split between facts and values—and, therefore, between science and morality—is an illusion. However, the discussion has taken place on at least two levels: I have reviewed scientific data that, I believe, supports my argument; but I have made a more basic, philosophical case, the validity of which does not narrowly depend on current data. Readers may wonder how these levels are related.

First, we should observe that a boundary between science and philosophy does not always exist. Einstein famously doubted Bohr's view of quantum mechanics, and yet both physicists were armed with the same experimental findings and mathematical techniques. Was their disagreement a matter of "philosophy" or "physics"? We cannot always draw a line between scientific thinking and "mere" philosophy because all data must be interpreted against a background theory, and different theories come bundled with a fair amount of contextual reasoning. A dualist who believes in the existence of immaterial souls might say that the entire field of neuroscience is beholden to the philosophy of *physicalism* (the view that mental events should be understood as physical events), and he would be right. The assumption that the mind is the product of the brain is integral to almost everything neuroscientists do. Is physicalism a matter of "philosophy" or "neuroscience"? The answer may depend upon where one happens to be standing on a university campus. Even if we grant that only philosophers tend to think about "physicalism" per se, it remains a fact that any argument or experiment that put this philosophical assumption in doubt would be a landmark finding *for* neuroscience—likely the most important in its history. So while there are surely some philosophical views that make no contact with science, science is often a matter of philosophy in practice. It is probably worth recalling that the original name for the physical sciences was, in fact, "natural philosophy."

Throughout the sections of this book that could be aptly described as "philosophical," I make many points that have scientific implications. Most scientists treat facts and values as though they were distinct and irreconcilable in principle. I have argued that they cannot be, as anything of value must be valuable *to* someone (whether actually or potentially)—and, therefore, its value should be attributable to facts about the well-being of conscious creatures. One could call this a "philosophical" position, but it is one that directly relates to the boundaries of science. If I am correct, science has a far wider purview than many of its practitioners suppose, and its findings may one day impinge upon culture in ways that they do not expect. If I am wrong, the boundaries of science are as narrow as most people assume. This difference of view might be ascribed to "philosophy," but it is a difference that will determine the practice of science in the years to come.

Recall the work of Jonathan Haidt, discussed at some length in chapter 2: Haidt has convinced many people, both inside and outside the scientific community, that there are two types of morality: liberal morality focuses on two primary concerns (harm and fairness), while conservative morality emphasizes five (harm, fairness, authority, purity, and group loyalty). As a result, many people believe that liberals and conservatives are bound to view human behavior in incompatible ways and that science will never be able to say that one approach to morality is "better" or "truer" or more "moral" than the other.

I think that Haidt is wrong, for at least two reasons. First, I suspect that the extra factors he attributes to conservatives can be understood as further concerns about harm. That is, I believe that conservatives have the same morality as liberals do, they just have different ideas about how harm accrues in this universe.[3] There is also some research to suggest that conservatives are more prone to feelings of disgust, and this seems to especially influence their moral judgments on the subject of sex.[4] More important, whatever the differences between liberals and conservatives may or may not be, if my argument about the moral landscape is correct, one approach to morality is likely more conducive to human flourishing than the other. While my disagreement with Haidt may be more a matter of argument than of experiment at present, whichever argument prevails will affect the progress of science, as well as science's impact on the rest of culture.

The Psychology of Happiness

I have said very little in this book about the current state of psychological science as it relates to human well-being. This research—which occasionally goes by the name of "positive psychology"—is in its infancy, especially when it comes to understanding the relevant details at the level of the brain. And given the difficulty of defining human well-being, coupled with the general reluctance of scientists to challenge anyone's beliefs about it, it is sometimes hard to know what is being studied in this research. What does it mean, for instance, to compare self-reported ratings of "happiness" or "life satisfaction" between individuals or across cultures? I'm not at all sure. Clearly, a person's conception of what is possible in human life will affect her judgment of whether she has made the best use of her opportunities, met her goals, developed deep friendships, etc. Some people will go to bed tonight proud to have merely reduced their daily consumption of methamphetamine; others will be frustrated that their rank on the Forbes 400 list has slipped into the triple digits. Where one is satisfied to be in life often has a lot to do with where one has been.

I once knew a very smart and talented man who sent an email to dozens of friends and acquaintances declaring his intention to kill himself. As you might expect, this communication prompted a flurry of responses. While I did not know him well, I sent several emails urging him to seek professional counseling, to try antidepressants, to address his sleep issues, and to do a variety of other obvious things to combat depression. In each of his replies, however, he insisted that he was not depressed. He believed himself to be acting on a philosophical insight: everyone dies eventually; life, therefore, is ultimately pointless; thus, there is no reason to keep on living if one doesn't want to.

We went back and forth on these topics, as I sought to persuade him that his "insight" was itself a symptom of depression or some other mood disorder. I argued that if he simply felt better, he wouldn't believe that his life was no longer worth living. No doubt many other people had similar exchanges with him. These communications seemed to nudge him away from the precipice for a while. Four years later, however, he committed suicide.

Experiences of this kind reveal how difficult it can be to discuss the subject of human well-being. Communication on any subject can be misleading, of course, because people often use the same words quite differently. Talking about states of mind poses special difficulties, however. Was my friend really "depressed" in my sense of the term? Did he even know what I meant by "depression"? Did *I* know what I should have meant by it? For instance, are there forms of depression that have yet to be differentiated which admit of distinct remedies? And is it possible that my friend suffered from none of these? Is it, in other words, possible for a person to see no point in living another day, and to be motivated to kill himself, without experiencing any disorder of mood? Two things seem quite clear to me at this point: such questions have answers, and yet we often do not know enough about human experience to even properly discuss the questions themselves.

We can mean many things when using words like "happiness" and "well-being." This makes it difficult to study the most positive aspects of human experience scientifically. In fact, it makes it difficult for many of us to even know what goals in life are worth seeking. Just how happy and fulfilled should we expect to be in our careers or intimate relationships? Much of the skepticism I encounter when speaking about these issues comes from people who think "happiness" is a superficial state of mind and that there are far more important things in life than "being happy." Some readers may think that concepts like "well-being" and "flourishing" are similarly effete. However, I don't know of any better terms with which to signify the most positive states of being to which we can aspire. One of the virtues of thinking about a moral landscape, the heights of which remain to be discovered, is that it frees us from these semantic difficulties. Generally speaking, we need only worry about what it will mean to move "up" as opposed to "down."

Some of what psychologists have learned about human well-being confirms what everyone already knows: people tend to be happier if they have good friends, basic control over their lives, and enough money to meet their needs. Loneliness, helplessness, and poverty are not recommended. We did not need science to tell us this.

But the best of this research also reveals that our intuitions about happiness are often quite wrong. For instance, most of us feel that having more choices available to us—when seeking a mate, choosing a career, shopping for a new stove, etc.—is always desirable. But while having *some* choice is generally good, it seems that having too many options tends to undermine our feelings of satisfaction, no matter which option we choose.[5] Knowing this, it could be rational to strategically limit one's choices. Anyone who has ever remodeled a home will know the glassy-eyed anguish of having gone to one too many stores in search of the perfect faucet.

One of the most interesting things to come out of the research on human happiness is the discovery that we are very bad judges of how we will feel in the future—an ability that the psychologist Daniel Gilbert has called "affective forecasting." Gilbert and others have shown that we systematically overestimate the degree to which good and bad experiences will affect us.[6] Changes in wealth, health, age, marital status, etc., tend not to matter as much as we think they will—and yet we make our most important decisions in life based on these inaccurate assumptions. It is useful to know that what we think will matter often matters much less than we think. Conversely, things we consider trivial can actually impact our lives greatly. If you have ever been impressed by how people often rise to the occasion while experiencing great hardship but can fall to pieces over minor inconveniences, you have seen this principle at work. The general finding of this research is now uncontroversial: we are poorly placed to accurately recall the past, to perceive the present, or to anticipate the future with respect to our own happiness. It seems little wonder, therefore, that we are so often unfulfilled.

Which Self Should We Satisfy?

If you ask people to report on their level of well-being moment-to-moment—by giving them a beeper that sounds at random intervals, prompting them to record their mental state—you get one measure of how happy they are. If, however, you simply ask them how satisfied they are with their lives generally, you often get a very different measure. The psychologist Daniel Kahneman calls the first source of information "the experiencing self" and the second "the remembering self." And his justification for partitioning the human mind in this way is that these two "selves" often disagree. Indeed, they can be experimentally shown to disagree, even across a relatively brief span of time. We saw this earlier with respect to Kahneman's data on colonoscopies: because "the remembering self" evaluates any experience by reference to its peak intensity and its final moments (the "peak/end rule"), it is possible to improve its lot, at the expense of "the experiencing self," by simply prolonging an unpleasant procedure at its lowest level of intensity (and thereby reducing the negativity of future memories).

What applies to colonoscopies seems to apply elsewhere in life. Imagine, for instance, that you want to go on vacation: You are deciding between a trip to Hawaii and a trip to Rome. On Hawaii, you envision yourself swimming in the ocean, relaxing on the beach, playing tennis, and drinking mai tais. Rome will find you sitting in cafés, visiting museums and ancient ruins, and drinking an impressive amount of wine. Which vacation should you choose? It is quite possible that your "experiencing self" would be much happier on Hawaii, as indicated by an hourly tally of your emotional and sensory pleasure, while your remembering self would give a much more positive account of Rome one year hence. Which self would be right? Does the question even make sense? Kahneman observes that while most of us think our "experiencing self" must be more important, it has no voice in our decisions about what to do in life. After all, we can't choose from among experiences; we must choose from among remembered (or imagined) experiences. And, according to Kahneman, we don't tend to think about the future as a set of experiences; we think of it as a set of "anticipated memories."[7] The problem, with regard to both doing science and living one's life, is that the "remembering self" is the only one who can think and speak about the past. It is, therefore, the only one who can consciously make decisions in light of past experience.

According to Kahneman, the correlation in well-being between these two "selves" is around 0.5.[8] This is essentially the same correlation observed between identical twins, or between a person and himself a decade later.[9] It would seem, therefore, that about half the information about a person's happiness is still left on the table whichever "self" we consult. What are we to make of a "remembering self" who claims to have a wonderful life, while his "experiencing self" suffers continuous marital stress, health complaints, and career anxiety? And what of a person whose "remembering self" claims to be deeply dissatisfied—having failed to reach his most important goals—but whose moment-to-moment state of happiness is quite high? Kahneman seems to think that there is no way to reconcile disparities of this sort. If true, this would appear to present a problem for any science of morality.

It seems clear, however, that the "remembering self" is simply the "experiencing self" in one of its modes. Imagine, for instance, that you are going about your day quite happily, experiencing one moment of contentment after the next, when you run into an old rival from school. Looking like the very incarnation of success, he asks what you have made of yourself in the intervening decades. At this point your "remembering self" steps forward and, feeling great chagrin, admits "not so much." Let us say that this encounter pitches you into a crisis of self-doubt that causes you to make some drastic decisions, affecting both your family and career. All of these moments are part of the fabric of your experience, however, whether recollected or not. Conscious memories and self-evaluations are themselves experiences that lay the foundation for future experiences. Making a conscious assessment of your life, career, or marriage feels a certain way in the present and leads to subsequent thoughts and behaviors. These changes will also feel a certain way and have further implications for your future. But none of these events occur outside the continuum of your experience in the present moment (i.e., the "experiencing self").

If we could take the 2.5 billion seconds that make up the average human life and assess a person's well-being at each point in time, the distinction between the "experiencing self" and the "remembering self" would disappear. Yes, the experience of recalling the past often determines what we decide to do in the future—and this greatly affects the character of one's future experience. But it would still be true to say that in each of the 2.5 billion seconds of an average life, certain moments were pleasant, and others were painful; some were later recalled with greater or lesser fidelity, and these memories had whatever effects they had later on. Consciousness and its ever-changing contents remain the only subjective reality.

Thus, if your "remembering self" claims to have had a wonderful time in Rome, while your "experiencing self" felt only boredom, fatigue, and despair, then your "remembering self" (i.e., your recollection of the trip) is simply wrong about what it was like to be you in Rome. This becomes increasingly obvious the more we narrow our focus: Imagine a "remembering self" who thinks that you were especially happy while sitting for fifteen minutes on the Spanish Steps; while your "experiencing self" was, in fact, plunged deeper into misery for every one of those minutes than at any other point on the trip. Do we need two selves to account for this disparity? No. The vagaries of memory suffice.

As Kahneman admits, the vast majority of our experiences in life never get recalled, and the time we spend actually remembering the past is comparatively brief. Thus, the quality of most of our lives can be assessed only in terms of whatever fleeting character it has as it occurs. But this includes the time we spend recalling the past. Amid this flux, the moments in which we construct a larger story about our lives appear like glints of sunlight on a dark river: they may seem special, but they are part of the current all the same.

On Being Right or Wrong

It is clear that we face both practical and conceptual difficulties when seeking to maximize human well-being. Consider, for instance, the tensions between freedom of speech, the right to privacy, and the duty of every government to keep its citizens safe. Each of these principles seems fundamental to a healthy society. The problem, however, is that at their extremes, each is hostile to the other two. Certain forms of speech painfully violate people's privacy and can even put society itself in danger. Should I be able to film my neighbor through his bedroom window and upload this footage onto YouTube as a work of "journalism"? Should I be free to publish a detailed recipe for synthesizing smallpox? Clearly, appropriate limits to free expression exist. Likewise, too much respect for privacy would make it impossible to gather the news or to prosecute criminals and terrorists. And too zealous a commitment to protecting innocent people can lead to unbearable violations of both privacy and freedom of expression. How should we balance our commitment to these various goods?

We may never be able to answer this question with absolute precision. It seems quite clear, however, that questions like this have answers. Even if there are a thousand different ways to optimally tune these three variables, given concomitant changes in the rest of culture, there must be many more ways that are less than optimal—and people will suffer as a result.

What would it mean for a couple to decide that they *should* have a child? It probably means they think that their own well-being will tend to increase for having brought another person into the world; it should also mean that they expect their child to have a life that is, on balance, worth living. If they didn't expect these things, it's hard to see why they would want to have a child in the first place.

However, most of the research done on happiness suggests that people actually become less happy when they have children and do not begin to approach their prior level of happiness until their children leave home.[10] Let us say that you are aware of this research but imagine that you will be an exception. Of course, another body of research shows that most people think that they are exceptions to rules of this sort: there is almost nothing more common than the belief that one is above average in intelligence, wisdom, honesty, etc. But you are aware of this research as well, and it does not faze you. Perhaps, in your case, all relevant exceptions are true, and you will be precisely as happy a parent as you hope to be. However, a famous study of human achievement suggests that one of the most reliable ways to diminish a person's contributions to society is for that person to start a family.[11] How would you view your decision to have a child if you knew that all the time you spent changing diapers and playing with Legos would prevent you from developing the cure for Alzheimer's disease that was actually within your reach?

These are not empty questions. But neither are they the sorts of questions that anyone is likely to answer. The decision to have a child may always be made in the context of reasonable (and not so reasonable) expectations about the future well-being of all concerned. It seems to me that thinking in this way is, nevertheless, to contemplate the moral landscape.

If we are not able to perfectly reconcile the tension between personal and collective well-being, there is still no reason to think that they are generally in conflict. Most boats will surely rise with the same tide. It is not at all difficult to envision the global changes that would improve life for everyone: We would all be better off in a world where we devoted fewer of our resources to preparing to kill one another. Finding clean sources of energy, cures for disease, improvements in agriculture, and new ways to facilitate human cooperation are general goals that are obviously worth striving for. What does such a claim mean? It means that we have every reason to believe that the pursuit of such goals will lead upward on the slopes of the moral landscape.

The claim that science could have something important to say about values (because values relate to facts about the well-being of conscious creatures) is an argument made on first principles. As such, it doesn't rest on any specific empirical results. That does not mean that this claim couldn't be falsified, however. Clearly, if there is a more important source of value that has nothing to do with the well-being of conscious creatures (in this life or a life to come), my thesis would be disproved. As I have said, however, I cannot conceive of what such a source of value could be: for if someone claimed to have found it somewhere, it could be of no possible interest to anyone, by definition.

There are other ways that my thesis could be falsified, however. There would be no future science of morality, for instance, if human well-being were completely haphazard and unrelated to states of the brain. If some people are made happiest by brain state X, while others are made miserable by it, there would be no neural correlate of human well-being. Alternately, a neural correlate of human well-being might exist, but it could be invoked to the same degree by antithetical states of the world. In this case, there would be no connection between a person's inner life and his or her outer circumstances. If either of these scenarios were true, we could not make any general claims about human flourishing. However, if this is the way the world works, the brain would seem to be little more than insulation for the skull, and the entire field of neuroscience would constitute an elaborate and very costly method of misunderstanding the world. Again, this is an intelligible claim, but that does not mean that intelligent people should take it seriously.

It is also conceivable that a science of human flourishing could be possible, and yet people could be made equally happy by very different "moral" impulses. Perhaps there is no connection between being good and feeling good—and, therefore, no connection between moral behavior (as generally conceived) and subjective well-being. In this case, rapists, liars, and thieves would experience the same depth of happiness as the saints. This scenario stands the greatest chance of being true, while still seeming quite far-fetched. Neuroimaging work already suggests what has long been obvious through introspection: human cooperation is rewarding.[12] However, if evil turned out to be as reliable a path to happiness as goodness is, my argument about the moral landscape would still stand, as would the likely utility of neuroscience for investigating it. It would no longer be an especially "moral" landscape; rather it would be a continuum of well-being, upon which saints and sinners would occupy equivalent peaks.

Worries of this kind seem to ignore some very obvious facts about human beings: we have all evolved from common ancestors and are, therefore, far more similar than we are different; brains and primary human emotions clearly transcend culture, and they are unquestionably influenced by states of the world (as anyone who has ever stubbed his toe can attest). No one, to my knowledge, believes that there is so much variance in the requisites of human well-being as to make the above concerns seem plausible.

Whether morality becomes a proper branch of science is not really the point. Is economics a true science yet? Judging from recent events, it wouldn't appear so. Perhaps a deep understanding of economics will always elude us. But does anyone doubt that there are better and worse ways to structure an economy? Would any educated person consider it a form of bigotry to criticize another society's response to a banking crisis? Imagine how terrifying it would be if great numbers of smart people became convinced that all efforts to prevent a global financial catastrophe must be either equally valid or equally nonsensical *in principle.* And yet this is precisely where we stand on the most important questions in human life.

Currently, most scientists believe that answers to questions of human value will fall perpetually beyond our reach—not because human subjectivity is too difficult to study, or the brain too complex, but because there is no intellectual justification for speaking about right and wrong, or good and evil, across cultures. Many people also believe that nothing much depends on whether we find a universal foundation for morality. It seems to me, however, that in order to fulfill our deepest interests in this life, both personally and collectively, we must first admit that some interests are more defensible than others. Indeed, some interests are so compelling that they need no defense at all.

This book was written in the hope that as science develops, we will recognize its application to the most pressing questions of human existence. For nearly a century, the moral relativism of science has given faith-based religion—that great engine of ignorance and bigotry—a nearly uncontested claim to being the only universal framework for moral wisdom. As a result, the most powerful societies on earth spend their time debating issues like gay marriage when they should be focused on problems like nuclear proliferation, genocide, energy security, climate change, poverty, and failing schools. Granted, the practical effects of thinking in terms of a moral landscape cannot be our only reason for doing so—we must form our beliefs about reality based on what we think is actually true. But few people seem to recognize the dangers posed by thinking that there are no true answers to moral questions.

If our well-being depends upon the interaction between events in our brains and events in the world, and there are better and worse ways to secure it, then some cultures will tend to produce lives that are more worth living than others; some political persuasions will be more enlightened than others; and some world views will be mistaken in ways that cause needless human misery. Whether or not we ever understand meaning, morality, and values in practice, I have attempted to show that there must be something to know about them in principle. And I am convinced that merely admitting this will transform the way we think about human happiness and the public good.

ACKNOWLEDGMENTS

The Moral Landscape is based, in part, on the dissertation I wrote for my PhD in neuroscience at the University of California, Los Angeles. Consequently, the book has benefited greatly from the vetting that this first manuscript received from my thesis committee. I am extremely grateful to Mark Cohen, Marco Iacoboni, Eran Zaidel, and Jerome ("Pete") Engel for their guidance and support—sustained, as it was, over many years during which the progress of my scientific research was difficult to discern. Each saved me from myself on several occasions—and, with unnerving frequency, from one another.

I am especially indebted to Mark Cohen, my dissertation advisor. Mark is an uncommonly gifted teacher and a model of caution in reporting scientific results. If our academic interests did not always coincide, I was surely the poorer for it. I would also like to thank Mark's wife and colleague, Susan Bookheimer: I always profited from Susan's advice—delivered, in my case, with the compassionate urgency of a mother rescuing a child from a busy intersection. I am also grateful to Suzie Vader, the smiling face of the Interdepartmental PhD Program for Neuroscience at UCLA, for providing generous encouragement and assistance over many years.

Sections of this book are based on two published papers: chapter 3 contains a discussion of Harris, S., Sheth, S. A., and Cohen, M. S. (2008), Functional neuroimaging of belief, disbelief, and uncertainty, *Annals of Neurology, 63*(2), 141–147; part of chapter 4 is drawn from Harris, S., Kaplan, J. T., Curiel, A., Bookheimer, S. Y., Iacoboni, M., Cohen, M. S. (2009), The neural correlates of religious and nonreligious belief, *PLoS ONE 4*(10). I gratefully acknowledge my coauthors on these works as well as their original publishers. I would especially like to thank Jonas T. Kaplan, now at the Brain and Creativity Institute at the University of Southern California, for partnering with me on the second paper. This study was a joint effort at every stage, and Jonas's involvement was essential to its completion.

In addition to my dissertation committee at UCLA, several outside scholars and scientists reviewed early drafts of this book. Paul Churchland, Daniel Dennett, Owen Flanagan, and Steven Pinker read the text, in whole or in part, and offered extremely helpful notes. A few sections contain cannibalized versions of essays that were first read by a larger circle of scientists and writers: including Jerry Coyne, Richard Dawkins, Daniel Dennett, Owen Flanagan, Anthony Grayling, Christopher Hitchens, and Steven Pinker. I am pleased to notice that with friends like these, it has become increasingly difficult to say something stupid. (Still, one does what one can.) It is an honor to be so deeply in their debt.

My editor at the Free Press, Hilary Redmon, greatly improved *The Moral Landscape* at every level, through several stages of revision. It was simply a joy to work with her. My agents, John Brockman, Katinka Matson, and Max Brockman, were extremely helpful in refining my initial conception of the book and in placing it with the right publisher. Of course, JB, as his friends, colleagues, and clients well know, is much more than an agent: he has become the world's preeminent wrangler of scientific opinion. We are all richer for his efforts to bring scientists and public intellectuals together through his Edge Foundation to discuss the most interesting questions of our time.

I have been greatly supported in all things by my family and friends—especially by my mother, who has always been a most extraordinary friend. She read the manuscript of *The Moral Landscape* more than once and offered extremely valuable notes and copyedits.

My wife, Annaka Harris, has continued to help me professionally on all fronts—editing my books, essays, and public talks, and helping to run our nonprofit foundation. If her abundant talent is not evident in every sentence I produce, it is because I remain a hard case. Annaka has also raised our daughter, Emma, while I've worked, and herein lies the largest debt of all: much of the time I spent researching and writing *The Moral Landscape* belonged to "my girls."

NOTES

Introduction: The Moral Landscape

1. Bilefsky, 2008; Mortimer & Toader, 2005.

2. For the purposes of this discussion, I do not intend to make a hard distinction between "science" and other intellectual contexts in which we discuss "facts"—e.g., history. For instance, it is a fact that John F. Kennedy was assassinated. Facts of this kind fall within the context of "science," broadly construed as our best effort to form a rational account of empirical reality. Granted, one doesn't generally think of events like assassinations as "scientific" facts, but the murder of President Kennedy is as fully corroborated a fact as can be found anywhere, and it would betray a profoundly unscientific frame of mind to deny that it occurred. I think "science," therefore, should be considered a specialized branch of a larger effort to form true beliefs about events in our world.

3. This is not to deny that cultural conceptions of health can play an important role in determining a person's experience of illness (more so with some illnesses than others). There is evidence that American notions of mental health have begun to negatively affect the way people in other cultures suffer (Waters, 2010). It has even been argued that, with a condition like schizophrenia, notions of spirit possession are palliative when compared to beliefs about organic brain disease. My point, however, is that whatever contributions cultural differences make to our experience of the world can themselves be understood, in principle, at the level of the brain.

4. Pollard Sacks, 2009.

5. In the interests of both simplicity and relevance, I tend to keep my references to religion focused on Christianity, Judaism, and Islam. Of course, most of what I say about these faiths applies to Hinduism, Buddhism, Sikhism, and to other religions as well.

6. There are many reasons to be pessimistic about the future of Europe: Ye'or, 2005; Bawer, 2006; Caldwell, 2009.

7. Gould, 1997.

8. *Nature 432,* 657 (2004).

9. I am not the first person to argue that morality can and should be integrated with our scientific understanding of the natural world. Of late, the philosophers William Casebeer and Owen Flanagan have each built similar cases (Casebeer, 2003; Flanagan, 2007). Both Casebeer and Flanagan have resurrected Aristotle's concept of *eudaimonia*, which is generally translated as "flourishing," "fulfillment," or "well-being." While I rely heavily on these English equivalents, I have elected not to pay any attention to Aristotle. While much of what Aristotle wrote in his *Nichomachean Ethics* is of great interest and convergent with the case I wish to make, some of it isn't. And I'd rather not be beholden to the quirks of the great man's philosophy. Both Casebeer and Flanagan also seem to place greater emphasis

on morality as a skill and a form of practical knowledge, arguing that living a good life is more a matter of "knowing how" than of "knowing that." While I think this distinction is often useful, I'm not eager to give up the fight for moral truth just yet. For instance, I believe that the compulsory veiling of women in Afghanistan tends to needlessly immiserate them and will breed a new generation of misogynistic, puritanical men. This is an instance of "knowing that," and it is a truth claim about which I am either right or wrong. I am confident that both Casebeer and Flanagan would agree. The difference in our approaches, therefore, seems to me to be more a matter of emphasis. In any case, both Casebeer and Flanagan go into greater philosophical detail than I have on many points, and both their books are well worth reading. Flanagan also offered very helpful notes on an early draft of this book.

10. E. O. Wilson, 1998.

11. Keverne & Curley, 2004; Pedersen, Ascher, Monroe, & Prange, 1982; Smeltzer, Curtis, Aragona, & Wang, 2006; Young & Wang, 2004.

12. Fries, Ziegler, Kurian, Jacoris, & Pollak, 2005.

13. Hume's argument was actually directed against religious apologists who sought to deduce morality from the existence of God. Ironically, his reasoning has since become one of the primary impediments to linking morality to the rest of human knowledge. However, Hume's is/ought distinction has always had its detractors (e.g., Searle, 1964); here is Dennett:

> If "ought" cannot be derived from "is," just what *can* it be derived from? . . . ethics must be *somehow* based on an appreciation of human nature—on a sense of what a human being is or might be, and on what a human being might want to have or want to be. If *that* is naturalism, then naturalism is no fallacy (Dennett, p. 468).

14. Moore [1903], 2004.

15. Popper, 2002, pp. 60–62.

16. The list of scientists who have followed Hume and Moore with perfect obedience is very long and defies citation. For a recent example within neuroscience, see Edelman (2006, pp. 84–91).

17. Fodor, 2007.

18. I recently had the pleasure of hearing the philosopher Patricia Churchland draw this same analogy. (Patricia, I did not steal it!)

19. De Grey & Rae, 2007.

20. The problem with using a strictly hedonic measure of the "good" grows more obvious once we consider some of the promises and perils of a maturing neuroscience. If, for instance, we can one day manipulate the brain so as to render specific behaviors and states of mind more pleasurable than they now are, it seems relevant to wonder whether such refinements would be "good." It might be good to make compassion more rewarding than sexual lust, but would it be good to make hatred the most pleasurable emotion of all? One can't appeal to pleasure as the measure of goodness in such cases, because pleasure is what we would be choosing to reassign.

21. Pinker, 2002, pp. 53–54.

22. It should be clear that the conventional distinction between "belief" and "knowledge" does not apply here. As will be made clear in chapter 3, our proposi-

tional knowledge about the world is entirely a matter of "belief" in the above sense. Whether one chooses to say that one "believes" X or that one "knows" X is merely a difference of emphasis, expressing one's degree of confidence. As discussed in this book, propositional knowledge is a form of belief. Understanding belief at the level of the brain has been the focus of my recent scientific research, using functional magnetic resonance imaging (fMRI) (S. Harris et al., 2009; S. Harris, Sheth, & Cohen, 2008).

23. Edgerton, 1992.

24. Cited in Edgerton, 1992, p. 26.

25. Though perhaps even this attributes too much common sense to the field of anthropology, as Edgerton (1992, p. 105) tells us: "A prevailing assumption among anthropologists who study the medical practices of small, traditional societies is that these populations enjoy good health and nutrition . . . Indeed, we are often told that seemingly irrational food taboos, once fully understood, will prove to be adaptive."

26. Leher, 2010.

27. Filkins, 2010.

28. For an especially damning look at the Bush administration's Council on Bioethics, see Steven Pinker's response to its 555-page report, *Human Dignity and Bioethics* (Pinker, 2008a).

29. S. Harris, 2004, 2006a, 2006b; S. Harris, 2006c; S. Harris, 2007a, 2007b.

30. Judson, 2008; Chris Mooney, 2005.

Chapter 1: Moral Truth

1. In February of 2010, I spoke at the TED conference about how we might one day understand morality in universal, scientific terms (www.youtube.com/watch?v=Hj9oB4zpHww). Normally, when one speaks at a conference the resulting feedback amounts to a few conversations in the lobby during a coffee break. As luck would have it, however, my TED talk was broadcast on the internet as I was in the final stages of writing this book, and this produced a blizzard of useful commentary.

Many of my critics fault me for not engaging more directly with the academic literature on moral philosophy. There are two reasons why I haven't done this: First, while I have read a fair amount of this literature, I did not arrive at my position on the relationship between human values and the rest of human knowledge by reading the work of moral philosophers; I came to it by considering the logical implications of our making continued progress in the sciences of mind. Second, I am convinced that every appearance of terms like "metaethics," "deontology," "noncognitivism," "antirealism," "emotivism," etc., directly increases the amount of boredom in the universe. My goal, both in speaking at conferences like TED and in writing this book, is to start a conversation that a wider audience can engage with and find helpful. Few things would make this goal harder to achieve than for me to speak and write like an academic philosopher. Of course, some discussion of philosophy will be unavoidable, but my approach is to generally make an end run around many of the views and conceptual distinctions that make academic discussions of human values so inaccessible. While this is guaranteed to annoy a few people, the professional philosophers I've consulted seem to understand and support what I am doing.

2. Given my experience as a critic of religion, I must say that it has been quite disconcerting to see the caricature of the overeducated, atheistic moral nihilist regularly appearing in my inbox and on the blogs. I sincerely hope that people like Rick Warren have not been paying attention.

3. Searle, 1995, p. 8.

4. There has been much confusion on this point, and most of it is still influential in philosophical circles. Consider the following from J. L. Mackie:

> If there were objective values, then they would be entities or qualities or relations of a very strange sort, utterly different from anything else in the universe. Correspondingly, if we were aware of them, it would have to be by some special faculty of moral perception or intuition, utterly different from our ordinary ways of knowing everything else (Mackie 1977, p. 38).

Clearly, Mackie has conflated the two senses of the term "objective." We need not discuss "entities or qualities or relations of a very strange sort, utterly different from anything else in the universe" in order to speak about moral truth. We need only admit that the experiences of conscious creatures are lawfully dependent upon states of the universe—and, therefore, that actions can cause more harm than good, more good than harm, or be morally neutral. Good and evil need only consist in this, and it makes no sense whatsoever to claim that an action that harms everyone affected by it (even its perpetrator) might still be "good." We do not require a metaphysical repository of right and wrong, or actions that are mysteriously right or wrong *in themselves,* for there to be right and wrong answers to moral questions; we simply need a landscape of possible experiences that can be traversed in *some* orderly way in light of how the universe actually is. The main criterion, therefore, is that misery and well-being not be completely random. It seems to me that we already know that they are not—and, therefore, that it is possible for a person to be right or wrong about how to move from one state to the other.

5. Is it always wrong to slice open a child's belly with a knife? No. One might be performing an emergency appendectomy.

6. One could respond by saying that scientists agree about science more than ordinary people agree about morality (I'm not sure this is true). But this is an empty claim, for at least two reasons: (1) it is circular, because anyone who insufficiently agrees with the majority opinion in any domain of science won't count as a "scientist" (so the definition of *scientist* is question begging); (2) Scientists are an elite group, by definition. "Moral experts" would also constitute an elite group, and the existence of such experts is completely in line with my argument.

7. Obvious exceptions include "socially constructed" phenomena that require some degree of consensus to be made real. The paper in my pocket really is "money"—but it is only money because a sufficient number of people are willing to treat it as such (see Searle, 1995).

8. Practically speaking, I think we have some very useful intuitions on this front. We care more about creatures that can experience a greater range of suffering and happiness—and we are right to, because suffering and happiness (defined in the widest possible sense) are all that can be cared about. Are all animal lives equiv-

alent? No. Do monkeys suffer more than mice from medical experiments? If so, all other things being equal, it is worse to run experiments on monkeys than on mice.

Are all human lives equivalent? No. I have no problem admitting that certain people's lives are more valuable than mine (I need only imagine a person whose death would create much greater suffering and prevent much greater happiness). However, it also seems quite rational for us to collectively act *as though* all human lives were equally valuable. Hence, most of our laws and social institutions generally ignore differences between people. I suspect that this is a very good thing. Of course, I could be wrong about this—and that is precisely the point. If we didn't behave this way, our world would be different, and these differences would either affect the totality of human well-being, or they wouldn't. Once again, there are answers to such questions, whether we can ever answer them in practice.

9. At bottom, this is purely a semantic point: I am claiming that whatever answer a person gives to the question "Why is religion important?" can be framed in terms of a concern about someone's well-being (whether misplaced or not).

10. I do not think that the moral philosophy of Immanuel Kant represents an exception either. Kant's categorical imperative only qualifies as a rational standard of morality given the assumption that it will be generally beneficial (as J. S. Mill pointed out at the beginning of *Utilitarianism*). One could argue, therefore, that what is serviceable in Kant's moral philosophy amounts to a covert form of consequentialism. I offer a few more remarks about Kant's categorical imperative below.

11. For instance, many people assume that an emphasis on human "well-being" would lead us to do terrible things like reinstate slavery, harvest the organs of the poor, periodically nuke the developing world, or nurture our children on a continuous drip of heroin. Such expectations are the result of not thinking about these issues seriously. There are rather clear reasons not to do these things—all of which relate to the immensity of suffering that such actions would cause and the possibilities of deeper happiness that they would foreclose. Does anyone really believe that the *highest possible* state of human flourishing is compatible with slavery, organ theft, and genocide?

12. Are there trade-offs and exceptions? Of course. There may be circumstances in which the very survival of a community requires that certain of these principles be violated. But this doesn't mean that they aren't generally conducive to human well-being.

13. Stewart, 2008.

14. I confess that, as a critic of religion, I have paid too little attention to the sexual abuse scandal in the Catholic Church. Frankly, it felt somehow unsportsmanlike to shoot so large and languorous a fish in so tiny a barrel. This scandal was one of the most spectacular "own goals" in the history of religion, and there seemed to be no need to deride faith at its most vulnerable and self-abased. Even in retrospect, it is easy to understand the impulse to avert one's eyes: Just imagine a pious mother and father sending their beloved child to the Church of a Thousand Hands for spiritual instruction, only to have him raped and terrified into silence by threats of hell. And then imagine this occurring to tens of thousands of children in our own time—and to children beyond reckoning for over a thousand years. The spectacle of faith so utterly misplaced, and so fully betrayed, is simply too depressing to think about.

But there was always more to this phenomenon that should have compelled my attention. Consider the ludicrous ideology that made it possible: the Catholic Church has spent two millennia demonizing human sexuality to a degree unmatched by any other institution, declaring the most basic, healthy, mature, and consensual behaviors taboo. Indeed, this organization *still* opposes the use of contraception: preferring, instead, that the poorest people on earth be blessed with the largest families and the shortest lives. As a consequence of this hallowed and incorrigible stupidity, the Church has condemned generations of decent people to shame and hypocrisy—or to Neolithic fecundity, poverty, and death by AIDS. Add to this inhumanity the artifice of cloistered celibacy, and you now have an institution—one of the wealthiest on earth—that preferentially attracts pederasts, pedophiles, and sexual sadists into its ranks, promotes them to positions of authority, and grants them privileged access to children. Finally, consider that vast numbers of children will be born out of wedlock, and their unwed mothers vilified, wherever Church teaching holds sway—leading boys and girls by the thousands to be abandoned to Church-run orphanages only to be raped and terrorized by the clergy. Here, in this ghoulish machinery set to whirling through the ages by the opposing winds of shame and sadism, we mortals can finally glimpse how strangely perfect are the ways of the Lord.

In 2009, the Irish Commission to Inquire into Child Abuse (CICA) investigated such of these events as occurred on Irish soil. Their report runs to 2,600 pages (www.childabusecommission.com/rpt/). Having read only an oppressive fraction of this document, I can say that when thinking about the ecclesiastical abuse of children, it is best not to imagine shades of ancient Athens and the blandishments of a "love that dare not speak its name." Yes, there have surely been polite pederasts in the priesthood, expressing anguished affection for boys who would turn eighteen the next morning. But behind these indiscretions there is a continuum of abuse that terminates in absolute evil. The scandal in the Catholic Church—one might now safely say the scandal *that is* the Catholic Church—includes the systematic rape and torture of orphaned and disabled children. Its victims attest to being whipped with belts and sodomized until bloody—sometimes by multiple attackers—and then whipped again and threatened with death and hellfire if they breathed a word about their abuse. And yes, many of the children who were desperate or courageous enough to report these crimes were accused of lying and returned to their tormentors to be raped and tortured again.

The evidence suggests that the misery of these children was facilitated and concealed by the hierarchy of the Catholic Church at every level, up to and including the prefrontal cortex of the current pope. In his former capacity as Cardinal Ratzinger, Pope Benedict personally oversaw the Vatican's response to reports of sexual abuse in the Church. What did this wise and compassionate man do upon learning that his employees were raping children by the thousands? Did he immediately alert the police and ensure that the victims would be protected from further torments? One still dares to imagine such an effulgence of basic human sanity might have been possible, even within the Church. On the contrary, repeated and increasingly desperate complaints of abuse were set aside, witnesses were pressured into silence, bishops were praised for their defiance of secular authority, and offending priests were relocated only to destroy fresh lives in unsuspecting parishes. It is no exaggeration to say that for decades (if not centuries) the Vatican has met the formal definition of a criminal organization devoted—not to gambling, prostitution, drugs, or any other venial sin—but to the sexual enslavement of children. Consider the following passages from the CICA report:

> 7.129 In relation to one School, four witnesses gave detailed accounts of sexual abuse, including rape in all instances, by two or more Brothers and on one occasion along with an older resident. A witness from the second School, from which there were several reports, described being raped by three Brothers: *"I was brought to the infirmary . . . they held me over the bed, they were animals. . . . They penetrated me, I was bleeding."* Another witness reported he was abused twice weekly on particular days by two Brothers in the toilets off the dormitory:
>
> *One Brother kept watch while the other abused me . . .* [sexually] *. . . then they changed over. Every time it ended with a severe beating. When I told the priest in Confession, he called me a liar. I never spoke about it again.*
>
> *I would have to go into his . . .* [Br X's] *. . . room every time he wanted. You'd get a hiding if you didn't, and he'd make me do it . . .* [masturbate] *. . . to him. One night I didn't . . .* [masturbate him] *. . . and there was another Brother there who held me down and they hit me with a hurley and they burst my fingers . . .* [displayed scar]. . . .
>
> 7.232 Witnesses reported being particularly fearful at night as they listened to residents screaming in cloakrooms, dormitories or in a staff member's bedroom while they were being abused. Witnesses were conscious that co-residents whom they described as orphans had a particularly difficult time:
>
> *The orphan children, they had it bad. I knew . . .* [who they were] *. . . by the size of them, I'd ask them and they'd say they come from . . . named institution. . . . They were there from an early age. You'd hear the screams from the room where Br . . . X . . . would be abusing them.*
>
> *There was one night, I wasn't long there and I seen one of the Brothers on the bed with one of the young boys . . . and I heard the young lad screaming crying and Br . . . X . . . said to me "if you don't mind your own business you'll get the same." . . . I heard kids screaming and you know they are getting abused and that's a nightmare in anybody's mind. You are going to try and break out. . . . So there was no way I was going to let that happen to me . . . I remember one boy and he was bleeding from the back passage and I made up my mind, there was no way it . . .* [anal rape] *. . . was going to happen to me. . . . That used to play on my mind.*

This is the kind of abuse that the Church has practiced and concealed since time out of memory. Even the CICA report declined to name the offending priests.

I have been awakened from my unconscionable slumber on this issue by recent press reports (Goodstein and Callender, 2010; Goodstein, 2010a, 2010b; Donadio, 2010a, 2010b; Wakin and McKinley Jr., 2010), and especially by the eloquence of my colleagues Christopher Hitchens (2010a, 2010b, 2010c, and 2010d), and Richard Dawkins (2010a, 2010b).

15. The Church even excommunicated the girl's mother (http://news.bbc.co.uk/2/hi/americas/7930380.stm).

16. The philosopher Hilary Putnam (2007) has argued that facts and values are "entangled." Scientific judgments presuppose "epistemic values"—coherence, simplicity, beauty, parsimony, etc. Putnam has pointed out, as I do here, that all the arguments against the existence of moral truth could be applied to scientific truth without any change.

17. Many people find the idea of "moral experts" abhorrent. Indeed, this ramification of my argument has been called "positively Orwellian" and a "recipe for fascism." Again, these concerns seem to arise from an uncanny reluctance to think about what the concept of "well-being" actually entails or how science might shed light on its causes and conditions. The analogy with health seems important to keep in view: Is there anything "Orwellian" about the scientific consensus on the link between smoking and lung cancer? Has the medical community's insistence that people should not smoke led to "fascism"? Many people's reflexive response to the notion of moral expertise is to say, "I don't want anyone telling me how to live my life." To which I can only respond, "If there were a way for you and those you care about to be much happier than you now are, would you want to know about it?"

18. This is the subject of that now infamous quotation from Albert Einstein, endlessly recycled by religious apologists, claiming that "science without religion is lame, religion without science is blind." Far from indicating his belief in God, or his respect for unjustified belief, Einstein was speaking about the primitive urge to understand the universe, along with the "faith" that such understanding is possible:

> Though religion may be that which determines the goal, it has, nevertheless, learned from science, in the broadest sense, what means will contribute to the attainment of the goals it has set up. But science can only be created by those who are thoroughly imbued with the aspiration toward truth and understanding. This source of feeling, however, springs from the sphere of religion. To this there also belongs the faith in the possibility that the regulations valid for the world of existence are rational, that is, comprehensible to reason. I cannot conceive of a genuine scientist without that profound faith. This situation may be expressed by an image: science without religion is lame, religion without science is blind (Einstein, 1954, p. 49).

19. These impasses are seldom as insurmountable as skeptics imagine. For instance, Creationist "scientists" can be led to see that the very standards of reasoning they use to vindicate scripture in light of empirical data also reveal hundreds of inconsistencies *within* scripture—thereby undermining their entire project. The same is true for moral impasses: those who claim to get their morality from God, without reference to any terrestrial concerns, are often susceptible to such concerns in the end. In an extreme case, the *New York Times* correspondent Thomas Friedman once reported meeting a Sunni militant who had begun fighting alongside the American military against al-Qaeda in Iraq, having been persuaded that the infidel troops were the lesser of two evils. What convinced him? He witnessed a member of al-Qaeda decapitate an eight-year-old girl (Friedman, 2007). It would seem,

therefore, that the boundary between the crazy values of Islam and the *utterly* crazy can be discerned when drawn in the spilled blood of little girls. This is a basis for hope, of sorts.

In fact, I think that morality will be on firmer ground than any other branch of science in the end, since scientific knowledge is only valuable because it contributes to our well-being. Of course, we must include among these contributions the claims of people who say that they value knowledge "for its own sake"—for they are merely describing the mental pleasure that comes with understanding the world, solving problems, etc. It is clear that well-being must take precedence over knowledge, because we can easily imagine situations in which it would be better not to know the truth, or when false knowledge would be desirable. No doubt, there are circumstances in which religious delusion functions in this way: where, for instance, soldiers are vastly outnumbered on the battlefield but, being ignorant of the odds against them and convinced that God is on their side, they manage to draw on emotional resources that would be unavailable to people with complete information and fully justified beliefs. However, the fact that a combination of ignorance and false knowledge can occasionally be helpful is no argument for the general utility of religious faith (much less for its truth). Indeed, the great weakness of religion, apart from the obvious implausibility of its doctrines, is that the cost of holding irrational and divisive beliefs on a global scale is extraordinarily high.

20. The physicist Sean Carroll finds Hume's analysis of facts and values so compelling that he elevates it to the status of mathematical truth:

> Attempts to derive ought from is are like attempts to reach an odd number by adding together even numbers. If someone claims that they've done it, you don't have to check their math; you know that they've made a mistake (Carroll, 2010a).

21. This spurious notion of "ought" can be introduced into any enterprise and seem to plant a fatal seed of doubt. Asking why we "ought" to value well-being makes even less sense than asking why we "ought" to be rational or scientific. And while it is possible to *say* that one can't move from "is" to "ought," we should be honest about how we get to "is" in the first place. Scientific "is" statements rest on implicit "oughts" all the way down. When I say, "Water is two parts hydrogen and one part oxygen," I have uttered a quintessential statement of scientific fact. But what if someone doubts this statement? I can appeal to data from chemistry, describing the outcome of simple experiments. But in so doing, I implicitly appeal to the values of empiricism and logic. What if my interlocutor doesn't share these values? What can I say then? As it turns out, this is the wrong question. The right question is, why should we care what such a person thinks about chemistry?

So it is with the linkage between morality and well-being: To say that morality is arbitrary (or culturally constructed, or merely personal) because we must first assume that the well-being of conscious creatures is good, is like saying that science is arbitrary (or culturally constructed, or merely personal) because we must first assume that a rational understanding of the universe is good. Yes, both endeavors rest on assumptions (and, as I have said, I think the former will prove to be more firmly grounded), but this is not a problem. No framework of knowledge can withstand utter skepticism, for none is perfectly self-justifying. Without being able to stand entirely outside of a framework, one is always open to the charge that the framework rests on nothing, that its axioms are wrong, or that there are foundational questions it cannot answer. Occasionally some of our basic assumptions do turn out to be wrong or limited in scope—e.g., the parallel postulate of Euclidean geometry does not apply to geometry as a whole—but these errors can be detected only by the light of other assumptions that stand firm.

Science and rationality generally are based on intuitions and concepts that cannot be reduced or justified. Just try defining "causation" in noncircular terms. Or try justifying transitivity in logic: if $A = B$ and $B = C$, then $A = C$. A skeptic could say, "This is nothing more than an assumption that we've built into the definition of 'equality.' Others will be free to define 'equality' differently." Yes, they will. And we will be free to call them "imbeciles." Seen in this light, moral relativism—the view that the difference between right and wrong has only local validity within a specific culture—should be no more tempting than physical, biological, mathematical, or logical relativism. There are better and worse ways to define our terms; there are more and less coherent ways to think about reality; and there are—is there any doubt about this?—many ways to seek fulfillment in this life and to not find it.

22. We can, therefore, let this metaphysical notion of "ought" fall away, and we will be left with a scientific picture of cause and effect. To the degree that it is in our power to produce the worst possible misery for everyone in this universe, we can say that if we don't want everyone to experience the worst possible misery, we shouldn't do X. Can we readily conceive of someone who might hold altogether different values and want all conscious beings, himself included, reduced to the state of worst possible misery? I don't think so. And I don't think we can intelligibly ask questions like, "What if the worst possible misery for everyone is actually good?" Such questions seem analytically confused. We can also pose questions like "What if the most perfect circle is really a square?" or "What if all true statements are actually false?" But if someone persists in speaking this way, I see no obligation to take his views seriously.

23. And even if minds were independent of the physical universe, we could still speak about facts relative to their well-being. But we would be speaking about some other basis for these facts (souls, disembodied consciousness, ectoplasm, etc.).

24. On a related point, the philosopher Russell Blackford wrote in response to my TED talk, "I've never yet seen an argument that shows that psychopaths are necessarily mistaken about some fact about the world. Moreover, I don't see how the argument could run." While I discuss psychopathy in greater detail in the next chapter, here is such an argument in brief: We already know that psychopaths have brain damage that prevents them from having certain deeply satisfying experiences (like empathy) that seem good for people both personally and collectively (in that they tend to increase well-being on both counts). Psychopaths, therefore, don't know what they are missing (but we do). The position of a psychopath also cannot be generalized; it is not, therefore, an alternative view of how human beings should live (this is one point Kant got right: even a psychopath couldn't want to live in a world filled with psychopaths). We should also realize that the psychopath we are envisioning is a straw man: watch interviews with real psychopaths, and you will find that they do not tend to claim to be in possession of an alternative morality or

to be living deeply fulfilling lives. These people are generally ruled by compulsions that they don't understand and cannot resist. It is absolutely clear that, whatever they might believe about what they are doing, psychopaths are seeking some form of well-being (excitement, ecstasy, feelings of power, etc.), but because of their neurological and social deficits, they are doing a very bad job of it. We can say that a psychopath like Ted Bundy takes satisfaction in the wrong things, because living a life purposed toward raping and killing women does not allow for deeper and more generalizable forms of human flourishing. Compare Bundy's deficits to those of a delusional physicist who finds meaningful patterns and mathematical significance in the wrong places. The mathematician John Nash, while suffering the symptoms of his schizophrenia, seems a good example: his "Eureka!" detectors were poorly calibrated; he saw meaningful patterns where his peers would not—and these patterns were a very poor guide to the proper goals of science (i.e., understanding the physical world). Is there any doubt that Ted Bundy's "Yes! I love this!" detectors were poorly coupled to the possibilities of finding deep fulfillment in this life, or that his obsession with raping and killing young women was a poor guide to the proper goals of morality (i.e., living a fulfilling life with others)?

While people like Bundy may want some very weird things out of life, no one wants utter, interminable misery. People with apparently different moral codes are still seeking forms of well-being that we recognize—like freedom from pain, doubt, fear, etc.—and their moral codes, however vigorously they might want to defend them, are undermining their well-being in obvious ways. And if someone *claims* to want to be truly miserable, we are free to treat them like someone who claims to believe that 2 + 2 = 5 or that all events are self-caused. On the subject of morality, as on every other subject, some people are not worth listening to.

25. From the White House press release: www.bioethics.gov/about/creation.html.

26. Oxytocin is a neuroactive hormone that appears to govern social recognition in animals and the experience of trust (and its reciprocation) in humans (Zak, Kurzban, & Matzner, 2005; Zak, Stanton, & Ahmadi, 2007).

27. Appiah, 2008, p. 41.

28. The *Stanford Encyclopedia of Philosophy* has this to say on the subject of moral relativism:

> In 1947, on the occasion of the United Nations debate about universal human rights, the American Anthropological Association issued a statement declaring that moral values are relative to cultures and that there is no way of showing that the values of one culture are better than those of another. Anthropologists have never been unanimous in asserting this, and in recent years human rights advocacy on the part of some anthropologists has mitigated the relativist orientation of the discipline. Nonetheless, prominent contemporary anthropologists such as Clifford Geertz and Richard A. Shweder continue to defend relativist positions. http://plato.stanford.edu/entries/moral-relativism/.

1947? Please note that this was the best the social scientists in the United States could do with the crematoria of Auschwitz still smoking. My spoken and written collisions with Richard Shweder, Scott Atran, Mel Konner, and other anthropologists have convinced me that awareness of moral diversity does not entail, and is a poor surrogate for, clear thinking about human well-being.

29. Pinker, 2002, p. 273.

30. Harding, 2001.

31. For a more complete demolition of feminist and multicultural critiques of Western science, see P. R. Gross, 1991; P. R. Gross & Levitt, 1994.

32. Weinberg, 2001, p. 105.

33. Dennett, 1995.

34. Ibid., p. 487.

35. See, for instance, M. D. Hauser, 2006. Experiments show that even eight-month-old infants want to see aggressors punished (Bloom, 2010).

36. www.gallup.com/poll/118378/Majority-Americans-Continue-Oppose-Gay-Marriage.aspx.

37. There is now a separate field called "neuroethics," formed by a confluence of neuroscience and philosophy, which loosely focuses on matters of this sort. Neuroethics is more than bioethics with respect to the brain (that is, it is more than an ethical framework for the conduct of neuroscience): it encompasses our efforts to understand ethics itself as a biological phenomenon. There is a quickly growing literature on neuroethics (recent, book-length introductions can be found in Gazzaniga, 2005, and Levy, 2007), and there are other neuroethical issues that are relevant to this discussion: concerns about mental privacy, lie detection, and the other implications of an advancing science of neuroimaging; personal responsibility in light of deterministic and random processes in the brain (neither of which lend any credence to common notions of "free will"); the ethics of emotional and cognitive enhancement; the implications of understanding "spiritual" experience in physical terms; etc.

Chapter 2: Good and Evil

1. Consider, for instance, how much time and money we spend to secure our homes, places of business, and cars against unwanted entry (and to have doors professionally unlocked when keys are lost). Consider the cost of internet and credit card security, and the time dissipated in the use and retrieval of passwords. When phone service is interrupted for five minutes in a modern society the cost is measured in billions of dollars. I think it safe to say that the costs of preventing theft are far higher. Add to the expense of locking doors, the pains we take to prepare formal contracts—locks of another sort—and the costs soar beyond all reckoning. Imagine a world that had no need for such prophylactics against theft (admittedly, it is difficult). It would be a world of far greater disposable wealth (measured in both time and money).

2. There are other ways of thinking about human cooperation, including politics and law, but I take the normative claims of ethics to be foundational.

3. Hamilton, 1964a, 1964b.

4. McElreath & Boyd, 2007, p. 82.

5. Trivers, 1971.

6. G. F. Miller, 2007.

7. For a recent review that also looks at the phenomenon of *indirect reciprocity*

(i.e., *A gives to B;* and then *B gives to C,* or *C gives to A,* or both), see Nowak, 2005. For doubts about the sufficiency of kin selection and reciprocal altruism to account for cooperation—especially among eusocial insects—see D. S. Wilson & Wilson, 2007; E. O. Wilson, 2005.

8. Tomasello, 2007.

9. Smith, [1759] 1853, p. 3.

10. Ibid. pp. 192–193.

11. Benedict, 1934, p. 172.

12. Consequentialism has undergone many refinements since the original *utilitarianism* of Jeremy Bentham and John Stuart Mill. My discussion will ignore most of these developments, as they are generally of interest only to academic philosophers. The *Stanford Encyclopedia of Philosophy* provides a good summary article (Sinnott-Armstrong, 2006).

13. J. D. Greene, 2007; J. D. Greene, Nystrom, Engell, Darley, & Cohen, 2004; J. D. Greene, Sommerville, Nystrom, Darley, & Cohen, 2001.

14. J. D. Greene, 2002, pp. 59–60.

15. Ibid., pp. 204–205.

16. Ibid., p. 264.

17. Let us briefly cover a few more philosophical bases: What would have to be true for a practice like the forced veiling of women to be objectively wrong? Would this practice have to cause unnecessary suffering in *all possible worlds*? No. It only need cause unnecessary suffering in this world. Must it be *analytically* true that compulsory veiling is immoral—that is, must the wrongness of the act be built into the meaning of the word "veil"? No. Must it be true *a priori*—that is, must this practice be wrong independent of human experience? No. The wrongness of the act very much depends on human experience. It is wrong to force women and girls to wear burqas because it is unpleasant and impractical to live fully veiled, because this practice perpetuates a view of women as being the property of men, and because it keeps the men who enforce it brutally obtuse to the possibility of real equality and communication between the sexes. Hobbling half of the population also directly subtracts from the economic, social, and intellectual wealth of a society. Given the challenges that face every society, this is a bad practice in almost every case. Must compulsory veiling be ethically unacceptable *without exception* in our world? No. We can easily imagine situations in which forcing one's daughter to wear a burqa could be perfectly moral—perhaps to escape the attention of thuggish men while traveling in rural Afghanistan. Does this slide from brute, analytic, *a priori,* and necessary truth to synthetic, *a posteriori,* contingent, exception-ridden truth pose a problem for moral realism? Recall the analogy I drew between morality and chess. Is it *always* wrong to surrender your Queen in a game of chess? No. But generally speaking, it is a terrible idea. Even granting the existence of an uncountable number of exceptions to this rule, there are still objectively good and objectively bad moves in every game of chess. Are we in a position to say that the treatment of women in traditional Muslim societies is generally bad? Absolutely we are. Should there be any doubt, I recommend that readers consult Ayaan Hirsi Ali's several fine books on the subject (A. Hirsi Ali, 2006, 2007, 2010).

18. J. D. Greene, 2002, pp. 287–288.

19. The philosopher Richard Joyce (2006) has argued that the evolutionary

origins of moral beliefs undermine them in ways that the evolutionary origins of mathematical and scientific beliefs do not. I do not find his reasoning convincing, however. For instance, Joyce asserts that our mathematical and scientific intuitions could have been selected for only by virtue of their accuracy, whereas our moral intuitions were selected for based on an entirely different standard. In the case of arithmetic (which he takes as his model), this may seem plausible. But science has progressed by violating many (if not most) of our innate, proto-scientific intuitions about the nature of reality. By Joyce's reasoning, we should view these violations as a likely step away from the Truth.

20. Greene's argument actually seems somewhat peculiar. Consequentialism is not true, because there is simply too much diversity of opinion about morality; but he seems to believe that most people will converge on consequentialist principles if given enough time to reflect.

21. Faison, 1996.

22. Dennett, 1995, p. 498.

23. Churchland, 2008a.

24. Slovic, 2007.

25. This seems related to a more general finding in the reasoning literature, in which people are often found to put more weight on a salient anecdote than on large-sample statistics (Fong, Krantz, & Nisbett, 1986/07; Stanovich & West, 2000). It also appears to be an especially perverse version of what Kahneman and Frederick call "extension neglect" (Kahneman & Frederick, 2005): where our valuations reliably fail to increase with the size of a problem. For instance, the value most people will place on saving 2,000 lives will be less than twice as large as the value they will place on 1,000 lives. Slovic's result, however, suggests that it could be *less* valuable (even if the larger group contained the smaller). If ever there were a nonnormative result in moral psychology, this is it.

26. There may be some exceptions to this principle: for instance, if you thought that either child would suffer intolerably if the other died, you might believe that both dying would be preferable than one dying. Whether such cases actually exist, they are clearly exceptions to the general rule that negative consequences should be additive.

27. Does this sound crazy? Jane McGonigal designs games with such real-world outcomes in mind: www.iftf.org/user/46.

28. Parfit, 1984.

29. While Parfit's argument is rightfully celebrated, and *Reasons and Persons* is a philosophical masterpiece, a very similar observation first appears in Rawls, [1971] 1999, pp. 140–141.

30. For instance:

> *How Only France Survives.* In one possible future, the worst-off people in the world soon start to have lives that are well worth living. The quality of life in different nations then continues to rise. Though each nation has its fair share of the world's resources, such things as climate and cultural traditions give to some nations a higher quality of life. The best-off people, for many centuries, are the French.
>
> In another possible future, a new infectious disease makes nearly everyone

> sterile. French scientists produce just enough of an antidote for all of France's population. All other nations cease to exist. This has some bad effects on the quality of life for the surviving French. Thus there is no new foreign art, literature, or technology that the French can import. These and other bad effects outweigh any good effects. Throughout this second possible future the French therefore have a quality of life that is slightly lower than it would be in the first possible future (Parfit, ibid., p. 421).

31. P. Singer, 2009, p. 139.
32. Graham Holm, 2010.
33. Kahneman, 2003.
34. LaBoeuf & Shafir, 2005.
35. Tom, Fox, Trepel, & Poldrack, 2007. But as the authors note, this protocol examined the brain's appraisal of potential loss (i.e., decision utility) rather than experienced losses, where other studies suggest that negative affect and associated amygdala activity can be expected.
36. Pizarro and Uhlmann make a similar observation (D. A. Pizarro & Uhlmann, 2008).
37. Redelmeier, Katz, & Kahneman, 2003.
38. Schreiber & Kahneman, 2000.
39. Kahneman, 2003.
40. Rawls, [1971] 1999; Rawls & Kelly, 2001.
41. S. Harris, 2004, 2006a, 2006d.
42. He later refined his view, arguing that justice as fairness must be understood as "a political conception of justice rather than as part of a comprehensive moral doctrine" (Rawls & Kelly, 2001, p. xvi).
43. Rawls, [1971] 1999, p. 27.
44. Tabibnia, Satpute, & Lieberman, 2008.
45. It is not unreasonable, therefore, to expect people who are seeking to maximize their well-being to also value fairness. Valuing fairness, they will tend to view its breach as less than ethical—that is, as not being conducive to their collective well-being. But what if they don't? What if the laws of nature allow for different and seemingly antithetical peaks on the moral landscape? What if there is a possible world in which the Golden Rule has become an unshakable instinct, while there is another world of equivalent happiness where the inhabitants reflexively violate it? Perhaps this is a world of perfectly matched sadists and masochists. Let's assume that in this world every person can be paired, one-for-one, with the saints in the first world, and while they are different in every other way, these pairs are identical in every way relevant to their well-being. Stipulating all these things, the consequentialist would be forced to say that these worlds are morally equivalent. Is this a problem? I don't think so. The problem lies in how many details we have been forced to ignore in the process of getting to this point. What possible reason do we have to worry that the principles of human well-being are this elastic? This is like worrying that there is a possible world in which the laws of physics, while as consistent as they are in our world, are completely antithetical to physics as we know it. Okay, what if? Exactly how much should this possibility concern us as we try to predict the behavior of matter in our world?

And the Kantian commitment to viewing people as ends in themselves, while a very useful moral principle, is difficult to map onto the world with precision. Not only are the boundaries between self and world hard to define, one's individuality with respect to one's own past and future is somewhat mysterious. For instance, we are each heirs to our actions and to our failures of action. Does this have any moral implications? If I am currently disinclined to do some necessary and profitable work, to eat well, to make regular visits to doctor and dentist, to avoid dangerous sports, to wear my seat belt, to save money, etc.—have I committed a series of *crimes* against the future self who will suffer the consequences of my negligence? Why not? And if I do live prudently, despite the pain it causes me, out of concern for the interests of my future self, is this an instance of *my* being used as a means to someone else's end? Am I merely a resource for the person I will be in the future?

46. Rawls's notion of "primary goods," access to which must be fairly allocated in any just society, seems parasitic upon a general notion of human well-being. Why are "basic rights and liberties," "freedom of movement and free choice of occupation," "the powers and prerogatives of offices and positions of authority," "income and wealth," and "the social bases of self-respect" of any interest to us at all if not as constituents of happy human lives? Of course, Rawls is at pains to say that his conception of the "good" is partial and merely political—but to the degree that it is good at all, it seems beholden to a larger conception of human well-being. See Rawls, 2001, pp. 58–60.

47. Cf. Pinker, 2008b.

48. Kant, [1785] 1995, p. 30.

49. As Patricia Churchland notes:

> Kant's conviction that detachment from emotions is essential in characterizing moral obligation is strikingly at odds with what we know about our biological nature. From a biological point of view, basic emotions are Mother Nature's way of getting us to do what we prudentially ought. The social emotions are a way of getting us to do what we socially ought, and the reward system is a way of learning to use past experiences to improve one's performance in both domains (Churchland, 2008b).

50. However, one problem that people often have with consequentialism is that it entails moral hierarchy: certain spheres of well-being (i.e., minds) will be more important than others. The philosopher Robert Nozick famously observed that this opens the door to "utility monsters": hypothetical creatures who could get enormously greater life satisfaction from devouring us than we would lose (Nozick 1974, p. 41). But, as Nozick observes, *we* are just such utility monsters. Leaving aside the fact that economic inequality allows many of us to profit from the drudgery of others, most of us pay others to raise and kill animals so that we can *eat* them. This arrangement works out rather badly for the animals. How much do these creatures actually suffer? How different is the happiest cow, pig, or chicken from those who languish on our factory farms? We seem to have decided, all things considered, that it is proper that the well-being of certain species be entirely sacrificed to our own. We might be right about this. Or we might not. For many people, eating meat is simply an unhealthy source of fleeting pleasure. It is very difficult to believe, therefore, that all of the suffering and death we impose on our fellow creatures is

ethically defensible. For the sake of argument, however, let's assume that allowing *some* people to eat *some* animals yields a net increase in well-being on planet earth.

In this context, would it be ethical for cows being led to slaughter to defend themselves if they saw an opportunity—perhaps by stampeding their captors and breaking free? Would it be ethical for a fish to fight against the hook in light of the fisherman's justified desire to eat it? Having judged some consumption of animals to be ethically desirable (or at least ethically acceptable), we appear to rule out the possibility of warranted resistance on their parts. We are their utility monsters.

Nozick draws the obvious analogy and asks if it would be ethical for our species to be sacrificed for the unimaginably vast happiness of some superbeings. Provided that we take the time to really imagine the details (which is not easy), I think the answer is clearly "yes." There seems no reason to suppose that we must occupy the highest peak on the moral landscape. If there are beings who stand in relation to us as we do to bacteria, it should be easy to admit that their interests must trump our own, and to a degree that we cannot possibly conceive. I do not think that the existence of such a moral hierarchy poses any problems for our ethics. And there is no compelling reason to believe that such superbeings exist, much less ones that want to eat us.

51. Traditional utility theory has been unable to explain why people so often behave in ways that they know they will later regret. If human beings were simply inclined to choose the path leading to their most satisfying option, then willpower would be unnecessary, and self-defeating behavior would be unheard of. In his fascinating book, *Breakdown of Will,* the psychiatrist George Ainslie examines the dynamics of human decision making in the face of competing preferences. To account for both the necessity of human will, along with its predictable failures, Ainslie presents a model of decision making in which each person is viewed as a community of present and future "selves" in competition, and each "self" discounts future rewards more steeply than seems strictly rational.

The multiplicity of competing interests in the human mind causes us each to function as a loose coalition of interests that may be unified only by resource limitations—like the fact that we have only one body with which to express our desires, moment to moment. This obvious constraint upon our fulfilling mutually incompatible ends keeps us bargaining with our "self" across time: "Ulysses planning for the Sirens must treat Ulysses hearing them as a separate person, to be influenced if possible and forestalled if not" (Ainslie, 2001, p. 40).

Hyperbolic discounting of future rewards leads to curiosities like "preference reversal": for example, most people prefer $10,000 today to $15,000 three years from now, but prefer $15,000 in thirteen years to $10,000 in ten years. Given that the latter scenario is simply the first seen at a distance of ten years, it seems clear that people's preferences reverse depending on the length of the delay. The deferral of a reward is less acceptable the closer one gets to the possibility of enjoying it.

52. I am also not as healthy or as well educated as I could be. I believe that such statements are *objectively* true (even where they relate to subjective facts about me).

53. Haidt, 2001, p. 821.

54. The wisdom of switching doors is seen more easily if you imagine having made your initial selection among a thousand doors, rather than three. Imagine

you picked Door #17, and Monty Hall then opens every door except for #562, revealing goats as far as the eye can see. What should you do next? Stick with Door #17 or switch to Door #562? It should be obvious that your initial choice was made in a condition of great uncertainty, with a 1-in-1,000 chance of success and a 999-in-1,000 chance of failure. The opening of 998 doors has given you an extraordinary amount of information—collapsing the remaining odds of 999-in-1,000 on door #562.

55. Haidt, 2008.

56. Haidt, 2001, p. 823.

57. http://newspolls.org/question.php?question_id=716. Incidentally, the same research found that 16 percent of Americans also believe that it is "very likely" that the "federal government is withholding proof of the existence of intelligent life from other planets" (http://newspolls.org/question.php? question_id=715).

58. This is especially obvious in split-brain research, when language areas in the left hemisphere routinely confabulate explanations for right-hemisphere behavior (Gazzaniga, 1998; M. S. Gazzaniga, 2005; Gazzaniga, 2008; Gazzaniga, Bogen, & Sperry, 1962).

59. Blow, 2009.

60. "Multiculturalism 'drives young Muslims to shun British values.'" *The Daily Mail* (January 29, 2007).

61. Moll, de Oliveira-Souza, & Zahn, 2008; 2005.

62. Moll et al., 2008, p. 162.

63. Including the nucleus accumbens, the caudate nucleus, the ventromedial and orbitofrontal cortex, and the rostral anterior cingulate (Rilling et al., 2002).

64. Though, as is often the case with neuroimaging work, the results do not divide as neatly as all that. In fact, one of Moll's earlier studies on disgust and moral indignation found medial regions also involved in these negative states (Moll, de Oliveira-Souza et al., 2005).

65. Koenigs et al., 2007.

66. J. D. Greene et al., 2001.

67. This thought experiment was first introduced by Foot (1967) and later elaborated by Thompson (1976).

68. J. D. Greene et al., 2001.

69. Valdesolo & DeSteno, 2006.

70. J. D. Greene, 2007.

71. Moll et al., 2008, p. 168. There is the additional concern, which bedevils much neuroimaging research: the regions that Greene et al. label as "emotional" have been implicated in other types of processing—memory and language, for instance (G. Miller, 2008b). This is an instance of the "reverse inference" problem raised by Poldrack (2006), discussed below in the context of my own research on belief.

72. While some researchers have sought to differentiate these terms, most use them interchangeably.

73. Salter, 2003, pp. 98–99. See also Stone, 2009.

74. www.missingkids.com.

75. Twenty percent of male and female prison inmates are psychopaths, and they are responsible for more than 50 percent of serious crimes (Hare, 1999, p. 87).

The recidivism rate of psychopaths is three times higher than that of other offenders (and the violent recidivism rate is three to five times higher) (Blair, Mitchell, & Blair, 2005, p. 16).

76. Nunez, Casey, Egner, Hare, & Hirsch, 2005. For reasons that may have something to do with the sensationalism just mentioned, psychopathy does not exist as a diagnostic category, or even as an index entry, in *The Diagnostic and Statistical Manual of Mental Disorders (DSM-IV)*. The two *DSM-IV* diagnoses that seek to address the behavioral correlates of psychopathy—antisocial personality disorder (ASPD) and conduct disorder—do not capture its interpersonal and emotional components at all. Antisocial behavior is common to several disorders, and people with ASPD may not score high on the PCL-R (de Oliveira-Souza et al., 2008; Narayan et al., 2007). The inadequacies of the *DSM-IV*'s treatment of the syndrome are very well brought out in Blair et al., 2005. There are many motives for antisocial behavior and many routes to becoming a violent felon. The hallmark of psychopathy isn't bad behavior per se, but an underlying spectrum of emotional and interpersonal impairments. And psychopathy, as a construct, is far more predictive of specific behaviors (e.g., recidivism) than the *DSM-IV* criteria are.

77. It would appear, however, that the same could be said of the great Erwin Schrödinger (Teresi, 2010).

78. Frontal lobe injury can result in a condition known as "acquired sociopathy," which shares some of the features of developmental psychopathy. While they are often mentioned in the same context, acquired sociopathy and psychopathy differ, especially with regard to the type of aggression they produce. *Reactive aggression* is triggered by an annoying or threatening stimuli and is often associated with anger. *Instrumental aggression* is purposed toward a goal. The man who lashes out after being jostled on the street has expressed reactive aggression; the man who attacks another man to steal his wallet or to impress his fellow gang members has displayed instrumental aggression. Subjects suffering from acquired sociopathy, who have generally sustained injuries to their orbitofrontal lobes, display poor impulse control and tend to exhibit increased levels of reactive aggression. However, they do not show a heightened tendency toward instrumental aggression. Psychopaths are prone to aggression of both types. Most important, instrumental aggression seems most closely linked to the callousness/unemotional (CU) trait that is the hallmark of the disorder. Studies of same-sex twins suggest that the CU trait is also most associated with heritable causes of antisocial behavior (Viding, Jones, Frick, Moffitt, & Plomin, 2008).

Moll, de Oliveira-Souza, and colleagues found that the correlation between gray matter reductions and psychopathy extends beyond the frontal cortex, and this would explain why acquired sociopathy and psychopathy are distinct disorders. Psychopathy was correlated with gray matter reductions in a wide network of structures: including the bilateral insula, the superior temporal sulci, the supramarginal/angular gyri, the caudate (head), the fusiform cortex, the middle frontal gyri, among others. It would be exceedingly unlikely to injure such a wide network selectively.

79. Kiehl et al., 2001; Glenn, Raine, & Schug, 2009. However, when given personal vs. impersonal moral dilemmas to solve, unlike MPFC patients, psycho-

paths tend to produce the same answers as normal controls, albeit without the same emotional response (Glenn, Raine, Schug, Young, & Hauser, 2009).

80. Hare, 1999, p. 76.

81. Ibid., p. 132.

82. Blair et al., 2005.

83. Buckholtz et al., 2010.

84. Richell et al., 2003.

85. Dolan & Fullam, 2004.

86. Dolan & Fullam, 2006; Blair et al., 2005.

87. Blair et al., 2005. The first book-length treatment of psychopathy appears to be Cleckley's *The Mask of Sanity*. While it is currently out of print, this book is still widely referenced and much revered. It is worth reading, if only for the author's highly (and often inadvertently) amusing prose. Hare, 1999, Blair et al., 2005, and Babiak & Hare, 2006, provide more recent book-length discussions of the disorder.

88. Blair et al., 2005. The developmental literature suggests that, because punishment (the unconditioned stimulus) rarely follows a specific transgression (the conditioned stimulus) closely in time, the aversive conditioning brought on by corporal punishment tends to get associated with the person who metes it out, rather than with the behavior in need of correction. Blair also observes that if punishment were the primary source of moral instruction, children would be unable to observe the difference between conventional transgressions (e.g., talking in class) and moral ones (e.g., hitting another student), as breaches of either sort tend to elicit punishment. And yet healthy children can readily distinguish between these forms of misbehavior. Thus, it would seem that they receive their correction directly from the distress that others exhibit when true moral boundaries have been crossed. Other mammals also find the suffering of their conspecifics highly aversive. We know this from work in monkeys (Masserman, Wechkin, & Terris, 1964) and rats (Church, 1959) that would seem scarcely ethical to perform today. For instance, the conclusion of the former study reads: "A majority of rhesus monkeys will consistently suffer hunger rather than secure food at the expense of electroshock to a conspecific."

89. Subsequent reviews of the neuroimaging literature have produced a somewhat muddled view of the underlying neurology of psychopathy (Raine & Yaling, 2006). While individual studies have found anatomical and functional abnormalities in a wide variety of brain regions—including the amygdala, hippocampus, corpus callosum, and putamen—the only result common to all studies is that psychopaths tend to show reduced gray matter in the prefrontal cortex (PFC). Reductions in gray matter in three regions of the PFC—the medial and lateral orbital areas and the frontal poles—correlate with psychopathy scores, and these regions have been shown in other work to be directly involved in the regulation of social conduct (de Oliveira-Souza et al., 2008). Recent findings suggest that the correlation between cortical thinning and psychopathy may be significant only for the right hemisphere (Yang, Raine, Colletti, Toga, & Narr, 2009). The brains of psychopaths also show reduced white matter connections between orbital frontal regions and the amygdala (M. C. Craig et al., 2009). In fact, the difference in the average volume of gray matter in orbitofrontal regions seems to account for half

of the variation in antisocial behavior between the sexes: men and women don't seem to differ in their experience of anger, but women tend to be both more fearful and more empathetic—and are thus better able to control their antisocial impulses (Jones, 2008).

90. Blair et al. hypothesize that the orbitofrontal deficits of psychopathy underlie the propensity for reactive aggression, while the amygdala dysfunction leads to "impairments in aversive conditioning, instrumental learning, and the processing of fearful and sad expressions" that allow for learned, instrumental aggression and make normal socialization impossible. Kent Kiehl, author of the first fMRI study on psychopathy, now believes that the functional neuroanatomy of the disorder includes a network of structures including the orbital frontal cortex, insula, anterior and posterior cingulate, amygdala, parahippocampal gyrus, and anterior superior temporal gyrus (Kiehl et al., 2001). He refers to this network as the "the paralimbic system" (Kiehl, 2006). Kiehl is currently engaged in a massive and ongoing fMRI study of incarcerated psychopaths, using a 1.5 Tesla scanner housed in a tractor-trailer that can be moved from prison to prison. He hopes to build a neuroimaging database of 10,000 subjects (G. Miller, 2008a; Seabrook, 2008).

91. Trivers, 2002, p. 53. For an extensive discussion of the details here, see Dawkins, [1976] 2006, pp. 202–233.

92. Jones, 2008.

93. Diamond, 2008. Pinker, 2007, makes the same point: "If the wars of the twentieth century had killed the same proportion of the population that die in the wars of a typical tribal society, there would have been two billion deaths, not 100 million."

It is easy to conclude that life is cheap in an honor culture, ruled by vengeance and the law of talion ("eye for an eye"), but, as William Ian Miller observes, by at least one measure these societies value life even more than we do. Our modern economies thrive because we tend to limit personal liability. If I sell you a defective ladder, and you fall and break your neck, I may have to pay you some compensation. But I will not have to pay you nearly as much as I would be willing to pay to avoid having my own neck broken. In our society we are constrained by the value a court places on the other guy's neck; in a culture ruled by talion law, we are constrained by the value we place on our own (W. I. Miller, 2006).

94. Bowles, 2006, 2008, 2009.

95. Churchland, 2008a.

96. Libet, Gleason, Wright, & Pearl, 1983.

97. Soon, Brass, Heinze, & Haynes, 2008. Libet later argued that while we don't have free will with respect to initiating behavior, we might have free will to veto an intention before it becomes effective (Libet, 1999, 2003). I think his reasoning was clearly flawed, as there is every reason to think that a conscious veto must also arise on the basis of unconscious neural events.

98. Fisher, 2001; Wegner, 2002; Wegner, 2004.

99. Heisenberg, 2009; Kandel, 2008; Karczmar, 2001; Libet, 1999; McCrone, 2003; Planck & Murphy, 1932; Searle, 2001; Sperry, 1976.

100. Heisenberg, 2009.

101. One problem with this approach is that quantum mechanical effects are

probably not, as a general rule, biologically salient. Quantum effects do drive evolution, as high-energy particles like cosmic rays cause point mutations in DNA, and the behavior of such particles passing through the nucleus of a cell is governed by the laws of quantum mechanics. Evolution, therefore, seems unpredictable in principle (Silver, 2006).

102. The laws of nature do not strike most of us as incompatible with free will because we have not imagined how human action would appear if all cause-and-effect relationships were understood. But imagine that a mad scientist has developed a means of controlling the human brain at a distance: What would it be like to watch him send a person to and fro on the wings of her "will"? Would there be even the slightest temptation to impute freedom to her? No. But this mad scientist is nothing more than causal determinism personified. What makes his existence so inimical to our notion of free will is that when we imagine him lurking behind a person's thoughts and actions—tweaking electrical potentials, manufacturing neurotransmitters, regulating genes, etc.—we cannot help but let our notions of freedom and responsibility travel up the puppet's strings to the hand that controls them. To see that the addition of randomness does nothing to change this situation, we need only imagine the scientist basing the inputs to his machine on a shrewd arrangement of roulette wheels. How would such unpredictable changes in the states of a person's brain constitute freedom?

Swapping any combination of randomness and natural law for a mad scientist, we can see that all the relevant features of a person's inner life would be conserved—thoughts, moods, and intentions would still arise and beget actions—and yet we are left with the undeniable fact that the conscious mind cannot be the source of its own thoughts and intentions. This discloses the real mystery of free will: if our experience is compatible with its utter *absence*, how can we say that we see any evidence for it in the first place?

103. Dennett, 2003.

104. The phrase "alien hand syndrome" describes a variety of neurological disorders in which a person no longer recognizes ownership of one of his hands. Actions of the nondominant hand in the split-brain patient can have this character, and in the acute phase after surgery this can lead to overt, intermanual conflict. Zaidel et al. (2003) prefer the phrase "autonomous hand," as patients typically experience their hand to be out of control but do not ascribe ownership of it to someone else. Similar anomalies can be attributed to other neurological causes: for instance, in *sensory alien hand syndrome* (following a stroke in the right posterior cerebral artery) the right arm will sometimes choke or otherwise attack the left side of the body (Pryse-Philips, 2003).

105. See S. Harris, 2004, pp. 272–274.

106. Burns & Bechara, 2007, p. 264.

107. Others have made a similar argument. See Burns & Bechara, 2007, p. 264; J. Greene & Cohen, 2004, p. 1776.

108. Cf. Levy, 2007.

109. The neuroscientist Michael Gazzaniga writes:

> Neuroscience will never find the brain correlate of responsibility, because that is something we ascribe to humans—to people—not to brains. It is a

> moral value we demand of our fellow, rule-following human beings. Just as optometrists can tell us how much vision a person has (20/20 or 20/200) but cannot tell us when someone is legally blind or has too little vision to drive a school bus, so psychiatrists and brain scientists might be able to tell us what someone's mental state or brain condition is but cannot tell us (without being arbitrary) when someone has too little control to be held responsible. The issue of responsibility (like the issue of who can drive school buses) is a social choice. In neuroscientific terms, no person is more or less responsible than any other for actions. We are all part of a deterministic system that someday, in theory, we will completely understand. Yet the idea of responsibility, a social construct that exists in the rules of a society, does not exist in the neuronal structures of the brain (Gazzaniga, 2005, pp. 101–102).

While it is true that responsibility is a social construct attributed to people and not to brains, it is a social construct that can make more or less sense given certain facts about a person's brain. I think we can easily imagine discoveries in neuroscience, as well as brain imaging technology, that would allow us to attribute responsibility to persons in a far more precise way than we do at present. A "Twinkie defense" would be entirely uncontroversial if we learned that there was something in the creamy center of every Twinkie that obliterated the frontal lobe's inhibitory control over the limbic system.

But perhaps "responsibility" is simply the wrong construct: for Gazzaniga is surely correct to say that "in neuroscientific terms, no person is more or less responsible than any other for actions." Conscious actions arise on the basis of neural events of which we are not conscious. Whether they are predictable or not, we do not cause our causes.

110. Diamond, 2008.

111. In the philosophical literature, one finds three approaches to the problem: determinism, libertarianism, and compatibilism. Both determinism and libertarianism are often referred to as "incompatibilist" views, in that both maintain that if our behavior is fully determined by background causes, free will is an illusion. Determinists believe that we live in precisely such a world; libertarians (no relation to the political view that goes by this name) believe that our agency rises above the field of prior causes—and they inevitably invoke some metaphysical entity, like a soul, as the vehicle for our freely acting wills. Compatibilists, like Daniel Dennett, maintain that free will is compatible with causal determinism (see Dennett, 2003; for other compatibilist arguments see Ayer, Chisholm, Strawson, Frankfurt, Dennett, and Watson—all in Watson, 1982). The problem with compatibilism, as I see it, is that it tends to ignore that people's moral intuitions are driven by deeper, metaphysical notions of free will. That is, the free will that people presume for themselves and readily attribute to others (whether or not this freedom is, in Dennett's sense, "worth wanting") is a freedom that slips the influence of impersonal, background causes. The moment you show that such causes are effective—as any detailed account of the neurophysiology of human thought and behavior would—proponents of free will can no longer locate a plausible hook upon which to hang their notions of moral responsibility. The neuroscientists Joshua Greene and Jonathan Cohen make the same point:

> Most people's view of the mind is implicitly dualist and libertarian and not materialist and compatibilist . . . [I]ntuitive free will is libertarian, not compatibilist. That is, it requires the rejection of determinism and an implicit commitment to some kind of magical mental causation . . . contrary to legal and philosophical orthodoxy, determinism really does threaten free will and responsibility as we intuitively understand them (J. Greene & Cohen, 2004, pp. 1779–1780).

Chapter 3: Belief

1. Brains do not fossilize, so we cannot examine the brains of our ancient ancestors. But comparing the neuroanatomy of living primates offers some indication of the types of physical adaptations that might have led to the emergence of language. For instance, diffusion-tensor imaging of macaque, chimpanzee, and human brains reveals a gradual increase in the connectivity of the arcuate fasciculus—the fiber tract linking the temporal and frontal lobes. This suggests that the relevant adaptations were incremental, rather than saltatory (Ghazanfar, 2008).

2. N. Patterson, Richter, Gnerre, Lander, & Reich, 2006, 2008.

3. Wade, 2006.

4. Sarmiento, Sawyer, Milner, Deak, & Tattersall, 2007; Wade, 2006.

5. It seems, however, that the Neanderthal copy of the FOXP2 gene carried the same two crucial mutations that distinguish modern humans from other primates (Enard et al., 2002; Krause et al., 2007). FOXP2 is now known to play a central role in spoken language, and its disruption leads to severe linguistic impairments in otherwise healthy people (Lai, Fisher, Hurst, Vargha-Khadem, & Monaco, 2001). The introduction of a human FOXP2 gene into mice changes their ultrasonic vocalizations, decreases exploratory behavior, and alters cortico-basal ganglia circuits (Enard et al., 2009). The centrality of FOXP2 for language development in humans has led some researchers to conclude that Neanderthals could speak (Yong, 2008). In fact, one could argue that the faculty of speech must precede *Homo sapiens,* as "it is difficult to imagine the emergence of complex subsistence behaviors and selection for a brain size increase of approximately 75 percent, both since about 800,000 years ago, without complex social communication" (Trinkaus, 2007).

Whether or not they could speak, the Neanderthals were impressive creatures. Their average cranial capacity was 1,520 cc, slightly larger than that of their *Homo sapien* contemporaries. In fact, human cranial capacity has *decreased* by about 150 cc over the millennia to its current average of 1,340 cc (Gazzaniga, 2008). Generally speaking, the correlation between brain size and cognitive ability is less than straightforward, as there are several species that have larger brains than we do (e.g., elephants, whales, dolphins) without exhibiting signs of greater intelligence. There have been many efforts to find some neuroanatomical measure that reliably tracks cognitive ability, including allometric brain size (brain size proportional to body mass), "encephalization quotient" (brain size proportional to the expected brain size for similar animals, corrected for body mass; for primates EQ = [brain weight] / [0.12 × body weight$^{0.67}$]), the size of the neocortex relative to the rest of the brain, etc. None of these metrics has proved especially useful. In fact, among primates, there is no better predictor of cognitive ability than absolute brain size, irrespective of body mass (Deaner, Isler, Burkart, & van Schaik, 2007). By this measure, our competition with Neanderthals looks especially daunting.

There are several genes involved in brain development that have been found to be differentially regulated in human beings compared to other primates; two of special interest are microcephalin and ASPM (the abnormal spindlelike microcephaly-associated gene). The modern variant of microcephalin, which regulates brain size, appeared approximately 37,000 years ago (more or less coincident with the ascendance of modern humans) and has increased in frequency under positive selection pressure ever since (P. D. Evans et al., 2005). One modern variant of ASPM, which also regulates brain size, has spread with great frequency in the last 5,800 years (Mekel-Bobrov et al., 2005). As these authors note, this can be loosely correlated with the spread of cities and the development of written language. The possible significance of these findings is also discussed in Gazzaniga (2008).

6. Fitch, Hauser, & Chomsky, 2005; Hauser, Chomsky, & Fitch, 2002; Pinker & Jackendoff, 2005.

7. Regrettably, language is also the basis of our ability to wage war effectively, to perpetrate genocide, and to render our planet uninhabitable.

8. While general information sharing has been undeniably useful, there is good reason to think that the communication of specifically *social* information has driven the evolution of language (Dunbar, 1998, 2003). Humans also transmit social information (i.e., gossip) in greater quantity and with higher fidelity than nonsocial information (Mesoudi, Whiten, & Dunbar, 2006).

9. Cf. S. Harris, 2004, pp. 243–244.

10. A. R. Damasio, 1999.

11. Westbury & Dennett, 1999.

12. Bransford & McCarrell, 1977.

13. Rumelhart, 1980.

14. Damasio draws a similar distinction (A. R. Damasio, 1999).

15. For the purposes of studying belief in the lab, therefore, there seems to be little problem in defining the phenomenon of interest: *believing* a proposition is the act of accepting it as "true" (e.g., marking it as "true" on a questionnaire); *disbelieving* a proposition is the act of rejecting it as "false"; and being *uncertain* about the truth value of a proposition is the disposition to do neither of these things, but to judge it, rather, as "undecidable."

In our search for the neural correlates of subjective states like belief and disbelief, we are bound to rely on behavioral reports. Therefore, having presented an experimental subject with a written statement—e.g., *the United States is larger than Guatemala*—and watched him mark it as "true," it may occur to us to wonder whether we can take him at his word. Does he *really* believe that the United States is larger than Guatemala? Does this statement, in other words, really *seem true* to him? This is rather like worrying, with reference to a subject who has just performed a lexical decision task, whether a given stimulus really *seems like a word* to him. While it may seem reasonable to worry that experimental subjects might be poor judges of what they believe, or that they might attempt to deceive experimenters, such concerns seem misplaced—or if appropriate here, they should haunt all studies of human perception and cognition. As long as we are content to rely on subjects to report their perceptual judgments (about when, or whether, a given stimulus appeared), or their cognitive ones (about what sort of stimulus it was), there seems to be no special problem taking reports of *belief, disbelief,* and *uncertainty* at face value. This does not ignore the possibility of deception (or self-deception), implicit cognitive conflict, motivated reasoning, and other sources of confusion.

16. Blakeslee, 2007.

17. These considerations run somewhat against David Marr's influential thesis that any complex information-processing system should be understood first at the level of "computational theory" (i.e., the level of highest abstraction) in terms of its "goals" (Marr, 1982). Thinking in terms of goals can be extremely useful, of course, in that it unifies (and ignores) a tremendous amount of bottom-up detail: the goal of "seeing," for instance, is complicated at the level of its neural realization and, what is more, it has been achieved by at least forty separate evolutionary routes (Dawkins, 1996, p. 139). Consequently, thinking about "seeing" in terms of abstract computational goals can make a lot of sense. In a structure like the brain, however, the "goals" of the system can never be fully specified in advance. We currently have no inkling what else a region like the insula might be "for."

18. There has been a long debate in neuroscience over whether the brain is best thought of as a collection of discrete modules or as a distributed, dynamical system. It seems clear, however, that both views are correct, depending on one's level of focus (J. D. Cohen & Tong, 2001). Some degree of modularity is now an undeniable property of brain organization, as damage to one brain region can destroy a specific ability (e.g., the recognition of faces) while sparing most others. There are also distinct differences in cell types and patterns of connectivity that articulate sharp borders between regions. And some degree of modularity is ensured by limitations on information transfer over large distances in the brain.

While regional specialization is a general fact of brain organization, strict partitioning generally isn't: as has already been said, most regions of the brain serve multiple functions. And even within functionally specific regions, the boundaries between their current function and their possible functions are provisional, fuzzy, and in the case of any individual brain, guaranteed to be idiosyncratic. For instance, the brain shows a general capacity to recover from focal injuries, and this entails the recruitment and repurposing of other (generally adjacent) brain areas. Such considerations suggest that we cannot expect true isomorphism between brains—or even between a brain and itself across time.

There is legitimate concern, however, that current methods of neuroimaging tend to beg the question in favor of the modularity thesis—leading, among uncritical consumers of this research, to a naïve picture of functional segregation in the brain. Consider functional magnetic resonance imaging (fMRI), which is the most popular method of neuroimaging at present. This technique does not give us an absolute measure of neural activity. Rather, it allows us to compare changes in blood flow throughout the brain between two experimental conditions. We can, for example, compare instances in which subjects believe statements to be true to instances in which they believe statements to be false. The resulting image reveals which regions of the brain are more active in one condition or the other. Because fMRI allows us to detect signal changes throughout the brain, it is not, in principle, blind to widely distributed or combinatorial processing. But its dependence on blood flow as a marker for neural activity reduces spatial and temporal resolution, and the statistical techniques we use to analyze our data require that we focus on relatively large clusters of activity. It is, therefore, in the very nature of the tool to deliver images that appear to confirm the modular organization of brain function (cf. Henson, 2005). The problem, as far as critics are concerned, is that this method of studying the brain ignores the fact that the whole brain is active in both experimental conditions (e.g., during belief and disbelief), and regions that don't survive this subtractive procedure may well be involved in the relevant information processing.

Functional magnetic resonance imaging (fMRI) also rests on the assumption that there is a more or less linear relationship between changes in blood flow, as measured by blood-oxygen-level-dependent (BOLD) changes in the MR signal, and changes in neuronal activity. While the validity of fMRI seems generally well supported (Logothetis, Pauls, Augath, Trinath, & Oeltermann, 2001), there is some uncertainty about whether the assumed linear relationship between blood flow and neuronal activity holds for all mental processes (Sirotin & Das, 2009). There are also potential problems with comparing one brain state to another on the assumption that changes in brain function are additive in the way that the components of an experimental task may be (this is often referred to as the problem of "pure insertion") (Friston et al., 1996). There are also questions about what "activity" is indicated by changes in the BOLD signal. The principal correlate of blood-flow changes in the brain appears to be presynaptic/neuromodulatory activity (as measured by local field potentials), not axonal spikes. This fact poses a few concerns related to the interpretation of fMRI data: fMRI cannot readily differentiate activity that is specific to a given task and neuromodulation; nor can it differentiate bottom-up from top-down processing. In fact, fMRI may be blind to the difference between excitatory and inhibitory signals, as metabolism also increases with inhibition. It seems quite possible, for instance, that increases in recurrent inhibition in a given region might be associated with greater BOLD signal but decreased neuronal firing. For a discussion of these and other limitations of the technology, see Logothetis, 2008; M. S. Cohen, 1996, 2001. Such concerns notwithstanding, fMRI remains the most important tool for studying brain function in human beings noninvasively.

A more sophisticated, neural network analysis of fMRI data has shown that representational content—which can appear, under standard methods of data analysis, to be strictly segregated (e.g., face-vs.-object perception in the ventral temporal lobe)—is actually intermingled and dispersed across a wider region of the cortex. Information encoding appears to depend not on strict localization, but on a combinatorial pattern of variations in the intensity of the neural response across regions once thought to be functionally distinct (Hanson, Matsuka, & Haxby, 2004).

There are also epistemological questions about what it means to correlate any mental state with physiological changes in the brain. And yet, while I consider the so-called "hard problem" of consciousness (Chalmers, 1996) a real barrier to scientific explanation, I do not think it will hinder the progress of cognitive neuroscience generally. The distinction between consciousness and its contents seems paramount. It is true that we do not understand how consciousness emerges from the unconscious activity of neural networks—or even how it *could* emerge. But we do not need such knowledge to compare states of mind through neuroimaging. To consider one among countless examples from the current literature: neuroscientists have begun to investigate how envy and schadenfreude are related in neuroanatomical terms. One group found activity in the ACC (anterior cingulate cortex) to be correlated with envy, and the magnitude of signal change was predictive of activity in the striatum (a region often associated with reward) when subjects witnessed those they envied experiencing misfortune (signifying the pleasure of schadenfreude) (Takahashi et al., 2009). This reveals something about the relationship between these mental states that may not be obvious by introspection. The finding that right-sided lesions in the MPFC impair the perception of envy (a negative emotion), while analogous left-sided lesions impair the perception of schadenfreude (a positive emotion) fills in a few more details (Shamay-Tsoory, Tibi-Elhanany, & Aharon-Peretz, 2007)—as there is a wider literature on the lateralization of positive and negative mental states. Granted, the relationship between envy and schadenfreude was somewhat obvious without our learning their neural correlates. But improvements in neuroimaging may one day allow us to understand the relationship between such mental states with great precision. This may deliver conceptual surprises and even personal epiphanies. And if the mental states and capacities most conducive to human well-being are ever understood in terms of their underlying neurophysiology, neuroimaging may become an integral part of any enlightened approach to ethics.

It seems to me that progress on this front does not require that we solve the "hard problem" of consciousness (or that it even admit of a solution). When comparing mental states, the reality of human consciousness is a given. We need not understand how consciousness relates to the behavior of atoms to investigate how emotions like love, compassion, trust, greed, fear, and anger differ (and interact) in neurophysiological terms.

19. Most inputs to cortical dendrites come from neurons in the same region of cortex: very few arrive from other cortical regions or from ascending pathways. For instance, only 5 percent to 10 percent of inputs to layer 4 of visual cortex arrive from the thalamus (R. J. Douglas & Martin, 2007).

20. The apparent (qualified) existence of "grandmother cells" notwithstanding (Quiroga, Reddy, Kreiman, Koch, & Fried, 2005). For a discussion of the limits of traditional "connectionist" accounts of mental representation, see Doumas & Hummel, 2005.

21. These data were subsequently published as Harris, S., Sheth, & Cohen 2008.

22. The *post-hoc* analysis of neuroimaging data is a limitation of many studies, and in our original paper we acknowledged the importance of distinguishing between results predicted by a specific model of brain function and those that arise in the absence of a prior hypothesis. This caveat notwithstanding, I believe that too much has been made of the distinction between descriptive and hypothesis-driven research in science generally and in neuroscience in particular. There must always be a first experimental observation, and one gets no closer to physical reality by running a follow-up study. To have been the first person to observe blood-flow changes in the right fusiform gyrus in response to visual stimuli depicting faces (Sergent,

Ohta, & MacDonald, 1992)—and to have concluded, on the basis of these data, that this region of cortex plays a role in facial recognition—was a perfectly legitimate instance of scientific induction. Subsequent corroboration of these results increased our collective confidence in this first set of data (Kanwisher, McDermott, & Chun, 1997) but did not constitute an epistemological advance over the first study. All subsequent hypothesis-driven research that has taken the fusiform gyrus as a region of interest derives its increased legitimacy from the descriptive study upon which it is based (or, as has often been the case in neuroscience, from the purely descriptive, clinical literature). If the initial descriptive study was in error, then any hypothesis based on it would be empty (or only accidentally correct); if the initial work was valid, then follow-up work would merely corroborate it and, perhaps, build upon it. The injuries suffered by Phineas Gage and H.M. were inadvertent, descriptive experiments, and the wealth of information learned from these cases—arguably more than was learned from any two experiments in the history of neuroscience—did not suffer for lack of prior hypothesis. Indeed, these clinical observations became the basis of all subsequent hypotheses about the function of the frontal and medial temporal lobes.

23. E. K. Miller & Cohen, 2001; Desimone & Duncan, 1995. While damage to the PFC can result in a range of deficits, the most common is haphazard, inappropriate, and impulsive behavior, along with the inability to acquire new behavioral rules (Bechara, Damasio, & Damasio, 2000). As many parents can attest, the human capacity for self-regulation does not fully develop until after adolescence; this is when the white-matter connections in the PFC finally mature (Sowell, Thompson, Holmes, Jernigan, & Toga, 1999).

24. Spinoza, [1677] 1982.

25. D. T. K. Gilbert, 1991; D. T. K. Gilbert, Douglas, & Malone, 1990; J. P. Mitchell, Dodson, & Schacter, 2005.

26. This truth bias may interact with (or underlie) what has come to be known as the "confirmation bias" or "positive test strategy" heuristic in reasoning (Klayman & Ha, 1987): people tend to seek evidence that confirms an hypothesis rather than evidence that refutes it. This strategy is known to produce frequent reasoning errors. Our bias toward belief may also explain the "illusory-truth effect," where mere exposure to a proposition, even when it was revealed to be false or attributed to an unreliable source, increases the likelihood that it will later be remembered as being true (Begg, Robertson, Gruppuso, Anas, & Needham, 1996; J. P. Mitchell et al., 2005).

27. This was due to a greater decrease in signal during disbelief trials than during belief trials. This region of the brain is known to have a high level of resting-state activity and to show reduced activity compared to baseline for a wide variety of cognitive tasks (Raichle et al., 2001).

28. Bechara et al., 2000. The MPFC is also activated by reasoning tasks that incorporate high emotional salience (Goel & Dolan, 2003b; Northoff et al., 2004). Individuals with MPFC lesions test normally on a variety of executive function tasks but often fail to integrate appropriate emotional responses into their reasoning about the world. They also fail to habituate normally to unpleasant somatosensory stimuli (Rule, Shimamura, & Knight, 2002). The circuitry in this region that links decision making to emotions seems rather specific, as MPFC lesions do not

disrupt fear conditioning or the normal modulation of memory by emotionally charged stimuli (Bechara et al., 2000). While reasoning appropriately about the likely consequences of their actions, these persons seem unable to feel the difference between good and bad choices.

29. Hornak et al., 2004; O'Doherty, Kringelbach, Rolls, Hornak, & Andrews, 2001.

30. Matsumoto & Tanaka, 2004.

31. Schnider, 2001.

32. Northoff et al., 2006.

33. Kelley et al., 2002.

34. When compared with both belief and uncertainty, disbelief was associated in our study with bilateral activation of the anterior insula, a primary region for the sensation of taste (Faurion, Cerf, Le Bihan, & Pillias, 1998; O'Doherty, Rolls, Francis, Bowtell, & McGlone, 2001). This area is widely thought to be involved with negatively valenced feelings like disgust (Royet, Plailly, Delon-Martin, Kareken, & Segebarth, 2003; Wicker et al., 2003), harm avoidance (Paulus, Rogalsky, Simmons, Feinstein, & Stein, 2003), and the expectation of loss in decision tasks (Kuhnen & Knutson, 2005). The anterior insula has also been linked to pain perception (Wager et al., 2004) and even to the perception of pain in others (T. Singer et al., 2004). The frequent association between activity in the anterior insula and negative affect appears to make at least provisional sense of the emotional tone of disbelief.

While disgust is regularly classed as a primary human emotion, infants and toddlers do not appear to feel it (Bloom, 2004, p. 155). This would account for some of their more arresting displays of incivility. Interestingly, people suffering from Huntington's disease, as well as presymptomatic carriers of the HD allele, exhibit reduced feelings of disgust and are generally unable to recognize the emotion in others (Calder, Keane, Manes, Antoun, & Young, 2000; Gray, Young, Barker, Curtis, & Gibson, 1997; Halligan, 1998; Hayes, Stevenson, & Coltheart, 2007; I. J. Mitchell, Heims, Neville, & Rickards, 2005; Sprengelmeyer, Schroeder, Young, & Epplen, 2006). The recognition deficit has been correlated with reduced activity in the anterior insula (Hennenlotter et al., 2004; Kipps, Duggins, McCusker, & Calder, 2007)—though other work has found that HD patients and carriers are impaired in processing a range of (predominantly negative) emotions: including disgust, anger, fear, sadness, and surprise (Henley et al., 2008; Johnson et al., 2007; Snowden et al., 2008).

We must be careful not to draw too strong a connection between disbelief and disgust (or any other mental state) on the basis of these data. While a connection between these states of mind seems intuitively plausible, equating disbelief with disgust represents a "reverse inference" of a sort known to be problematic in the field of neuroimaging (Poldrack, 2006). One cannot reliably infer the presence of a mental state on the basis of brain data alone, unless the brain regions in question are known to be truly selective for a single mental state. If it were known, for instance, that the anterior insulae were active if and only if subjects experienced disgust, then we could draw quite a strong inference about the role of disgust in disbelief. But there are very few regions of the brain whose function is so selective as to justify inferences of this kind. The anterior insula, for instance, appears to be involved in a wide range of neutral/positive states—including time perception, music appreciation, self-recognition, and smiling (A. D. Craig, 2009).

And there may also be many forms of disgust: While subjects tend to rate a wide range of stimuli as equivalently "disgusting," one group found that disgust associated with pathogen-related acts, social-sexual acts (e.g., incest), and nonsexual moral violations activated different (but overlapping) brain networks (J. S. Borg, Lieberman, & Kiehl, 2008). To further complicate matters, they did not find the insula implicated in any of this disgust processing, with the exception of the subjects' response to incest. This group is not alone in suggesting that the insula may not be selective for disgust and may be more generally sensitive to other factors, including self-monitoring and emotional salience. As the authors note, the difficulty in interpreting these results is compounded by the fact that their subjects were engaged in a memory task and not required to explicitly evaluate how disgusting a stimulus was until after the scanning session. This may have selected against insular activity; at least one other study suggests that the insula may only be preferentially active in response to attended stimuli (Anderson, Christoff, Panitz, De Rosa, & Gabrieli, 2003).

35. These results seem to pull the rug out from under one widely subscribed view in moral philosophy, generally described as "non-cognitivism." Non-cognitivists hold that moral claims lack propositional content and, therefore, do not express genuine beliefs about the world. Unfortunately for this view, our brains appear to be unaware of this breakthrough in metaethics: we seem to accept the truth of moral assertions in the same way as we accept any other statements of fact.

In this first experiment on belief, we also analyzed the brain's response to uncertainty: the mental state in which the truth value of a proposition cannot be judged. Not knowing what one believes to be true—*Is the hotel north of Main Street, or south of Main Street? Was he talking to me, or to the man behind me?*—has obvious behavioral/emotional consequences. Uncertainty prevents the link between thought and subsequent behavior/emotion from forming. It can be distinguished readily from belief and disbelief in this regard, because in the latter states, the mind has settled upon a specific, actionable representation of the world. The results of our study suggest two mechanisms that might account for this difference.

The contrasts—*uncertainty minus belief* and *uncertainty minus disbelief*—yielded signal in the anterior cingulate cortex (ACC). This region of the brain has been widely implicated in error detection (Schall, Stuphorn, & Brown, 2002) and response conflict (Gehring & Fencsik, 2001), and it regularly responds to increases in cognitive load and interference (Bunge, Ochsner, Desmond, Glover, & Gabrieli, 2001). It has also been shown to play a role in the perception of pain (Coghill, McHaffie, & Yen, 2003).

The opposite contrasts, *belief minus uncertainty* and *disbelief minus uncertainty*, showed increased signal in the caudate nucleus, which is part of the basal ganglia. One of the primary functions of the basal ganglia is to provide a route by which cortical association areas can influence motor action. The caudate has displayed context-specific, anticipatory, and reward-related activity in a variety of animal studies (Mink, 1996) and has been associated with cognitive planning in humans (Monchi, Petrides, Strafella, Worsley, & Doyon, 2006). It has also been shown to respond to feedback in both reasoning and guessing tasks when compared to the same tasks without feedback (Elliott, Frith, & Dolan, 1997).

In cognitive terms, one of the principal features of feedback is that it systematically removes uncertainty. The fact that both belief and disbelief showed highly localized signal changes in the caudate, when compared to uncertainty, appears to implicate basal ganglia circuits in the acceptance or rejection of linguistic representations of the world. Delgado et al. showed that the caudate response to feedback can be modulated by prior expectations (Delgado, Frank, & Phelps, 2005). In a trust game played with three hypothetical partners (neutral, bad, and good), they found that the caudate responded strongly to violations of trust by a neutral partner, to a lesser degree with a bad partner, but not at all when the partner was assumed to be morally good. On their account, it seems that the assumption of moral goodness in a partner led subjects to ignore or discount feedback. This result seems convergent with our own: one might say that subjects in their study were uncertain of what to conclude when a trusted collaborator failed to cooperate.

The ACC and the caudate display an unusual degree of connectivity, as the surgical lesioning of the ACC (a procedure known as a *cingulotomy*) causes atrophy of the caudate, and the disruption of this pathway is thought to be the basis of the procedure's effect in treating conditions like obsessive-compulsive disorder (Rauch et al., 2000; Rauch et al., 2001).

There are, however, different types of uncertainty. For instance, there is a difference between expected uncertainty—where one knows that one's observations are unreliable—and unexpected uncertainty, where something in the environment indicates that things are not as they seem. The difference between these two modes of cognition has been analyzed within a Bayesian statistical framework in terms of their underlying neurophysiology. It appears that expected uncertainty is largely mediated by acetylcholine and unexpected uncertainty by norepinephrine (Yu & Dayan, 2005). Behavioral economists sometimes distinguish between "risk" and "ambiguity": the former being a condition where probability can be assessed, as in a game of roulette, the latter being the uncertainty borne of missing information. People are generally more willing to take even very low-probability bets in a condition of risk than they are to act in a condition of missing information. One group found that ambiguity was negatively correlated with activity in the dorsal striatum (caudate/putamen) (Hsu, Bhatt, Adolphs, Tranel, & Camerer, 2005). This result fits very well with our own, as the uncertainty provoked by our stimuli would have taken the form of "ambiguity" rather than "risk."

36. There are many factors that bias our judgment, including: arbitrary anchors on estimates of quantity, availability biases on estimates of frequency, insensitivity to the prior probability of outcomes, misconceptions of randomness, nonregressive predictions, insensitivity to sample size, illusory correlations, overconfidence, valuing of worthless evidence, hindsight bias, confirmation bias, biases based on ease of imaginability, as well as other nonnormative modes of thinking. See Baron, 2008; J. S. B. T. Evans, 2005; Kahneman, 2003; Kahneman, Krueger, Schkade, Schwarz, & Stone, 2006; Kahneman, Slovic, & Tversky, 1982; Kahneman & Tversky, 1996; Stanovich & West, 2000; Tversky & Kahneman, 1974.

37. Stanovich & West, 2000.

38. Fong et al., 1986/07. Once again, asking whether something is rationally or

morally normative is distinct from asking whether it has been evolutionarily adaptive. Some psychologists have sought to minimize the significance of the research on cognitive bias by suggesting that subjects make decisions using heuristics that conferred adaptive fitness on our ancestors. As Stanovich and West (2000) observe, what serves the genes does not necessarily advance the interests of the individual. We could also add that what serves the individual in one context may not serve him in another. The cognitive and emotional mechanisms that may (or may not) have optimized us for face-to-face conflict (and its resolution) have clearly not prepared us to negotiate conflicts waged from afar—whether with email or other long-range weaponry.

39. Ehrlinger, Johnson, Banner, Dunning, & Kruger, 2008; Kruger & Dunning, 1999.

40. Jost, Glaser, Kruglanski, & Sulloway, 2003. Amodio et al. (2007) used EEG to look for differences in neurocognitive function between liberals and conservatives on a Go/No-Go task. They found that liberalism correlated with increased event-related potentials in the anterior cingulate cortex (ACC). Given the ACC's well-established role in mediating cognitive conflict, they concluded that this difference might, in part, explain why liberals are less set in their ways than conservatives, and more aware of nuance, ambiguity, etc. Inzlicht (2009) found a nearly identical result for religious nonbelievers versus believers.

41. Rosenblatt, Greenberg, Solomon, Pyszczynski, & Lyon, 1989.

42. Jost et al., 2003, p. 369.

43. D. A. Pizarro & Uhlmann, 2008.

44. Kruglanski, 1999. The psychologist Drew Westen describes motivated reasoning as "a form of implicit affect regulation in which the brain converges on solutions that minimize negative and maximize positive affect states" (Westen, Blagov, Harenski, Kilts, & Hamann, 2006). This seems apt.

45. The fact that this principle often breaks down, spectacularly and unselfconsciously, in the domain of religion is precisely why one can reasonably question whether the world's religions are in touch with reality at all.

46. Bechara et al., 2000; Bechara, Damasio, Tranel, & Damasio, 1997; A. Damasio, 1999.

47. S. Harris et al., 2008.

48. Burton, 2008.

49. Frith, 2008, p. 45.

50. Silver, 2006, pp. 77–78.

51. But this allele has also been linked to a variety of psychological traits, like novelty seeking and extraversion, which might also account for its persistence in the genome (Benjamin et al., 1996).

52. Burton, 2008, pp. 188–195.

53. Joseph, 2009.

54. Houreld, 2009; LaFraniere, 2007; Harris, 2009.

55. Mlodinow, 2008.

56. Wittgenstein, 1969, p. 206.

57. Analogical reasoning is generally considered a form of induction (Holyoak, 2005).

58. Sloman & Lagnado, 2005; Tenenbaum, Kemp, & Shafto, 2007.

59. For a review of the literature on deductive reasoning see Evans, 2005.

60. Cf. J. S. B. T. Evans, 2005, pp. 178–179.

61. For example, Canessa et al., 2005; Goel, Gold, Kapur, & Houle, 1997; Osherson et al., 1998; Prabhakaran, Rypma, & Gabrieli, 2001; Prado, Noveck, & Van Der Henst, 2009; Rodriguez-Moreno & Hirsch, 2009; Strange, Henson, Friston, & Dolan, 2001. Goel and Dolan (2003a) found that when syllogistic reasoning was modulated by a strong belief bias, the ventromedial prefrontal cortex was preferentially engaged, while such reasoning without an effective belief bias appeared to be driven by a greater activation of the (right) lateral prefrontal cortex. Elliot et al. (1997) found that guessing appears to be mediated by the ventromedial prefrontal cortex. Bechara et al. (1997) report that patients suffering ventromedial prefrontal damage fail to act according to their correct conceptual beliefs while engaged in a gambling task. Prior to our 2008 study, it was unclear how these findings would relate to belief and disbelief per se. They suggested, however, that the medial prefrontal cortex would be among our regions of interest.

While decision making is surely related to belief processing, the "decisions" that neuroscientists have tended to study are those that precede voluntary movements in tests of sensory discrimination (Glimcher, 2002). The initiation of such movements requires the judgment that a target stimulus has appeared—we might even say that this entails the "belief" that an event has occurred—but such studies are not designed to examine belief as a propositional attitude. Decision making in the face of potential reward is obviously of great interest to anyone who would understand the roots of human and animal behavior, but the link to belief per se appears tenuous. For instance, in a visual-decision task (in which monkeys were trained to detect the coherent motion of random dots and signal their direction with eye movements), Gold and Shadlen found that the brain regions responsible for this sensory judgment were the very regions that subsequently initiated the behavioral response (Gold & Shadlen, 2000, 2002; Shadlen & Newsome, 2001). Neurons in these regions appear to act as integrators of sensory information, initiating the trained behavior whenever a threshold of activation has been reached. We might be tempted to say, therefore, that the "belief" that a stimulus is moving to the left is located in the lateral intraparietal area, the frontal eye fields, and the superior colliculus—as these are the brain regions responsible for initiating eye movements. But here we are talking about the "beliefs" of a monkey—a monkey that has been trained to reproduce a stereotyped response to a specific stimulus in expectation of an immediate reward. This is not the kind of "belief" that has been the subject of my research.

The literature on decision making has generally sought to address the link between voluntary action, error detection, and reward. Insofar as the brain's reward system involves a prediction that a specific behavior will lead to future reward, we might say that this is a matter of belief formation—but there is nothing to indicate that such beliefs are explicit, linguistically mediated, or propositional. We know that they cannot be, as most studies of reward processing have been done in rodents, monkeys, titmice, and pigeons. This literature has investigated the link between sensory judgments and motor responses, not the difference between belief and disbelief in matters of propositional truth. This is not to minimize the fascinating progress that has occurred in this field. In fact, the same economic modeling that allows behavioral ecologists to account for the foraging behavior of animal groups also allows neurophysiologists to describe the activity of the neuronal assemblies that govern an individual animal's response to differential rewards (Glimcher, 2002). There is also a growing literature on neuroeconomics, which examines human decision making (as well as trust and reciprocity) using neuroimaging. Some of these findings are discussed here.

62. This becomes especially feasible using more sophisticated techniques of data analysis, like multivariate pattern classification (Cox & Savoy, 2003; P. K. Douglas, Harris, & Cohen, 2009). Most analyses of fMRI data are univariate and merely look for correlations between the activity at each point in the brain and the task paradigm. This approach ignores the interrelationships that surely exist between regions. Cox and Savoy demonstrated that a multivariate approach, in which statistical pattern recognition methods are used to look for correlations across all regions, allows for a very subtle analysis of fMRI data in a way that is far more sensitive to distributed patterns of activity (Cox & Savoy, 2003). With this approach, they were able to determine which visual stimulus a subject was viewing (out of ten possible types) by examining a mere 20 seconds of his experimental run.

Pamela Douglas, a graduate student in Mark Cohen's cognitive neuroscience lab at UCLA, recently took a similar approach to analyzing my original belief data (P. K. Douglas, Harris, & Cohen, 2009). She created an unsupervised machine-learning classifier by first performing an independent component (IC) analysis on each of our subjects' three scanning sessions. She then selected the IC time-course values that corresponded to the maximum value of the hemodynamic response function (HRF) following either "belief" or "disbelief" events. These values were fed into a selection process, whereby ICs that were "good predictors" were promoted as features in a classification network for training a Naïve Bayes classifier. To test the accuracy of her classification, Douglas performed a leave-one-out cross-validation. Using this criterion, her Naïve Bayes classifier correctly labeled the "left out" trial 90 percent of the time. Given such results, it does not seem far-fetched that, with further refinements in both hardware and techniques of data analysis, fMRI could become a means for accurate lie detection.

63. Holden, 2001.

64. Broad, 2002.

65. Pavlidis, Eberhardt, & Levine, 2002.

66. Allen & Iacono, 1997; Farwell & Donchin, 1991. Spence et al. (2001) appear to have published the first neuroimaging study on deception. Their research suggests that "deception" is associated with bilateral increases in activity in the ventrolateral prefrontal cortex (BA 47), a region often associated with response inhibition and the suppression of inappropriate behavior (Goldberg, 2001).

The results of the Spence study were susceptible to some obvious limitations, however—perhaps most glaring was the fact that the subjects were told precisely when to lie by being given a visual cue. Needless to say, this did much to rob the experiment of verisimilitude. The natural ecology of deception is one in which a potential liar must notice when questions draw near to factual terrain that he is committed to keeping hidden, and he must lie as the situation warrants, while respecting the criteria for logical coherence and consistency that he and his interlocutor share. (It is worth noting that unless one respects the norms of reasoning and belief formation, it is impossible to lie successfully. This is not an accident.) To be asked to lie automatically in response to a visual cue simply does not simulate ordinary acts of deception. Spence et al. did much to remedy this problem in a subsequent study, where subjects could lie at their own discretion and on subjects related to their personal histories (Spence, Kaylor-Hughes, Farrow, & Wilkinson, 2008). This study largely replicated their findings with respect to the primary involvement of the ventrolateral PFC (though now almost entirely in the left hemisphere). There have been other neuroimaging studies of deception—as "guilty knowledge" (Langleben et al., 2002), "feigned memory impairment" (Lee et al., 2005), etc.—but the challenge, apart from reliably finding the neural correlates of any of these states, is to find a result that generalizes to all forms of deception.

It is not entirely obvious that these studies have given us a sound basis for detecting deception through neuroimaging. Focusing on the neural correlates of belief and disbelief might obviate whatever differences exist between types of deception, the mode of stimulus presentation, etc. Is there a difference, for instance, between denying what is true and asserting what is false? Recasting the question in terms of a proposition to be believed or disbelieved might circumvent any problem posed by the "directionality" of a lie. Another group (Abe et al., 2006) took steps to address the directionality issue by asking subjects to alternately deny true knowledge and assert false knowledge. However, this study suffered from the usual limitations, in that subjects were directed when to lie, and their lies were limited to whether they had previously viewed an experimental stimulus.

A functional neuroanatomy of belief might also add to our understanding of the placebo response—which can be both profound and profoundly unhelpful to the process of vetting pharmaceuticals. For instance, 65 percent to 80 percent of the effect of antidepressant medication seems attributable to positive expectation (Kirsch, 2000). There are even forms of surgery that, while effective, are no more effective than sham procedures (Ariely, 2008). While some neuroimaging work has been done in this area, the placebo response is currently operationalized in terms of symptom relief, without reference to a subject's underlying state of mind (Lieberman et al., 2004; Wager et al., 2004). Finding the neural correlates of belief might allow us to eventually control for this effect during the process of drug design.

67. Stoller & Wolpe, 2007.

68. Grann, 2009.

69. There are, however, reasons to doubt that our current methods of neuroimaging, like fMRI, will yield a practical mind-reading technology. Functional MRI studies as a group have several important limitations. Perhaps first and most important are those of statistical power and sensitivity. If one chooses to analyze one's data at extremely conservative thresholds to exclude the possibility of type I (false positive) detection errors, this necessarily increases one's type II (false negative) error. Further, most studies implicitly assume uniform detection sensitivity throughout the brain, a condition known to be violated for the low-bandwidth, fast-imaging scans used for fMRI. Field inhomogeneity also tends to increase the magnitude of motion artifacts. When motion is correlated to the stimuli, this can produce false positive activations, especially in the cortex.

We may also discover that the underlying physics of neuroimaging grants only so much scope for human ingenuity. If so, an era of cheap, covert lie detection might never dawn, and we will be forced to rely upon some relentlessly costly, cumbersome technology. Even so, I think it safe to say that the time is not far off when lying, on the weightiest matters—in court, before a grand jury, during important business negotiations, etc.—will become a practical impossibility. This fact will be widely publicized, of course, and the relevant technology will be expected to be in place, or accessible, whenever the stakes are high. This very assurance, rather than the incessant use of these machines, will change us.

70. Ball, 2009.

71. Pizarro & Uhlmann, 2008.

72. Kahneman, 2003.

73. Rosenhan, 1973.

74. McNeil, Pauker, Sox, & Tversky, 1982.

75. There are other reasoning biases that can affect medical decisions. It is well known, for instance, that the presence of two similar options can create "decisional conflict," biasing a choice in favor of a third alternative. In one experiment, neurologists and neurosurgeons were asked to determine which patients to admit to surgery first. Half the subjects were given a choice between a woman in her early fifties and a man in his seventies. The other half were given the same two patients, plus another woman in her fifties who was difficult to distinguish from the first: 38 percent of doctors chose to operate on the older man in the first scenario; 58 percent chose him in the second (LaBoeuf & Shafir, 2005). This is a bigger change in outcomes than might be apparent at first glance: in the first case, the woman's chance of getting the surgery is 62 percent; in the second it is 21 percent.

Chapter 4: Religion

1. Marx, [1843] 1971.

2. Freud, [1930] 1994; Freud & Strachey, [1927] 1975.

3. Weber, [1922] 1993.

4. Zuckerman, 2008.

5. Norris & Inglehart, 2004.

6. Finke & Stark, 1998.

7. Norris & Inglehart, 2004, p. 108.

8. It does not seem, however, that socioeconomic inequality explains religious extremism in the Muslim world, where radicals are, on average, wealthier and more educated than moderates (Atran, 2003; Esposito, 2008).

9. http://pewglobal.org/reports/display.php?ReportID=258.

10. http://pewforum.org/surveys/campaign08/.

11. Pyysiäinen & Hauser, 2010.

12. Zuckerman, 2008.

13. Paul, 2009.

14. Hall, Matz, & Wood, 2010.

15. Decades of cross-cultural research on "subjective well-being" (SWB) by the World Values Survey (www.worldvaluessurvey.org) indicate that religion may make an important contribution to human happiness and life satisfaction at low levels of societal development, security, and freedom. The happiest and most secure societies, however, tend to be the most secular. The greatest predictors of a society's

mean SWB are social tolerance (of homosexuals, gender equality, other religions, etc.) and personal freedom (Inglehart, Foa, Peterson, & Welzel, 2008). Of course, tolerance and personal freedom are directly linked, and neither seems to flourish under the shadow of orthodox religion.

16. Paul, 2009.

17. Culotta, 2009.

18. Buss, 2002.

19. I am indebted to the biologist Jerry Coyne for pointing this out (personal communication). The neuroscientist Mark Cohen has further observed (personal communication), however, that many traditional societies are far more tolerant of male promiscuity than female—for instance, the sanction for being raped has often been as bad, or worse, than for initiating a rape. Cohen speculates that in such cases religion may offer a post-hoc justification for a biological imperative. This may be so. I would only add that here, as elsewhere, the task of maximizing human well-being is clearly separable from Pleistocene biological imperatives.

20. Foster & Kokko, 2008.

21. Fincher, Thornhill, Murray, & Schaller, 2008.

22. Dawkins, 1994; D. Dennett, 1994; D. C. Dennett, 2006; D. S. Wilson & Wilson, 2007; E. O. Wilson, 2005; E. O. Wilson & Holldobler, 2005, pp. 169–172; Dawkins, 2006.

23. Boyer, 2001; Durkheim & Cosman, [1912] 2001.

24. Stark, 2001, pp. 180–181.

25. Livingston, 2005.

26. Dennett, 2006.

27. http://pewforum.org/docs/?DocID=215.

28. http://pewforum.org/docs/?DocID=153.

29. Boyer, 2001, p. 302.

30. Barrett, 2000.

31. Bloom, 2004.

32. Brooks, 2009.

33. E. M. Evans, 2001.

34. Hood, 2009.

35. D'Onofrio, Eaves, Murrelle, Maes, & Spilka, 1999.

36. Previc, 2006.

37. In addition, the densities of a specific type of serotonin receptor have been inversely correlated with high scores on the "spiritual acceptance" subscale of the Temperament and Character Inventory (J. Borg, Andree, Soderstrom, & Farde, 2003).

38. Asheim, Hansen & Brodtkorb, 2003; Blumer, 1999; Persinger & Fisher, 1990.

39. Brefczynski-Lewis, Lutz, Schaefer, Levinson, & Davidson, 2007; Lutz, Brefczynski-Lewis, Johnstone, & Davidson, 2008; Lutz, Greischar, Rawlings, Ricard, & Davidson, 2004; Lutz, Slagter, Dunne, & Davidson, 2008; A. Newberg et al., 2001.

40. Anastasi & Newberg, 2008; Azari et al., 2001; A. Newberg, Pourdehnad, Alavi, & d'Aquili, 2003; A. B. Newberg, Wintering, Morgan, & Waldman, 2006; Schjoedt, Stodkilde-Jorgensen, Geertz, & Roepstorff, 2008, 2009.

41. S. Harris et al., 2008.

42. Kapogiannis et al., 2009.

43. S. Harris et al., 2009.

44. D'Argembeau et al., 2008; Moran, Macrae, Heatherton, Wyland, & Kelley, 2006; Northoff et al., 2006; Schneider et al., 2008.

45. Bechara et al., 2000.

46. Hornak et al., 2004; O'Doherty et al., 2003; Rolls, Grabenhorst, & Parris, 2008.

47. Matsumoto & Tanaka, 2004.

48. A direct comparison of *belief minus disbelief* in Christians and nonbelievers did not show any significant group differences for nonreligious stimuli. For religious stimuli, there were additional regions of the brain that did differ by group; however, these results seem best explained by a common reaction in both groups to statements that violate religious doctrines (i.e., "blasphemous" statements).

The opposite contrast, *disbelief minus belief,* yielded increased signal in the superior frontal sulcus and the precentral gyrus. The engagement of these areas is not readily explained on the basis of prior work. However, a region-of-interest analysis revealed increased signal in the insula for this contrast. This partially replicates our previous finding for this contrast and supports the work of Kapogiannis et al., who also found signal in the insula to be correlated with the rejection of religious statements deemed false. The significance of the anterior insula for negative affect/appraisal has been discussed above. Because Kapogiannis et al. did not include a nonreligious control condition in their experiment, they interpreted the insula's recruitment as a sign that violations of religious doctrine might provoke "aversion, guilt, or fear of loss" in people of faith. Whereas, our prior work suggests that the insula is active for disbelief generally.

In our study, Christians appeared to make the largest contribution to the insula signal bilaterally, while the pooled data from both groups produced signal in the left hemisphere exclusively. Kapogiannis et al. also found that religious subjects produced bilateral insula signal on disbelief trials, while data from both believers and nonbelievers yielded signal only on the left. Taken together, these findings suggest that there may be a group difference between religious believers and nonbelievers with respect to insular activity. In fact, Inbar et al. found that heightened feelings of disgust are predictive of social conservatism (as measured by self-reported disgust in response to homosexuality) (Inbar, Pizarro, Knobe, & Bloom, 2009). Our finding of bilateral insula signal for this contrast in our first study might be explained by the fact that we did not control for religious belief (or political orientation) during recruitment. Given the rarity of nonbelievers in the United States, even on college campuses, one would expect that most of the subjects in our first study possessed some degree of religious faith.

49. We obtained these results, despite the fact that our two groups accepted and rejected diametrically opposite statements in half of our experimental trials. This would seem to rule out the possibility that our data could be explained by any property of the stimuli apart from their being deemed "true" or "false" by the participants in our study.

50. Wager et al., 2004.

51. T. Singer et al., 2004.

52. Royet et al., 2003; Wicker et al., 2003.

53. Izuma, Saito, & Sadato, 2008.

54. Another key region that appears to be preferentially engaged by religious thinking is the posterior medial cortex. This area is part of the "resting state" network that shows greater activity during both rest and self-referential tasks (Northoff et al., 2006). It is possible that one difference between responding to religious and nonreligious stimuli is that, for both groups, a person's answers serve to affirm his or her identity: i.e., for every religious trial, Christians were explicitly affirming their religious worldview, while nonbelievers were explicitly denying the truth claims of religion.

The opposite contrast, *nonreligious minus religious statements,* produced greater signal in left hemisphere memory networks, including the hippocampus, the parahippocampal gyrus, middle temporal gyrus, temporal pole, and retrosplenial cortex. It is well known that the hippocampus and the parahippocampal gyrus are involved in memory retrieval (Diana, Yonelinas, & Ranganath, 2007). The anterior temporal lobe is also engaged by semantic memory tasks (K. Patterson, Nestor, & Rogers, 2007), and the retrosplenial cortex displays especially strong reciprocal connectivity with structures in the medial temporal lobe (Buckner, Andrews-Hanna, & Schacter, 2008). Thus, judgments about the nonreligious stimuli presented in our study seemed more dependent upon those brain systems involved in accessing stored knowledge.

Among our religious stimuli, the subset of statements that ran counter to Christian doctrine yielded greater signal for both groups in several brain regions, including the ventral striatum, paracingulate cortex, middle frontal gyrus, the frontal poles, and inferior parietal cortex. These regions showed greater signal both when Christians rejected stimuli contrary to their doctrine (e.g., *The Biblical god is a myth*) and when nonbelievers affirmed the truth of those same statements. In other words, these brain areas responded preferentially to "blasphemous" statements in both subject groups. The ventral striatum signal in this contrast suggests that decisions about these stimuli may have been more rewarding for both groups: Nonbelievers may take special pleasure in making assertions that explicitly negate religious doctrine, while Christians may enjoy rejecting such statements as false.

55. Festinger, Riecken, & Schachter, [1956] 2008.

56. Atran, 2006a.

57. Atran, 2007.

58. Bostom, 2005; Butt, 2007; Ibrahim, 2007; Oliver & Steinberg, 2005; Rubin, 2009; Shoebat, 2007.

59. Atran, 2006b.

60. Gettleman, 2008.

61. Ariely, 2008, p. 177.

62. Pierre, 2001.

63. Larson & Witham, 1998.

64. Twenty-one percent of American adults (and 14 percent of those born on American soil) are functionally illiterate (www.nifl.gov/nifl/facts/reading_facts.html), while only 3 percent of Americans agree with the statement "I don't believe in God." Despite their near invisibility, atheists are the most stigmatized minority

in the United States—beyond homosexuals, African Americans, Jews, Muslims, Asians, or any other group. Even after September 11, 2001, more Americans would vote for a Muslim for president than would vote for an atheist (Edgell, Geteis, & Hartmann, 2006).

65. Morse, 2009.

66. And if there were a rider to this horse, he would be entirely without structure and oblivious to the details of perception, cognition, emotion, and intention that owe their existence to electrochemical activity in specific regions of the brain. If there is a "pure consciousness" that might occupy such a role, it will bear little resemblance to what most religious people mean by a "soul." A soul this diaphanous would be just as at home in the brain of a hyena (and seems just as likely to be there) as it would in the brain of a human being.

67. Levy (2007) poses the same question.

68. Collins, 2006.

69. It is worth recalling in this context that it is, in fact, possible for an established scientist to destroy his career by saying something stupid. James Watson, the codiscoverer of the structure of DNA, a Nobel laureate, and the original head of the Human Genome Project, recently accomplished this feat by asserting in an interview that people of African descent appear to be innately less intelligent than white Europeans (Hunte-Grubbe, 2007). A few sentences, spoken off the cuff, resulted in academic defenestration: lecture invitations were revoked, award ceremonies canceled, and Watson was forced to immediately resign his post as chancellor of Cold Spring Harbor Laboratory.

Watson's opinions on race are disturbing, but his underlying point was not, in principle, unscientific. There may very well be detectable differences in intelligence between races. Given the genetic consequences of a population living in isolation for tens of thousands of years, it would be very surprising if there were *no* differences between racial or ethnic groups waiting to be discovered. I say this not to defend Watson's fascination with race, or to suggest that such race-focused research might be worth doing. I am merely observing that there is, at least, a *possible* scientific basis for his views. While Watson's statement was obnoxious, one cannot say that his views are utterly irrational or that, by merely giving voice to them, he has repudiated the scientific worldview and declared himself immune to its further discoveries. Such a distinction would have to be reserved for Watson's successor at the Human Genome Project, Dr. Francis Collins.

70. Collins, 2006, p. 225.

71. Van Biema, 2006; Paulson, 2006.

72. Editorial, 2006.

73. Collins, 2006, p. 178.

74. Ibid., pp. 200–201.

75. Ibid., p. 119.

76. It is true that the mysterious effectiveness of mathematics for describing the physical world has lured many scientists to mysticism, philosophical Platonism, and religion. The physicist Eugene Wigner famously posed the problem in a paper entitled "The Unreasonable Effectiveness of Mathematics in the Natural Sciences" (Wigner, 1960). While I'm not at all sure that it exhausts this mystery, I think there is something to be said for Craik's idea (Craik, 1943) that an isomorphism between

brain processes and the processes in the world that they represent might account for the utility of numbers and certain mathematical operations. Is it really so surprising that certain patterns of brain activity (i.e., numbers) can map reliably onto the world?

77. Collins also has a terrible tendency of cherry-picking and misrepresenting the views of famous scientists like Stephen Hawking and Albert Einstein. For instance he writes:

> Even Albert Einstein saw the poverty of a purely naturalistic worldview. Choosing his words carefully, he wrote, "science without religion is lame, religion without science is blind."

The one choosing words carefully here is Collins. As we saw above, when read in context (Einstein, 1954, pp. 41–49), this quote reveals that Einstein did not in the least endorse theism and that his use of the word "God" was a poetical way of referring to the laws of nature. Einstein had occasion to complain about such deliberate distortions of his work:

> It was, of course, a lie what you read about my religious convictions, a lie which is being systematically repeated. I do not believe in a personal God and I have never denied this but have expressed it clearly. If something is in me which can be called religious then it is the unbounded admiration for the structure of the world so far as our science can reveal it (cited in R. Dawkins, 2006, p. 36).

78. Wright, 2003, 2008.

79. Polkinghorne, 2003; Polkinghorne & Beale, 2009.

80. Polkinghorne, 2003, pp. 22–23.

81. In 1996, the physicist Alan Sokal submitted the nonsense paper "Transgressing the Boundaries: Towards a Transformative Hermeneutics of Quantum Gravity" to the journal *Social Text*. While the paper was patently insane, this journal, which still stands "at the forefront of cultural theory," avidly published it. The text is filled with gems like following:

> [T]he discourse of the scientific community, for all its undeniable value, cannot assert a privileged epistemological status with respect to counterhegemonic narratives emanating from dissident or marginalized communities . . . In quantum gravity, as we shall see, the space-time manifold ceases to exist as an objective physical reality; geometry becomes relational and contextual; and the foundational conceptual categories of prior science—among them, existence itself—become problematized and relativized. This conceptual revolution, I will argue, has profound implications for the content of a future postmodern and liberatory science (Sokal, 1996, p. 218).

82. Ehrman, 2005. Bible scholars agree that the earliest Gospels were written decades after the life of Jesus. We don't have the original texts of any of the Gospels. What we have are copies of copies of copies of ancient Greek manuscripts that differ from one another in literally thousands of places. Many show signs of later interpolation—which is to say that people have added passages to these texts over the centuries, and these passages have found their way into the canon. In fact,

there are whole sections of the New Testament, like the Book of Revelation, that were long considered spurious, that were included in the Bible only after many centuries of neglect; and there are other books, like the Shepherd of Hermas, that were venerated as part of the Bible for hundreds of years only to be rejected finally as false scripture. Consequently, it is true to say that generations of Christians lived and died having been guided by scripture that is now deemed to be both mistaken and incomplete by the faithful. In fact, to this day, Roman Catholics and Protestants cannot agree on the full contents of the Bible. Needless to say, such a haphazard and all-too-human process of cobbling together the authoritative word of the Creator of the Universe seems a poor basis for believing that the miracles of Jesus actually occurred.

The philosopher David Hume made a very nice point about believing in miracles on the basis of testimony: "No testimony is sufficient to establish a miracle, unless the testimony be of such a kind, that its falsehood would be more miraculous, than the fact, which it endeavours to establish . . ." (Hume, 1996, vol. IV, p. 131). This is a good rule of thumb. Which is more likely, that Mary, the mother of Jesus, would have sex outside of wedlock and then feel the need to lie about it, or that she would conceive a child through parthenogenesis the way aphids and Komodo dragons do? On the one hand, we have the phenomenon of lying about adultery—in a context where the penalty for adultery is death—and on the other, we have a woman spontaneously mimicking the biology of certain insects and reptiles. Hmm . . .

83. Editorial, 2008.

84. Maddox, 1981.

85. Sheldrake, 1981.

86. I have publicly lamented this double standard on a number of occasions (S. Harris, 2007a; S. Harris & Ball, 2009)

87. Collins, 2006, p. 23.

88. Langford et al., 2006.

89. Masserman et al., 1964.

90. Our picture of chimp notions of fairness is somewhat muddled. There is no question that they notice inequity, but they do not seem to care if they profit from it (Brosnan, 2008; Brosnan, Schiff, & de Waal, 2005; Jensen, Call, & Tomasello, 2007; Jensen, Hare, Call, & Tomasello, 2006; Silk et al., 2005).

91. Range et al., 2009.

92. Siebert, 2009.

93. Silver, 2006, p. 157.

94. Ibid., p. 162.

95. Collins, 2006.

96. Of course, I also received much support, especially from scientists, and even from scientists at the NIH.

97. Miller, it should be noted, is also a believing Christian and the author of *Finding Darwin's God* (K. R. Miller, 1999). For all its flaws, this book contains an extremely useful demolition of "intelligent design."

98. C. Mooney & S. Kirshenbaum, 2009, pp. 97–98.

99. The claim is ubiquitous, even at the highest levels of scientific discourse. From a recent editorial in *Nature,* insisting on the reality of human evolution:

> The vast majority of scientists, and the majority of religious people, see little potential for pleasure or progress in the conflicts between religion and science that are regularly fanned into flame by a relatively small number on both sides of the debate. Many scientists are religious, and perceive no conflict between the values of their science—values that insist on disinterested, objective inquiry into the nature of the Universe—and those of their faith (Editorial, 2007).

From the National Academy of Sciences:

> Science can neither prove nor disprove religion . . . Many scientists have written eloquently about how their scientific studies have increased their awe and understanding of a creator . . . The study of science need not lessen or compromise faith (National Academy of Sciences [U.S.] & Institute of Medicine [U.S.], 2008, p. 54).

Chapter 5: The Future of Happiness

1. Allen, 2000.
2. *Los Angeles Times,* July 5, 1910.
3. As indicated above, I think it is reasonably clear that concerns about angering God and/or suffering an eternity in hell are based on specific notions of harm. Not believing in God or hell leaves one blissfully unconcerned about such liabilities. Under Haidt's analysis, concerns about God and the afterlife would seem to fall under the categories of "authority" and/or "purity." I think such assignments needlessly parcel what is, at bottom, a more general concern about harm.
4. Inbar et al., 2009.
5. Schwartz, 2004.
6. D. T. Gilbert, 2006.
7. www.ted.com/talks/daniel_kahneman_the_riddle_of_experience_vs_memory.html.
8. Ibid.
9. Lykken & Tellegen, 1996.
10. D. T. Gilbert, 2006, pp. 220–222.
11. Simonton, 1994.
12. Rilling et al., 2002.

REFERENCES

Aaronovitch, D. (2010). *Voodoo histories: The role of the conspiracy theory in shaping modern history.* New York: Riverhead Books.

Abe, N., Suzuki, M., Tsukiura, T., Mori, E., Yamaguchi, K., Itoh, M., et al. (2006). Dissociable roles of prefrontal and anterior cingulate cortices in deception. *Cereb Cortex, 16*(2), 192–199.

Abraham, A., & von Cramon, D. Y. (2009). Reality = relevance? Insights from spontaneous modulations of the brain's default network when telling apart reality from fiction. *PLoS ONE, 4*(3), e4741.

Abraham, A., von Cramon, D. Y., & Schubotz, R. I. (2008). Meeting George Bush versus meeting Cinderella: The neural response when telling apart what is real from what is fictional in the context of our reality. *J Cogn Neurosci, 20*(6), 965–976.

Adolphs, R., Tranel, D., Koenigs, M., & Damasio, A. R. (2005). Preferring one taste over another without recognizing either. *Nat Neurosci, 8*(7), 860–861.

Ainslie, G. (2001). *Breakdown of will.* Cambridge, UK: Cambridge University Press.

Allen, J. (2000). *Without sanctuary: Lynching photography in America.* Santa Fe, NM: Twin Palms.

Allen, J. J., & Iacono, W. G. (1997). A comparison of methods for the analysis of event-related potentials in deception detection. *Psychophysiology, 34*(2), 234–240.

Amodio, D. M., Jost, J. T., Master, S. L., & Yee, C. M. (2007). Neurocognitive correlates of liberalism and conservatism. *Nat Neurosci, 10*(10), 1246–1247.

Anastasi, M. W., & Newberg, A. B. (2008). A preliminary study of the acute effects of religious ritual on anxiety. *J Altern Complement Med, 14*(2), 163–165.

Anderson, A. K., Christoff, K., Panitz, D., De Rosa, E., & Gabrieli, J. D. (2003). Neural correlates of the automatic processing of threat facial signals. *J Neurosci, 23*(13), 5627–5633.

Andersson, J. L. R., Jenkinson, M., & Smith, S. M. (2007). Non-linear registration, aka spatial normalisation. *FMRIB technical report, TR07JA2.*

Andersson, J. L. R., Jenkinson, M., & Smith, S. M. (2007). Non-linear optimisation. *FMRIB technical report, TR07JA1.*

Appiah, A. (2008). *Experiments in ethics.* Cambridge, MA: Harvard University Press.

Ariely, D. (2008). *Predictably irrational.* New York: Harper Collins.

Asheim Hansen, B., & Brodtkorb, E. (2003). Partial epilepsy with "ecstatic" seizures. *Epilepsy Behav, 4*(6), 667–673.

Atchley, R. A., Ilardi, S. S., & Enloe, A. (2003). Hemispheric asymmetry in the processing of emotional content in word meanings: The effect of current and past depression. *Brain Lang, 84*(1), 105–119.

Atran, S. (2003, May 5). Who wants to be a martyr? *New York Times.*

Atran, S. (2006a). Beyond belief: Further discussion. Retrieved June 11, 2008, from www.edge.org/discourse/bb.html.

Atran, S. (2006b). What would Gandhi do today? Nonviolence in an age of terrorism. Retrieved from http://sitemaker.umich.edu/satran/relevant_articles_on_terrorism.

Atran, S. (2007). Paper presented at the Beyond Belief: Enlightenment 2.0. Retrieved from http://thesciencenetwork.org/programs/beyond-belief-enlightenment-2-0/scott-atran.

Azari, N. P., Nickel, J., Wunderlich, G., Niedeggen, M., Hefter, H., Tellmann, L., et al. (2001). Neural correlates of religious experience. *Eur J Neurosci, 13*(8), 1649–1652.

Baars, B. J., & Franklin, S. (2003). How conscious experience and working memory interact. *Trends Cogn Sci, 7*(4), 166–172.

Babiak, P., & Hare, R. D. (2006). *Snakes in suits: When psychopaths go to work* (1st ed.). New York: Regan Books.

Ball, P. (2009, June 25). And another thing . . . Retrieved July 6, 2009, from http://philipball.blogspot.com.

Baron, A. S., & Banaji, M. R. (2006). The development of implicit attitudes. Evidence of race evaluations from ages 6 and 10 and adulthood. *Psychol Sci, 17*(1), 53–58.

Baron, J. (2008). *Thinking and deciding* (4th ed.). New York: Cambridge University Press.

Baron-Cohen, S. (1995). *Mindblindness: An essay on autism and theory of mind.* Cambridge, MA: MIT Press.

Barrett, J. L. (2000). Exploring the natural foundations of religion. *Trends Cogn Sci, 4*(1), 29–34.

Bauby, J.-D. (1997). *The diving bell and the butterfly* (1st U.S. ed.). New York: A. A. Knopf.

Baumeister, R. F. (2001). Violent pride. *Sci Am, 284*(4), 96–101.

Baumeister, R. F., Campbell, J. D., Krueger, J. I., & Vohs, K. D. (2005). Exploding the self-esteem myth. *Sci Am, 292*(1), 70–77.

Bawer, B. (2006). *While Europe slept: How radical Islam is destroying the West from within* (1st ed.). New York: Doubleday.

Bechara, A., Damasio, H., & Damasio, A. R. (2000). Emotion, decision making and the orbitofrontal cortex. *Cereb Cortex, 10*(3), 295–307.

Bechara, A., Damasio, H., Tranel, D., & Damasio, A. R. (1997). Deciding advantageously before knowing the advantageous strategy. *Science, 275*(5304), 1293–1295.

Begg, I. M., Robertson, R. K., Gruppuso, V., Anas, A., & Needham, D. R. (1996). The Illusory-knowledge effect. *Journal of Memory and Language, 35*, 410–433.

Benedetti, F., Mayberg, H. S., Wager, T. D., Stohler, C. S., & Zubieta, J. K. (2005). Neurobiological mechanisms of the placebo effect. *J Neurosci, 25*(45), 10390–10402.

Benedict, R. (1934). *Patterns of culture.* Boston, New York: Houghton Mifflin.

Benjamin, J., Li, L., Patterson, C., Greenberg, B. D., Murphy, D. L., & Hamer, D. H. (1996). Population and familial association between the D4 dopamine receptor gene and measures of novelty seeking. *Nat Genet, 12*(1), 81–84.

Bilefsky, D. (2008, July 10). In Albanian feuds, isolation engulfs families. *New York Times.*

Blackmore, S. J. (2006). *Conversations on consciousness: What the best minds think about the brain, free will, and what it means to be human.* Oxford, UK; New York: Oxford University Press.

Blair, J., Mitchell, D. R., & Blair, K. (2005). *The psychopath: Emotion and the brain.* Malden, MA: Blackwell.

Blakemore, S. J., & Frith, C. (2003). Self-awareness and action. *Curr Opin Neurobiol, 13*(2), 219–224.

Blakemore, S. J., Oakley, D. A., & Frith, C. D. (2003). Delusions of alien control in the normal brain. *Neuropsychologia, 41*(8), 1058–1067.

Blakemore, S. J., Rees, G., & Frith, C. D. (1998). How do we predict the consequences of our actions? A functional imaging study. *Neuropsychologia, 36*(6), 521–529.

Blakeslee, S. (2007, February 6). A small part of the brain, and its profound effects. *New York Times.*

Block, N. (1995). On a confusion about the function of consciousness. *Behavioral and Brain Sciences, 18*, 227–247.

Block, N., Flanagan, O., & Güzeldere, G. (1997). *The Nature of Consciousness: Philosophical Debates.* Cambridge, MA: The MIT Press.

Bloom, P. (2004). *Descartes' baby: How the science of child development explains what makes us human.* New York: Basic Books.

Bloom, P. (2010, May 9). The moral life of babies. *New York Times Magazine.*

Blow, C. M. (2009, June 26). The prurient trap. *New York Times.*

Blumer, D. (1999). Evidence supporting the temporal lobe epilepsy personality syndrome. *Neurology, 53*(5 Suppl 2), S9–12.

Bogen, G. M., & Bogen, J. E. (1986). On the relationship of cerebral duality to creativity. *Bull Clin Neurosci, 51*, 30–32.

Bogen, J. E. (1986). Mental duality in the intact brain. *Bull Clin Neurosci, 51*, 3–29.

Bogen, J. E. (1995a). On the neurophysiology of consciousness: Pt. II. Constraining the semantic problem. *Conscious Cogn, 4*(2), 137–158.

Bogen, J. E. (1995b). On the neurophysiology of consciousness: Pt. I. An overview. *Conscious Cogn, 4*(1), 52–62.

Bogen, J. E. (1997). Does cognition in the disconnected right hemisphere require right hemisphere possession of language? *Brain Lang, 57*(1), 12–21.

Bogen, J. E. (1998). My developing understanding of Roger Wolcott Sperry's philosophy. *Neuropsychologia, 36*(10), 1089–1096.

Bogen, J. E., Sperry, R. W., & Vogel, P. J. (1969). Addendum: Commissural section and propagation of seizures. In Jasper et al. (Ed.), *Basic mechanisms of the epilepsies.* Boston: Little, Brown and Company, 439.

Bok, H. (2007). The implications of advances in neuroscience for freedom of the will. *Neurotherapeutics, 4*(3), 555–559.

Borg, J., Andree, B., Soderstrom, H., & Farde, L. (2003). The serotonin system and spiritual experiences. *Am J Psychiatry, 160*(11), 1965–1969.

Borg, J. S., Lieberman, D., & Kiehl, K. A. (2008). Infection, incest, and iniquity: investigating the neural correlates of disgust and morality. *J Cogn Neurosci, 20*(9), 1529–1546.

Bostom, A. G. (2005). *The legacy of Jihad: Islamic holy war and the fate of non-Muslims.* Amherst, NY: Prometheus Books.

Bostrom, N. (2003). Are we living in a computer simulation? *Philosophical Quarterly, 53*(211), 243–255.

Bostrom, N., & Ord, T. (2006). The reversal test: Eliminating status quo bias in applied ethics. *Ethics 116*, 656–679.

Bouchard, T. J., Jr. (1994). Genes, environment, and personality. *Science, 264*(5166), 1700–1701.

Bouchard, T. J., Jr., Lykken, D. T., McGue, M., Segal, N. L., & Tellegen, A. (1990). Sources of human psychological differences: The Minnesota study of twins reared apart. *Science, 250*(4978), 223–228.

Bouchard, T. J., Jr., McGue, M., Lykken, D., & Tellegen, A. (1999). Intrinsic and extrinsic religiousness: genetic and environmental influences and personality correlates. *Twin Res, 2*(2), 88–98.

Bowles, S. (2006). Group competition, reproductive leveling, and the evolution of human altruism. *Science, 314*(5805), 1569–1572.

Bowles, S. (2008). Being human: Conflict: Altruism's midwife. *Nature, 456*(7220), 326–327.

Bowles, S. (2009). Did warfare among ancestral hunter-gatherers affect the evolution of human social behaviors? *Science, 324*(5932), 1293–1298.

Boyer, P. (2001). *Religion explained: The evolutionary origins of religious thought.* New York: Basic Books.

Boyer, P. (2003). Religious thought and behaviour as by-products of brain function. *Trends Cogn Sci, 7*(3), 119–124.

Bransford, J. D., & McCarrell, N. S. (1977). A sketch of a cognitive approach to comprehension: Some thoughts about understanding what it means to comprehend. In P. N. Johnson-Laird & P. C. Wason (Eds.), *Thinking* (pp. 377–399). Cambridge, UK: Cambridge University Press.

Brefczynski-Lewis, J. A., Lutz, A., Schaefer, H. S., Levinson, D. B., & Davidson, R. J. (2007). Neural correlates of attentional expertise in long-term meditation practitioners. *Proc Natl Acad Sci USA, 104*(27), 11483–11488.

Broad, W. J. (2002, October, 9). Lie-detector tests found too flawed to discover spies. *New York Times.*

Broks, P. (2004). *Into the silent land: Travels in neuropsychology.* New York: Atlantic Monthly Press.

Brooks, M. (2009). Born believers: How your brain creates God. *New Scientist* (2694) Feb. 4, 30–33.

Brosnan, S. F. (2008). How primates (including us!) respond to inequity. *Adv Health Econ Health Serv Res, 20*, 99–124.

Brosnan, S. F., Schiff, H. C., & de Waal, F. B. (2005). Tolerance for inequity may increase with social closeness in chimpanzees. *Proc Biol Sci, 272*(1560), 253–258.

Buckholtz, J. W., Treadway, M. T., Cowan, R. L., Woodward, N. D., Benning, S. D., Li, R., et al. (2010). Mesolimbic dopamine reward system hypersensitivity in individuals with psychopathic traits. *Nat Neurosei, 13*(4), 419–421.

Buckner, R. L., Andrews-Hanna, J. R., & Schacter, D. L. (2008). The brain's default network: Anatomy, function, and relevance to disease. *Ann NY Acad Sci, 1124*, 1–38.

Buehner, M. J., & Cheng, P. W. (2005). Causal learning. In K. J. Holyoak & R. G. Morrison (Eds.), *The Cambridge handbook of thinking and reasoning* (pp. 143–168). New York: Cambridge University Press.

Bunge, S. A., Ochsner, K. N., Desmond, J. E., Glover, G. H., & Gabrieli, J. D. (2001). Prefrontal regions involved in keeping information in and out of mind. *Brain, 124*(Pt. 10), 2074–2086.

Burgess, P. W., & McNeil, J. E. (1999). Content-specific confabulation. *Cortex, 35*(2), 163–182.

Burns, K., & Bechara, A. (2007). Decision making and free will: a neuroscience perspective. *Behav Sci Law, 25*(2), 263–280.

Burton, H., Snyder, A. Z., & Raichle, M. E. (2004). Default brain functionality in blind people. *Proc Natl Acad Sci USA, 101*(43), 15500–15505.

Burton, R. A. (2008). *On being certain: Believing you are right even when you're not* (1st ed.). New York: St. Martin's Press.

Buss, D. (2002). Sex, marriage, and religion: What adaptive problems do religious phenomena solve? *Psychological Inquiry, 13*(3), 201–203.

Butt, H. (2007, July 2). I was a fanatic . . . I know their thinking, says former radical Islamist. *Daily Mail.*

Calder, A. J., Keane, J., Manes, F., Antoun, N., & Young, A. W. (2000). Impaired recognition and experience of disgust following brain injury. *Nat Neurosci, 3*(11), 1077–1078.

Caldwell, C. (2009). *Reflections on the revolution in Europe: Immigration, Islam, and the West.* New York: Doubleday.

Camerer, C. F. (2003). Psychology and economics. Strategizing in the brain. *Science, 300*(5626), 1673–1675.

Canessa, N., Gorini, A., Cappa, S. F., Piattelli-Palmarini, M., Danna, M., Fazio, F., et al. (2005). The effect of social content on deductive reasoning: An fMRI study. *Hum Brain Mapp, 26*(1), 30–43.

Canli, T., Brandon, S., Casebeer, W., Crowley, P. J., Du Rousseau, D., Greely, H. T., et al. (2007a). Neuroethics and national security. *Am J Bioeth, 7*(5), 3–13.

Canli, T., Brandon, S., Casebeer, W., Crowley, P. J., Durousseau, D., Greely, H. T., et al. (2007b). Response to open peer commentaries on "Neuroethics and national security." *Am J Bioeth, 7*(5), W1–3.

Canli, T., Sivers, H., Whitfield, S. L., Gotlib, I. H., & Gabrieli, J. D. (2002). Amygdala response to happy faces as a function of extraversion. *Science, 296*(5576), 2191.

Carroll, S. (2010). Science and morality: You can't derive "ought" from "is." *NPR: 13.7 Cosmos and Culture,* www.npr.org/templates/story/story.php?storyId=126504492.

Carroll, S. (2010a). The moral equivalent of the parallel postulate. Cosmic Variance, (March 24) http://blogs.discovermagazine.com/cosmicvariance/2010/03/24/the-moral-equivalent-of-the-parallel-postulate/.

Carson, A. J., MacHale, S., Allen, K., Lawrie, S. M., Dennis, M., House, A., et al. (2000). Depression after stroke and lesion location: a systematic review. *Lancet, 356*(9224), 122–126.

Carter, C. S., Braver, T. S., Barch, D. M., Botvinick, M. M., Noll, D., & Cohen, J. D. (1998). Anterior cingulate cortex, error detection, and the online monitoring of performance. *Science, 280*(5364), 747–749.

Casebeer, W. D. (2003). *Natural ethical facts: Evolution, connectionism, and moral cognition.* Cambridge, MA: MIT Press.

Chalmers, D. J. (1995). The puzzle of conscious experience. *Sci Am, 273*(6), 80–86.

Chalmers, D. J. (1996). *The conscious mind: In search of a fundamental theory.* New York: Oxford University Press.

Chalmers, D. J. (1997). Moving forward on the problem of consciousness. *Journal of Consciousness Studies, 4*(1), 3–46.

Choi, J. K., & Bowles, S. (2007). The coevolution of parochial altruism and war. *Science, 318*(5850), 636–640.

Christoff, K., Gordon, A. M., Smallwood, J., Smith, R., & Schooler, J. W. (2009). Experience sampling during fMRI reveals default network and executive system contributions to mind wandering. *Proc Natl Acad Sci USA* (May 26) *106*(21), 8719–24.

Church, R. M. (1959). Emotional reactions of rats to the pain of others. *J Comp Physiol Psychol, 52*(2), 132–134.

Churchland, P. M. (1979). *Scientific realism and the plasticity of mind.* Cambridge, UK: Cambridge University Press.

Churchland, P. M. (1988). *Matter and consciousness.* Cambridge, MA: MIT Press.

Churchland, P. M. (1995). *The engine of reason, the seat of the soul: A philosophical journey into the brain.* Cambridge, MA: MIT Press.

Churchland, P. M. (1997). Knowing qualia: A reply to Jackson. In N. Block, O. Flanagan, & G. Güzeldere (Eds.), *The nature of consciousness: Philosophical debates* (pp. 571–578). Cambridge, MA: MIT Press.

Churchland, P. S. (2008b). *Morality & the social brain.* Unpublished manuscript.

Churchland, P. S. (2009). Inference to the best decision. In J. Bickle (Ed.), *Oxford Handbook of philosophy and neuroscience.* Oxford: Oxford University Press, 419–430.

Cleckley, H. M. ([1941] 1982). *The mask of sanity* (Rev. ed.). New York: New American Library.

Coghill, R. C., McHaffie, J. G., & Yen, Y. F. (2003). Neural correlates of interindividual differences in the subjective experience of pain. *Proc Natl Acad Sci USA, 100*(14), 8538–8542.

Cohen, J. D., & Blum, K. I. (2002). Reward and decision. *Neuron, 36*(2), 193–198.

Cohen, J. D., & Tong, F. (2001). Neuroscience. The face of controversy. *Science, 293*(5539), 2405–2407.

Cohen, M. (1996). Functional MRI: a phrenology for the 1990's? *J Magn Reson Imaging, 6*(2), 273–274.

Cohen, M. S. (1999). Echo-planar imaging and functional MRI. In C. Moonen & P. Bandettini (Eds.), *Functional MRI* (pp. 137–148). Berlin: Springer-Verlag.

Cohen, M. S. (2001). Practical aspects in the design of mind reading instruments. *American Journal of Neuroradiology.*

Cohen, M. S. (2001). Real-time functional magnetic resonance imaging. *Methods, 25*(2), 201–220.

Collins, F. S. (2006). *The language of God: A scientist presents evidence for belief.* New York: Free Press.

Comings, D. E., Gonzales, N., Saucier, G., Johnson, J. P., & MacMurray, J. P. (2000). The DRD4 gene and the spiritual transcendence scale of the character temperament index. *Psychiatr Genet, 10*(4), 185–189.

Cooney, J. W., & Gazzaniga, M. S. (2003). Neurological disorders and the structure of human consciousness. *Trends Cogn Sci, 7*(4), 161–165.

Corballis, M. C. (1998). Sperry and the age of Aquarius: Science, values and the split brain. *Neuropsychologia, 36*(10), 1083–1087.

Cox, D. D., & Savoy, R. L. (2003). Functional magnetic resonance imaging (fMRI) "brain reading": Detecting and classifying distributed patterns of fMRI activity in human visual cortex. *Neuroimage, 19*(2 Pt. 1), 261–270.

Craig, A. D. (2002). How do you feel? Interoception: the sense of the physiological condition of the body. *Nat Rev Neurosci, 3*(8), 655–666.

Craig, A. D. (2009). How do you feel—now? The anterior insula and human awareness. *Nat Rev Neurosci, 10*(1), 59–70.

Craig, M. C., Catani, M., Deeley, Q., Latham, R., Daly, E., Kanaan, R., et al. (2009). Altered connections on the road to psychopathy. *Mol Psychiatry, 14*(10), 946–953.

Craik, K. (1943). Hypothesis on the nature of thought. *The nature of explanation.* Cambridge, UK: Cambridge University Press.

Crick, F. (1994). *The astonishing hypothesis: The scientific search for the soul.* New York: Charles Scribner's Sons.

Crick, F., & Koch, C. (1998). Consciousness and neuroscience. *Cereb. Cortex, 8,* 97–107.

Crick, F., & Koch, C. (1999). The unconscious homunculus. In T. Metzinger (Ed.), *The neural correlates of consciousness* (pp. 103–110). Cambridge, MA: MIT Press.

Crick, F., & Koch, C. (2003). A framework for consciousness. *Nat Neurosci, 6*(2), 119–126.

Culotta, E. (2009). Origins. On the origin of religion. *Science, 326*(5954), 784–787.

D'Argembeau, A., Feyers, D., Majerus, S., Collette, F., Van der Linden, M., Maquet, P., et al. (2008). Self-reflection across time: Cortical midline structures differentiate between present and past selves. *Soc Cogn Affect Neurosci, 3*(3), 244–252.

D'Onofrio, B. M., Eaves, L. J., Murrelle, L., Maes, H. H., & Spilka, B. (1999). Understanding biological and social influences on religious affiliation, attitudes, and behaviors: A behavior genetic perspective. *J Pers, 67*(6), 953–984.

Damasio, A. (1999). *The feeling of what happens: Body and emotion in the making of consciousness.* New York: Harcourt Brace.

Damasio, A. R. (1999). Thinking about belief: Concluding remarks. In D. L. Schacter & E. Scarry (Eds.), *Memory, brain, and belief* (pp. 325–333). Cambridge, MA: Harvard University Press.

Davidson, D. (1987). Knowing one's own mind. *Proceedings and addresses of the American Philosophical Association, 61*, 441–458.

Dawkins, R. (1994). Burying the vehicle. *Behavioural and Brain Sciences, 17*(4), 616–617.

Dawkins, R. (1996). *Climbing mount improbable.* New York: Norton.

Dawkins, R. (2006). *The God delusion.* New York: Houghton Mifflin.

Dawkins, R. ([1976] 2006). *The selfish gene.* Oxford, UK: New York: Oxford University Press.

Dawkins, R. (2010a, March 28). Ratzinger is the perfect pope. *Washington Post: On Faith.*

Dawkins, R. (2010b, April 13). The pope should stand trial. *The Guardian.*

De Grey, A. D. N. J., & Rae, M. (2007). *Ending aging: The rejuvenation breakthroughs that could reverse human aging in our lifetime.* New York: St. Martin's Press.

De Neys, W., Vartanian, O., & Goel, V. (2008). Smarter than we think: When our brains detect that we are biased. *Psychol Sci, 19*(5), 483–489.

de Oliveira-Souza, R., Hare, R. D., Bramati, I. E., Garrido, G. J., Azevedo Ignacio, F., Tovar-Moll, F., et al. (2008). Psychopathy as a disorder of the moral brain: Fronto-temporo-limbic grey matter reductions demonstrated by voxel-based morphometry. *Neuroimage, 40*(3), 1202–1213.

Deaner, R. O., Isler, K., Burkart, J., & van Schaik, C. (2007). Overall brain size, and not encephalization quotient, best predicts cognitive ability across non-human primates. *Brain Behav Evol, 70*(2), 115–124.

Delacour, J. (1995). An introduction to the biology of consciousness. *Neuropsychologia, 33*(9), 1061–1074.

Delgado, M. R., Frank, R. H., & Phelps, E. A. (2005). Perceptions of moral character modulate the neural systems of reward during the trust game. *Nat Neurosci, 8*(11), 1611–1618.

Dennett, D. (1990). Quining qualia. In W. Lycan (Ed.), *Mind and cognition: A reader* (pp. 519–547). Oxford: Blackwell.

Dennett, D. (1994). E pluribus unum? Commentary on Wilson & Sober: Group selection. *Behavioural and Brain Sciences, 17*(4), 617–618.

Dennett, D. (1996). Facing backwards on the problem of consciousness. *Journal of Consciousness Studies, 3*(1), 4–6.

Dennett, D. C. (1987). *The intentional stance.* Cambridge, Mass.: MIT Press.

Dennett, D. C. (1991). *Consciousness explained* (1st Ed.). Boston: Little, Brown & Co.

Dennett, D. C. (1995). *Darwin's dangerous idea: Evolution and the meanings of life* (1st ed.). New York: Simon & Schuster.

Dennett, D. C. (2003). *Freedom evolves.* New York: Viking.

Dennett, D. C. (2006). *Breaking the spell: Religion as a natural phenomenon.* London: Allen Lane.

Desimone, R., & Duncan, J. (1995). Neural mechanisms of selective visual attention. *Annu Rev Neurosci, 18*, 193–222.

Diamond, J. (2008, April 21). Vengeance is ours. *New Yorker*, 74–87.

Diamond, J. M. (1997). *Guns, germs, and steel: The fates of human societies* (1st ed.). New York: W.W. Norton & Co.

Diamond, J. M. (2005). *Collapse: How societies choose to fail or succeed.* New York: Viking.

Diana, R. A., Yonelinas, A. P., & Ranganath, C. (2007). Imaging recollection and familiarity in the medial temporal lobe: a three-component model. *Trends Cogn Sci, 11*(9), 379–386.

Diener, E., Oishi, S., & Lucas, R. E. (2003). Personality, culture, and subjective well-being: Emotional and cognitive evaluations of life. *Annu Rev Psychol, 54*, 403–425.

Ding, Y. C., Chi, H. C., Grady, D. L., Morishima, A., Kidd, J. R., Kidd, K. K., et al. (2002). Evidence of positive selection acting at the human dopamine receptor D4 gene locus. *Proc Natl Acad Sci USA, 99*(1), 309–314.

Dolan, M., & Fullam, R. (2004). Theory of mind and mentalizing ability in antisocial personality disorders with and without psychopathy. *Psychol Med, 34*(6), 1093–1102.

Dolan, M., & Fullam, R. (2006). Face affect recognition deficits in personality-disordered offenders: Association with psychopathy. *Psychol Med, 36*(11), 1563–1569.

Donadio, R. (2010a, March 26). Pope may be at crossroads on abuse, forced to reconcile policy and words. *New York Times.*

Donadio, R. (2010b, April 29). In abuse crisis, a church is pitted against society and itself. *New York Times.*

Doty, R. W. (1998). The five mysteries of the mind, and their consequences. *Neuropsychologia, 36*(10), 1069–1076.

Douglas, P. K., Harris, S., & Cohen, M. S. (2009). *Naïve Bayes classification of belief versus disbelief using event related neuroimaging data.* Paper presented at the Organization for Human Brain Mapping 2009 (July) Annual Meeting.

Douglas, R. J., & Martin, K. A. (2007). Recurrent neuronal circuits in the neocortex. *Curr Biol, 17*(13), R496–500.

Doumas, L. A. A., & Hummel, J. E. (2005). Approaches to modeling human mental representations: What works, what doesn't, and why. In K. J. Holyoak & R. G. Morrison (Eds.), *The Cambridge handbook of thinking and reasoning* (pp. 73–91). New York: Cambridge University Press.

Dressing, H., Sartorius, A., & Meyer-Lindenberg, A. (2008). Implications of fMRI and genetics for the law and the routine practice of forensic psychiatry. *Neurocase, 14*(1), 7–14.

Dronkers, N. F. (1996). A new brain region for coordinating speech articulation. *Nature, 384*(6605), 159–161.

Dunbar, R. (1998). The social brain hypothesis. *Evolutionary Anthropology, 6,* 178–190.

Dunbar, R. (2003). Psychology. Evolution of the social brain. *Science, 302*(5648), 1160–1161.

Dunbar, R. (2006). We believe. *New Scientist, 189*(2536), 30–33.

Duncan, J., & Owen, A. M. (2000). Common regions of the human frontal lobe recruited by diverse cognitive demands. *Trends Neurosci, 23*(10), 475–483.

Durkheim, E. (2001 [1912]). *The elementary forms of religious life.* (C. Cosmen, Trans.) Oxford, UK; New York: Oxford University Press.

Dyson, F. (2002). The conscience of physics. *Nature, 420*(12 December), 607–608.

Eddington, A. S. (1928). *The nature of the physical world.* Cambridge, UK: Cambridge University Press.

Edelman, G. M. (1989). *The remembered present: A biological theory of consciousness.* New York: Basic Books.

Edelman, G. M. (2004). *Wider than the sky: The phenomenal gift of consciousness.* New Haven: Yale University Press.

Edelman, G. M. (2006). *Second nature: Brain science and human knowledge.* New Haven: Yale University Press.

Edelman, G. M., & Tononi, G. (2000). *A universe of consciousness: How matter becomes imagination* (1st ed.). New York, NY: Basic Books.

Edgell, P., Geteis, J., & Hartmann, D. (2006). Atheists as "other": Moral boundaries and cultural membership in American society. *American Sociological Review, 71*(April), 211–234.

Edgerton, R. B. (1992). *Sick societies: Challenging the myth of primitive harmony.* New York: Free Press.

Editorial, N. (2006a). Neuroethics needed. *Nature, 441*(7096), 907.

Editorial, N. (2006b). Building bridges. *Nature, 442*(7099), 110.

Editorial, N. (2007). Evolution and the brain. *Nature, 447*(7146), 753.

Editorial, N. (2008). Templeton's legacy. *Nature, 454*(7202), 253–254.

Egnor, S. E. (2001). Effects of binaural decorrelation on neural and behavioral processing of interaural level differences in the barn owl (*Tyto alba*). *J Comp Physiol [A], 187*(8), 589–595.

Ehrlinger, J., Johnson, K., Banner, M., Dunning, D., & Kruger, J. (2008). Why the unskilled are unaware: Further explorations of (absent) self-insight among the incompetent. *Organ Behav Hum Decis Process, 105*(1), 98–121.

Ehrman, B. D. (2005). *Misquoting Jesus: The Story Behind Who Changed the Bible and Why* (1st ed.). New York: HarperSanFrancisco.

Ehrsson, H. H., Spence, C., & Passingham, R. E. (2004). That's my hand! Activity in premotor cortex reflects feeling of ownership of a limb. *Science, 305*(5685), 875–877.

Einstein, A. (1954). *Ideas and opinions. Based on* Mein Weltbild. New York: Crown Publishers.

Eisenberger, N. I., Lieberman, M. D., & Satpute, A. B. (2005). Personality from a controlled processing perspective: An fMRI study of neuroticism, extraversion, and self-consciousness. *Cogn Affect Behav Neurosci, 5*(2), 169–181.

Elliott, R., Frith, C. D., & Dolan, R. J. (1997). Differential neural response to positive and negative feedback in planning and guessing tasks. *Neuropsychologia, 35*(10), 1395–1404.

Enard, W., Gehre, S., Hammerschmidt, K., Holter, S. M., Blass, T., Somel, M., et al. (2009). A humanized version of FOXP2, affects cortico-basal ganglia circuits in mice. *Cell, 137*(5), 961–971.

Enard, W., Przeworski, M., Fisher, S. E., Lai, C. S., Wiebe, V., Kitano, T., et al. (2002). Molecular evolution of FOXP2, a gene involved in speech and language. *Nature, 418*(6900), 869–872.

Esposito, J. L. (2008). *Who speaks for Islam?: What a billion Muslims really think.* New York, NY: Gallup Press.

Evans, E. M. (2001). Cognitive and contextual factors in the emergence of diverse belief systems: Creation versus evolution. *Cogn Psychol, 42*(3), 217–266.

Evans, J. S. B. T. (2005). Deductive reasoning. In K. J. Holyoak & R. G. Morrison (Eds.), *The Cambridge handbook of thinking and reasoning* (pp. 169–184). New York: Cambridge University Press.

Evans, P. D., Gilbert, S. L., Mekel-Bobrov, N., Vallender, E. J., Anderson, J. R., Vaez-Azizi, L. M., et al. (2005). Microcephalin, a gene regulating brain size, continues to evolve adaptively in humans. *Science, 309*(5741), 1717–1720.

Evers, K. (2005). Neuroethics: A philosophical challenge. *Am J Bioeth, 5*(2), 31–33; discussion W33–34.

Faison, S. (1996, December 20). The death of the last emperor's last eunuch. *New York Times.*

Farah, M. J. (2005). Neuroethics: the practical and the philosophical. *Trends Cogn Sci, 9*(1), 34–40.

Farah, M. J. (2007). Social, legal, and ethical implications of cognitive neuroscience: "Neuroethics" for short. *J Cogn Neurosci, 19*(3), 363–364.

Farah, M. J., Illes, J., Cook-Deegan, R., Gardner, H., Kandel, E., King, P., et al. (2004). Neurocognitive enhancement: What can we do and what should we do? *Nat Rev Neurosci, 5*(5), 421–425.

Farah, M. J., & Murphy, N. (2009). Neuroscience and the soul. *Science, 323*(5918), 1168.

Farrer, C., & Frith, C. D. (2002). Experiencing oneself vs. another person as being the cause of an action: the neural correlates of the experience of agency. *Neuroimage, 15*(3), 596–603.

Farwell, L. A., & Donchin, E. (1991). The truth will out: Interrogative polygraphy ("lie detection") with event-related brain potentials. *Psychophysiology, 28*(5), 531–547.

Faurion, A., Cerf, B., Le Bihan, D., & Pillias, A. M. (1998). fMRI study of taste cortical areas in humans. *Ann NY Acad Sci, 855*, 535–545.

Feigl, H. (1967). *The "mental" and the "physical": The essay and a postcript.* Minneapolis, MN.: University of Minnesota Press.

Festinger, L., Riecken, H. W., & Schachter, S. ([1956] 2008). *When prophecy fails.* Minneapolis, MN: University of Minnesota Press.

Filkins, D. (2010, February 7). On Afghan road, scenes of beauty and death. *New York Times.*

Fincher, C. L., Thornhill, R., Murray, D. R., & Schaller, M. (2008). Pathogen prevalence predicts human cross-cultural variability in individualism/collectivism. *Proc Biol Sci, 275*(1640), 1279–1285.

Finkbeiner, M., & Forster, K. I. (2008). Attention, intention and domain-specific processing. *Trends Cogn Sci, 12*(2), 59–64.

Finke, R., & Stark, R. (1998). Religious choice and competition. *American Sociological Review, 63*(5), 761–766.

Fins, J. J., & Shapiro, Z. E. (2007). Neuroimaging and neuroethics: Clinical and policy considerations. *Curr Opin Neurol, 20*(6), 650–654.

Fisher, C. M. (2001). If there were no free will. *Med Hypotheses, 56*(3), 364–366.

Fitch, W. T., Hauser, M. D., & Chomsky, N. (2005). The evolution of the language faculty: Clarifications and implications. *Cognition, 97*(2), 179–210; discussion 211–225.

Flanagan, O. J. (2002). *The problem of the soul: Two visions of mind and how to reconcile them.* New York: Basic Books.

Flanagan, O. J. (2007). *The really hard problem: Meaning in a material world.* Cambridge, MA: MIT Press.

Fletcher, P. C., Happé, F., Frith, U., Baker, S. C., Dolan, R. J., Frackowiak, R. S., et al. (1995). Other minds in the brain: A functional imaging study of "theory of mind" in story comprehension. *Cognition, 57*(2), 109–128.

Fodor, J. (2000). *The mind doesn't work that way.* Cambridge, MA: MIT Press.

Fodor, J. (2007, October 18). Why pigs don't have wings. *London Review of Books.*

Fong, G. T., Krantz, D. H., & Nisbett, R. E. (1986/07). The effects of statistical training on thinking about everyday problems. *Cognitive Psychology, 18*(3), 253–292.

Foot, P. (1967). The problem of abortion and the doctrine of double effect. *Oxford Review, 5*, 5–15.

Foster, K. R., & Kokko, H. (2009). The evolution of superstitious and superstition-like behavior. *Proc Biol Sci* 276(1654), 31–37.

Frank, M. J., D'Lauro, C., & Curran, T. (2007). Cross-task individual differences in error processing: Neural, electrophysiological, and genetic components. *Cogn Affect Behav Neurosci, 7*(4), 297–308.

Frederico Marques, J., Canessa, N., & Cappa, S. (2009). Neural differences in the processing of true and false sentences: Insights into the nature of 'truth' in language comprehension. *Cortex*, 45(6), 759–68.

Freeman, W. J. (1997). Three centuries of category errors in studies of the neural basis of consciousness and intentionality. *Neural Networks, 10*(7), 1175–1183.

Freud, S. ([1930] 2005). *Civilization and its discontents.* New York: W. W. Norton.

Freud, S., & Strachey, J. ([1927] 1975). *The future of an illusion.* New York: Norton.

Friedman, T. L. (2007, September 5). Letter from Baghdad. *New York Times.*

Fries, A. B., Ziegler, T. E., Kurian, J. R., Jacoris, S., & Pollak, S. D. (2005). Early experience in humans is associated with changes in neuropeptides critical for regulating social behavior. *Proc Natl Acad Sci USA, 102*(47), 17237–17240.

Friston, K. J., Price, C. J., Fletcher, P., Moore, C., Frackowiak, R. S., & Dolan, R. J. (1996). The trouble with cognitive subtraction. *Neuroimage, 4*(2), 97–104.

Frith, C. (2008). No one really uses reason. *New Scientist*, (2666) (July 26), 45.

Frith, C. D., & Frith, U. (2006). The neural basis of mentalizing. *Neuron, 50*(4), 531–534.

Frith, U., Morton, J., & Leslie, A. M. (1991). The cognitive basis of a biological disorder: Autism. *Trends Neurosci, 14*(10), 433–438.

Fromm, E. (1973). *The anatomy of human destructiveness* (1st ed.). New York: Holt.

Fuchs, T. (2006). Ethical issues in neuroscience. *Curr Opin Psychiatry, 19*(6), 600–607.

Fuster, J. M. (2003). *Cortex and mind: Unifying cognition.* Oxford, UK: New York: Oxford University Press.

Gallea, C., Graaf, J. B., Pailhous, J., & Bonnard, M. (2008). Error processing during online motor control depends on the response accuracy. *Behav Brain Res*, 193(1), 117–125.

Garavan, H., Ross, T. J., Murphy, K., Roche, R. A., & Stein, E. A. (2002). Dissociable executive functions in the dynamic control of behavior: Inhibition, error detection, and correction. *Neuroimage, 17*(4), 1820–1829.

Gazzaniga, M. S. (1998). The split brain revisited. *Sci Am, 279*(1), 50–55.

Gazzaniga, M. S. (2005). Forty-five years of split-brain research and still going strong. *Nat Rev Neurosci, 6*(8), 653–659.

Gazzaniga, M. S. (2005). *The ethical brain.* New York: Dana Press.

Gazzaniga, M. S. (2008). *Human: The science behind what makes us unique.* New York: Ecco.

Gazzaniga, M. S., Bogen, J. E., & Sperry, R. W. (1962). Some functional effects of sectioning the cerebral commissures in man. *Proc Natl Acad Sci USA, 48*, 1765–1769.

Gazzaniga, M. S., Bogen, J. E., & Sperry, R. W. (1965). Observations on visual perception after disconnexion of the cerebral hemispheres in man. *Brain, 88*(2), 221–236.

Gazzaniga, M. S., Ivry, R. B. and Mangun, G. R. (1998). *Cognitive neuroscience: The biology of the mind.* New York: W. W. Norton.

Gehring, W. J., & Fencsik, D. E. (2001). Functions of the medial frontal cortex in the processing of conflict and errors. *J Neurosci, 21*(23), 9430–9437.

Geschwind, D. H., Iacoboni, M., Mega, M. S., Zaidel, D. W., Cloughesy, T., & Zaidel, E. (1995). Alien hand syndrome: Interhemispheric motor disconnection due to a lesion in the midbody of the corpus callosum. *Neurology, 45*(4), 802–808.

Gettleman, J. (2008, June 8). Albinos, long shunned, face threat in Tanzania. *New York Times.*

Ghazanfar, A. A. (2008). Language evolution: Neural differences that make a difference. *Nat Neurosci, 11*(4), 382–384.

Gilbert, D. T. (1991). How mental systems believe. *American Psychologist, 46*(2), 107–119.

Gilbert, D. T. (2006). *Stumbling on happiness* (1st ed.). New York: A. A. Knopf.

Gilbert, D. T., Brown, R. P., Pinel, E. C., & Wilson, T. D. (2000). The illusion of external agency. *J Pers Soc Psychol, 79*(5), 690–700.

Gilbert, D. T., Lieberman, M. D., Morewedge, C. K., & Wilson, T. D. (2004). The peculiar longevity of things not so bad. *Psychol Sci, 15*(1), 14–19.

Gilbert, D. T., Morewedge, C. K., Risen, J. L., & Wilson, T. D. (2004). Looking forward to looking backward: The misprediction of regret. *Psychol Sci, 15*(5), 346–350.

Gilbert, D. T., Krull, D. S., Malone, S. (1990). Unbelieving the unbelievable: Some problems in the rejection of false information. *Journal of Personality and Social Psychology, 59*(4), 601–613.

Glannon, W. (2006). Neuroethics. *Bioethics, 20*(1), 37–52.

Glenn, A. L., Raine, A., & Schug, R. A. (2009). The neural correlates of moral decision-making in psychopathy. *Mol Psychiatry, 14*(1), 5–6.

Glenn, A. L., Raine, A., Schug, R. A., Young, L., & Hauser, M. (2009). Increased DLPFC activity during moral decision-making in psychopathy. *Mol Psychiatry, 14*(10), 909–911.

Glimcher, P. (2002). Decisions, decisions, decisions: Choosing a biological science of choice. *Neuron, 36*(2), 323–332.

Goel, V., & Dolan, R. J. (2003a). Explaining modulation of reasoning by belief. *Cognition, 87*(1), B11–22.

Goel, V., & Dolan, R. J. (2003b). Reciprocal neural response within lateral and ventral medial prefrontal cortex during hot and cold reasoning. *Neuroimage, 20*(4), 2314–2321.

Goel, V., Gold, B., Kapur, S., & Houle, S. (1997). The seats of reason? An imaging study of deductive and inductive reasoning. *Neuroreport, 8*(5), 1305–1310.

Goffman, E. (1967). *Interaction ritual: Essays on face-to-face behavior.* New York: Pantheon Books.

Gold, J. I., & Shadlen, M. N. (2000). Representation of a perceptual decision in developing oculomotor commands. *Nature, 404*(6776), 390–394.

Gold, J. I., & Shadlen, M. N. (2002). Banburismus and the brain: Decoding the relationship between sensory stimuli, decisions, and reward. *Neuron, 36*(2), 299–308.

Gold, J. I., & Shadlen, M. N. (2007). The neural basis of decision making. *Annu Rev Neurosci, 30*, 535–574.

Goldberg, E. (2001). *The executive brain: Frontal lobes and the civilized mind.* Oxford, UK; New York: Oxford University Press.

Goldberg, I., Ullman, S., & Malach, R. (2008). Neuronal correlates of "free will" are associated with regional specialization in the human intrinsic/default network. *Conscious Cogn, 17*(3), 587–601.

Gomes, G. (2007). Free will, the self, and the brain. *Behav Sci Law, 25*(2), 221–234.

Goodstein, L. (2010a, March 24). Vatican declined to defrock U.S. priest who abused boys. *New York Times.*

Goodstein, L. (2010b, April 21). Invitation to cardinal is withdrawn. *New York Times.*

Goodstein, L., & Callender, D. (2010, March 26). For years, deaf boys tried to tell of priest's abuse. *New York Times.*

Gould, S. J. (1997). Nonoverlapping magisteria. *Natural History, 106*(March), 16–22.

Graham Holm, N. (2010, January 4). Prejudiced Danes provoke fanaticism. *The Guardian.*

Grann, D. (2009, September 7). Trial by Fire. *New Yorker.*

Gray, J. M., Young, A. W., Barker, W. A., Curtis, A., & Gibson, D. (1997). Impaired recognition of disgust in Huntington's disease gene carriers. *Brain, 120* (Pt. 11), 2029–2038.

Gray, J. R., Burgess, G. C., Schaefer, A., Yarkoni, T., Larsen, R. J., & Braver, T. S. (2005). Affective personality differences in neural processing efficiency confirmed using fMRI. *Cogn Affect Behav Neurosci, 5*(2), 182–190.

Greely, H. (2007). On neuroethics. *Science, 318*(5850), 533.

Greene, J., & Cohen, J. (2004). For the law, neuroscience changes nothing and everything. *Philos Trans R Soc Lond B Biol Sci, 359*(1451), 1775–1785.

Greene, J. D. (2002). *The terrible, horrible, no good, very bad truth about morality and what to do about it.* Princeton, NJ: Princeton University.

Greene, J. D. (2007). Why are VMPFC patients more utilitarian? A dual-process theory of moral judgment explains. *Trends Cogn Sci, 11*(8), 322–323; author reply 323–324.

Greene, J. D., Nystrom, L. E., Engell, A. D., Darley, J. M., & Cohen, J. D. (2004). The neural bases of cognitive conflict and control in moral judgment. *Neuron, 44*(2), 389–400.

Greene, J. D., Sommerville, R. B., Nystrom, L. E., Darley, J. M., & Cohen, J. D. (2001). An fMRI investigation of emotional engagement in moral judgment. *Science, 293*(5537), 2105–2108.

Gregory, R. L. (1987). *The Oxford companion to the mind.* Oxford, UK: Oxford University Press.

Grim, P. (2007). Free will in context: A contemporary philosophical perspective. *Behav Sci Law, 25*(2), 183–201.

Gross, P. R. (1991). On the "gendering" of science. *Academic Questions, 5*(2), 10–23.

Gross, P. R., & Levitt, N. (1994). *Higher superstition: The academic left and its quarrels with science.* Baltimore: Johns Hopkins University Press.

Gusnard, D. A., Akbudak, E., Shulman, G. L., & Raichle, M. E. (2001). Medial prefrontal cortex and self-referential mental activity: Relation to a default mode of brain function. *Proc Natl Acad Sci USA, 98*(7), 4259–4264.

Gutchess, A. H., Welsh, R. C., Boduroglu, A., & Park, D. C. (2006). Cultural differences in neural function associated with object processing. *Cogn Affect Behav Neurosci, 6*(2), 102–109.

Guttenplan, S. (1994). *A companion to the philosophy of mind.* Oxford, UK: Blackwell.

Haber, S. N., Kunishio, K., Mizobuchi, M., & Lynd-Balta, E. (1995). The orbital and medial prefrontal circuit through the primate basal ganglia. *J Neurosci, 15*(7 Pt. 1), 4851–4867.

Haggard, P. (2001). The psychology of action. *Br J Psychol, 92*(Pt. 1), 113–128.

Haggard, P., Clark, S., & Kalogeras, J. (2002). Voluntary action and conscious awareness. *Nat Neurosci, 5*(4), 382–385.

Haggard, P., & Eimer, M. (1999). On the relation between brain potentials and the awareness of voluntary movements. *Exp Brain Res, 126*(1), 128–133.

Haggard, P., & Magno, E. (1999). Localising awareness of action with transcranial magnetic stimulation. *Exp Brain Res, 127*(1), 102–107.

Haidt, J. (2001). The emotional dog and its rational tail: A social intuitionist approach to moral judgment. *Psychol Rev, 108*(4), 814–834.

Haidt, J. (2003). The emotional dog does learn new tricks: A reply to Pizarro and Bloom (2003). *Psychol Rev, 110*(1), 197–198.

Haidt, J. (2007). The new synthesis in moral psychology. *Science, 316*(5827), 998–1002.

Haidt, J. (2008). What makes people vote Republican? Retrieved from www.edge.org/3rd_culture/haidt08/haidt08_index.html.

Haidt, J. (2009). Faster evolution means more ethnic differences. *The Edge Annual Question 2009.* Retrieved from www.edge.org/q2009/q09_4.html#haidt.

Hajcak, G., & Simons, R. F. (2008). Oops! . . . I did it again: An ERP and behavioral study of double-errors. *Brain Cogn, 68*(1), 15–21.

Hall, D. L., Matz, D. C., & Wood, W. (2010). Why don't we practice what we preach? A meta-analytic review of religious racism. *Personality and Social Psychology Review, 14*(1), 126–139.

Halligan, P. W. (1998). Inability to recognise disgust in Huntington's disease. *Lancet, 351*(9101), 464.

Hameroff, S., Kaszniak, A. W., and Scott, A. C. (1996). *Toward a science of consciousness: The first Tucson discussions and debates.* Cambridge, MA: MIT Press.

Hamilton, W. D. (1964a). The genetical evolution of social behaviour. Pt. I. *J Theor Biol, 7*(1), 1–16.

Hamilton, W. D. (1964b). The genetical evolution of social behaviour. Pt. II. *J Theor Biol, 7*(1), 17–52.

Han, S., Mao, L., Gu, X., Zhu, Y., Ge, J., & Ma, Y. (2008). Neural consequences of religious belief on self-referential processing. *Soc Neurosci, 3*(1), 1–15.

Hanson, S. J., Matsuka, T., & Haxby, J. V. (2004). Combinatorial codes in ventral temporal lobe for object recognition: Haxby (2001) revisited: Is there a "face" area? *Neuroimage, 23*(1), 156–166.

Happé, F. (2003). Theory of mind and the self. *Ann NY Acad Sci, 1001*, 134–144.

Hardcastle, V. G. (1993). The naturalists versus the skeptics: The debate over a scientific understanding of consciousness. *J Mind Behav, 14*(1), 27–50.

Hardcastle, V. G., & Flanagan, O. (1999). Multiplex vs. multiple selves: Distinguishing dissociative disorders. *The Monist, 82*(4), 645–657.

Harding, S. (2001). *Gender, democracy, and philosophy of science.* Paper presented at the Science, Engineering and Global Responsibility lectures, Stockholm (June 14–18, 2000).

Hare, R. D. (1999). *Without conscience: The disturbing world of the psychopaths among us.* New York: Guilford Press.

Hare, T. A., Tottenham, N., Galvan, A., Voss, H. U., Glover, G. H., & Casey, B. J. (2008). Biological substrates of emotional reactivity and regulation in adolescence during an emotional go-nogo task. *Biol Psychiatry, 63*(10), 927–934.

Harris, D., & Karamehmedovic, A. (2009, March 2). Child witches: Accused in the name of Jesus. *Nightline:* ABC News.

Harris, S. (2004). *The end of faith: Religion, terror, and the future of reason* (1st ed.). New York: W. W. Norton.

Harris, S. (2006a). *Letter to a Christian nation.* New York: Knopf.

Harris, S. (2006b). Science must destroy religion. In J. Brockman (Ed.), *What is your dangerous idea?* New York: Simon & Schuster.

Harris, S. (2006c). Reply to Scott Atran. *An Edge discussion of BEYOND BELIEF: Science, religion, reason and survival,* from www.edge.org/discourse/bb.html.

Harris, S. (2006d). Do we really need bad reasons to be good? *Boston Globe*, Oct. 22.

Harris, S. (2007b). Response to Jonathan Haidt. *Edge.org*, from www.edge.org/discourse/moral_religion.html.

Harris, S. (2007a). Scientists should unite against threat from religion. *Nature, 448*(7156), 864.

Harris, S. (2009, July 27). Science is in the details. *New York Times.*

Harris, S., & Ball, P. (2009, June 26). What should science do? Sam Harris v. Philip Ball, from www.project-reason.org/archive/item/what_should_science_dosam_harris_v_philip_ball/.

Harris, S., Kaplan, J. T., Curiel, A., Bookheimer, S. Y., Iacoboni, M., & Cohen, M. S. (2009). The neural correlates of religious and nonreligious belief. *PLoS ONE, 4*(10), e7272.

Harris, S., Sheth, S. A., & Cohen, M. S. (2008). Functional neuroimaging of belief, disbelief, and uncertainty. *Ann Neurol, 63*(2), 141–147.

Hauser, M. D. (2000). *Wild minds: What animals really think* (1st ed.). New York: Henry Holt.

Hauser, M. D. (2006). *Moral minds: How nature designed our universal sense of right and wrong* (1st ed.). New York: Ecco.

Hauser, M. D., Chomsky, N., & Fitch, W. T. (2002). The faculty of language: What is it, who has it, and how did it evolve? *Science, 298*(5598), 1569–1579.

Hayes, C. J., Stevenson, R. J., & Coltheart, M. (2007). Disgust and Huntington's disease. *Neuropsychologia, 45*(6), 1135–1151.

Haynes, J. D. (2009). Decoding visual consciousness from human brain signals. *Trends Cogn Sci*, 13(5), 194–202.

Haynes, J. D., & Rees, G. (2006). Decoding mental states from brain activity in humans. *Nat Rev Neurosci, 7*(7), 523–534.

Heisenberg, M. (2009). Is free will an illusion? *Nature, 459*(7244), 164–165.

Heisenberg, W. (1958). The representation of Nature in contemporary physics. *Daedalus, 87*(Summer), 95–108.

Henley, S. M., Wild, E. J., Hobbs, N. Z., Warren, J. D., Frost, C., Scahill, R. I., et al. (2008). Defective emotion recognition in early HD is neuropsychologically and anatomically generic. *Neuropsychologia, 46*(8), 2152–2160.

Hennenlotter, A., Schroeder, U., Erhard, P., Haslinger, B., Stahl, R., Weindl, A., et al. (2004). Neural correlates associated with impaired disgust processing in pre-symptomatic Huntington's disease. *Brain, 127*(Pt. 6), 1446–1453.

Henson, R. (2005). What can functional neuroimaging tell the experimental psychologist? *Q J Exp Psychol A, 58*(2), 193–233.

Hirsi Ali, A. (2006). *The caged virgin: An emancipation proclamation for women and Islam* (1st Free Press ed.). New York: Free Press.

Hirsi Ali, A. (2007). *Infidel.* New York: Free Press.

Hirsi Ali, A. (2010). *Nomad.* New York: Free Press.

Hitchens, C. (2007). *God is not great: How religion poisons everything.* New York: Twelve.

Hitchens, C. (2010, March 15). The great Catholic cover-up. *Slate.*

Hitchens, C. (2010, March 22). Tear down that wall. *Slate.*

Hitchens, C. (2010, March 29). The pope is not above the law. *Slate.*

Hitchens, C. (2010, May 3). Bring the pope to justice. *Newsweek.*

Holden, C. (2001). Polygraph screening. Panel seeks truth in lie detector debate. *Science, 291*(5506), 967.

Holyoak, K. J. (2005). Analogy. In K. J. Holyoak & R. G. Morrison (Eds.), *The Cambridge handbook of thinking of reasoning* (pp. 117–142). New York: Cambridge University Press.

Holyoak, K. J., & Morrison, R. G. (2005). *The Cambridge handbook of thinking and reasoning.* New York: Cambridge University Press.

Hood, B. M. (2009). *Supersense: Why we believe in the unbelievable.* New York: HarperOne.

Hornak, J., O'Doherty, J., Bramham, J., Rolls, E. T., Morris, R. G., Bullock, P. R., et al. (2004). Reward-related reversal learning after surgical excisions in orbito-frontal or dorsolateral prefrontal cortex in humans. *J Cogn Neurosci, 16*(3), 463–478.

Houreld, K. (2009, October 20). Church burns "witchcraft" children. *Daily Telegraph.*

Hsu, M., Bhatt, M., Adolphs, R., Tranel, D., & Camerer, C. F. (2005). Neural systems responding to degrees of uncertainty in human decision-making. *Science, 310*(5754), 1680–1683.

Hume, D. (1996). *The philosophical works of David Hume.* Bristol, U.K.: Thoemmes Press.

Hunte-Grubbe, C. (2007, October 14). The elementary DNA of Dr. Watson. *Sunday Times.*

Hutchison, W. D., Davis, K. D., Lozano, A. M., Tasker, R. R., & Dostrovsky, J. O. (1999). Pain-related neurons in the human cingulate cortex. *Nat Neurosci, 2*(5), 403–405.

Iacoboni, M. (2008). *Mirroring people: The new science of how we connect with others* (1st ed.). New York: Farrar, Straus and Giroux.

Iacoboni, M., & Dapretto, M. (2006). The mirror neuron system and the consequences of its dysfunction. *Nat Rev Neurosci, 7*(12), 942–951.

Iacoboni, M., & Mazziotta, J. C. (2007). Mirror neuron system: Basic findings and clinical applications. *Ann Neurol, 62*(3), 213–218.

Iacoboni, M., Rayman, J., & Zaidel, E. (1996). Left brain says yes, right brain says no: Normative duality in the split brain. In S. Hameroff, A. W. Kaszniak, & A. C. Scott (Eds.), *Toward a science of consciousness: The first Tucson discussions and debates* (pp. 197–202). Cambridge, MA: MIT Press.

Ibrahim, R. (Ed.)(2007). *The Al Qaeda reader* (1st pbk. ed.). New York: Broadway Books.

Illes, J. (2003). Neuroethics in a new era of neuroimaging. *AJNR Am J Neuroradiol, 24*(9), 1739–1741.

Illes, J. (2004). Medical imaging: A hub for the new field of neuroethics. *Acad Radiol, 11*(7), 721–723.

Illes, J. (2007). Empirical neuroethics. Can brain imaging visualize human thought? Why is neuroethics interested in such a possibility? *EMBO Rep. 8 Spec No.* S57–60.

Illes, J., & Bird, S. J. (2006). Neuroethics: A modern context for ethics in neuroscience. *Trends Neurosci, 29*(9), 511–517.

Illes, J., Blakemore, C., Hansson, M. G., Hensch, T. K., Leshner, A., Maestre, G., et al. (2005). International perspectives on engaging the public in neuroethics. *Nat Rev Neurosci, 6*(12), 977–982.

Illes, J., Kirschen, M. P., & Gabrieli, J. D. (2003). From neuroimaging to neuroethics. *Nat Neurosci, 6*(3), 205.

Illes, J., & Racine, E. (2005). Imaging or imagining? A neuroethics challenge informed by genetics. *Am J Bioeth, 5*(2), 5–18.

Illes, J., & Raffin, T. A. (2002). Neuroethics: An emerging new discipline in the study of brain and cognition. *Brain Cogn, 50*(3), 341–344.

Inbar, Y., Pizarro, D. A., Knobe, J., & Bloom, P. (2009). Disgust sensitivity predicts intuitive disapproval of gays. *Emotion, 9*(3), 435–439.

Inglehart, R., Foa, R., Peterson, C., & Welzel, C. (2008). Development, freedom, and rising happiness. *Perspectives on Psychological Science, 3*(4), 264–285.

Inzlicht, M., McGregor, I., Hirsh, J. B., & Nash, K. (2009). Neural markers of religious conviction. *Psychol Sci, 20*(3), 385–392.

Izuma, K., Saito, D. N., & Sadato, N. (2008). Processing of social and monetary rewards in the human striatum. *Neuron, 58*(2), 284–294.

James, W. ([1890] 1950). *The principles of psychology* (Authorized ed.). Mineola, NY: Dover Publications.

James, W. ([1912] 1996). *Essays in radical empiricism.* Lincoln, NE: University of Nebraska Press.

Jeannerod, M. (1999). The 25th Bartlett Lecture. To act or not to act: Perspectives on the representation of actions. *Q J Exp Psychol A, 52*(1), 1–29.

Jeannerod, M. (2001). Neural simulation of action: A unifying mechanism for motor cognition. *Neuroimage, 14*(1 Pt. 2), S103–109.

Jeannerod, M. (2003). The mechanism of self-recognition in humans. *Behav Brain Res, 142*(1–2), 1–15.

Jeans, J. (1930). *The mysterious universe.* Cambridge, UK: Cambridge University Press.

Jedlicka, P. (2005). Neuroethics, reductionism and dualism. *Trends Cogn Sci, 9*(4), 172; author reply, 173.

Jenkinson, M., Bannister, P., Brady, M., & Smith, S. (2002). Improved optimization for the robust and accurate linear registration and motion correction of brain images. *Neuroimage, 17*(2), 825–841.

Jenkinson, M., & Smith, S. (2001). A global optimisation method for robust affine registration of brain images. *Med Image Anal, 5*(2), 143–156.

Jensen, K., Call, J., & Tomasello, M. (2007). Chimpanzees are rational maximizers in an ultimatum game. *Science, 318*(5847), 107–109.

Jensen, K., Hare, B., Call, J., & Tomasello, M. (2006). What's in it for me? Self-regard precludes altruism and spite in chimpanzees. *Proc Biol Sci, 273*(1589), 1013–1021.

Johnson, S. A., Stout, J. C., Solomon, A. C., Langbehn, D. R., Aylward, E. H., Cruce, C. B., et al. (2007). Beyond disgust: Impaired recognition of negative emotions prior to diagnosis in Huntington's disease. *Brain, 130*(Pt. 7), 1732–1744.

Jones, D. (2008). Human behaviour: killer instincts. *Nature, 451*(7178), 512–515.

Joseph, O. (2009). Horror of Kenya's "witch," lynchings. Retrieved June 27, 2009, from http://news.bbc.co.uk/2/hi/africa/8119201.stm.

Joseph, R. (1999). Frontal lobe psychopathology: Mania, depression, confabulation, catatonia, perseveration, obsessive compulsions, and schizophrenia. *Psychiatry, 62*(2), 138–172.

Jost, J. T., Glaser, J., Kruglanski, A. W., & Sulloway, F. J. (2003). Political conservatism as motivated social cognition. *Psychol Bull, 129*(3), 339–375.

Joyce, R. (2006). Metaethics and the empirical sciences. *Philosophical Explorations, 9* (Special issue: Empirical research and the nature of moral judgment), 133–148.

Judson, O. (2008, December 2). Back to reality. *New York Times.*

Justo, L., & Erazun, F. (2007). Neuroethics and human rights. *Am J Bioeth, 7*(5), 16–18.

Kahane, G., & Shackel, N. (2008). Do abnormal responses show utilitarian bias? *Nature, 452*(7185), E5; author reply E5–6.

Kahneman, D. (2003a). Experiences of collaborative research. *Am Psychol, 58*(9), 723–730.

Kahneman, D. (2003b). A perspective on judgment and choice: Mapping bounded rationality. *Am Psychol, 58*(9), 697–720.

Kahneman, D., & Frederick, S. (2005). A model of heuristic judgment. In K. J. Holyoak & R. G. Morrison (Eds.), *The Cambridge handbook of thinking and reasoning* (pp. 267–293). New York: Cambridge University Press.

Kahneman, D., Krueger, A. B., Schkade, D., Schwarz, N., & Stone, A. A. (2006). Would you be happier if you were richer? A focusing illusion. *Science, 312*(5782), 1908–1910.

Kahneman, D., Slovic, P., & Tversky, A. (1982). *Judgment under uncertainty: Heuristics and biases.* New York: Cambridge University Press.

Kahneman, D., & Tversky, A. (1979). Prospect theory: An analysis of decision under risk. *Econometrica, 47*(2), 263–292.

Kahneman, D., & Tversky, A. (1996). On the reality of cognitive illusions. *Psychol Rev, 103*(3), 582–591; discussion 592–586.

Kandel, E. R. (2008). Interview with Eric R. Kandel: From memory, free will, and the problem with Freud to fortunate decisions. *J Vis Exp*(15), April 24, p. 762.

Kant, I. ([1785] 1995). *Ethical philosophy: Grounding for the metaphysics of morals and metaphysical principles of virtue* (J. W. Ellington, Trans.). Indianapolis, IN: Hackett Publishing.

Kanwisher, N., McDermott, J., & Chun, M. M. (1997). The fusiform face area: A module in human extrastriate cortex specialized for face perception. *J Neurosci, 17*(11), 4302–4311.

Kaplan, J. T., Freedman, J., & Iacoboni, M. (2007). Us versus them: Political attitudes and party affiliation influence neural response to faces of presidential candidates. *Neuropsychologia, 45*(1), 55–64.

Kaplan, J. T., & Iacoboni, M. (2006). Getting a grip on other minds: Mirror neurons, intention understanding, and cognitive empathy. *Soc Neurosci, 1*(3–4), 175–183.

Kapogiannis, D., Barbey, A. K., Su, M., Zamboni, G., Krueger, F., & Grafman, J. (2009). Cognitive and neural foundations of religious belief. *Proc Natl Acad Sci USA, 106*(12), 4876–4881.

Karczmar, A. G. (2001). Sir John Eccles, 1903–1997. Pt. 2. The brain as a machine or as a site of free will? *Perspect Biol Med, 44*(2), 250–262.

Keane, M. M., Gabrieli, J. D., Monti, L. A., Fleischman, D. A., Cantor, J. M., & Noland, J. S. (1997). Intact and impaired conceptual memory processes in amnesia. *Neuropsychology, 11*(1), 59–69.

Kelley, W. M., Macrae, C. N., Wyland, C. L., Caglar, S., Inati, S., & Heatherton, T. F. (2002). Finding the self? An event-related fMRI study. *J Cogn Neurosci, 14*(5), 785–794.

Kennedy, D. (2004). Neuroscience and neuroethics. *Science, 306*(5695), 373.

Kertesz, A. (2000). Alien hand, free will and Arnold Pick. *Can J Neurol Sci, 27*(3), 183.

Keverne, E. B., & Curley, J. P. (2004). Vasopressin, oxytocin and social behaviour. *Curr Opin Neurobiol, 14*(6), 777–783.

Kiehl, K. A. (2006). A cognitive neuroscience perspective on psychopathy: Evidence for paralimbic system dysfunction. *Psychiatry Res, 142*(2–3), 107–128.

Kiehl, K. A., Smith, A. M., Hare, R. D., Mendrek, A., Forster, B. B., Brink, J., et al. (2001). Limbic abnormalities in affective processing by criminal psychopaths as revealed by functional magnetic resonance imaging. *Biol Psychiatry, 50*(9), 677–684.

Kihlstrom, J. F. (1996). Unconscious processes in social interaction. In S. Hameroff, A. W. Kaszniak, & A. C. Scott (Eds.), *Toward a science of consciousness: The first Tucson discussions and debates* (pp. 93–104). Cambridge, MA: MIT Press.

Kim, J. ([1984] 1991). Epiphenomenal and supervenient causation. In D. Rosenthal (Ed.), *The nature of mind* (pp. 257–265). Oxford: Oxford University Press.

Kim, J. (1993). The myth of nonreductive materialism. In *Supervenience and mind* (pp. 265–283). Cambridge, UK: Cambridge University Press.

King-Casas, B., Tomlin, D., Anen, C., Camerer, C. F., Quartz, S. R., & Montague, P. R. (2005). Getting to know you: Reputation and trust in a two-person economic exchange. *Science, 308*(5718), 78–83.

Kipps, C. M., Duggins, A. J., McCusker, E. A., & Calder, A. J. (2007). Disgust and happiness recognition correlate with anteroventral insula and amygdala volume respectively in preclinical Huntington's disease. *J Cogn Neurosci, 19*(7), 1206–1217.

Kircher, T. T., Senior, C., Phillips, M. L., Benson, P. J., Bullmore, E. T., Brammer, M., et al. (2000). Towards a functional neuroanatomy of self processing: Effects of faces and words. *Brain Res Cogn Brain Res, 10*(1–2), 133–144.

Kircher, T. T., Senior, C., Phillips, M. L., Rabe-Hesketh, S., Benson, P. J., Bullmore, E. T., et al. (2001). Recognizing one's own face. *Cognition, 78*(1), B1–B15.

Kirsch, I. (2000). Are drug and placebo effects in depression additive? *Biol Psychiatry, 47*(8), 733–735.

Klayman, J., & Ha, Y. W. (1987). Confirmation, disconfirmation, and information in hypothesis testing. *Psychological Review, 94*(2), 211–228.

Koenig, L. B., McGue, M., Krueger, R. F., & Bouchard, T. J., Jr. (2005). Genetic and environmental influences on religiousness: Findings for retrospective and current religiousness ratings. *J Pers, 73*(2), 471–488.

Koenig, L. B., McGue, M., Krueger, R. F., & Bouchard, T. J., Jr. (2007). Religiousness, antisocial behavior, and altruism: Genetic and environmental mediation. *J Pers, 75*(2), 265–290.

Koenigs, M., Young, L., Adolphs, R., Tranel, D., Cushman, F., Hauser, M., et al. (2007). Damage to the prefrontal cortex increases utilitarian moral judgements. *Nature, 446*(7138), 908–911.

Kolb, B., & Whishaw, I. Q. (2008). *Fundamentals of human neuropsychology* (6th ed.). New York: Worth Publishers.

Kosik, K. S. (2006). Neuroscience gears up for duel on the issue of brain versus deity. *Nature, 439*(7073), 138.

Krause, J., Lalueza-Fox, C., Orlando, L., Enard, W., Green, R. E., Burbano, H. A., et al. (2007). The derived FOXP2 variant of modern humans was shared with Neandertals. *Curr Biol, 17*(21), 1908–1912.

Kripke, S. ([1970] 1991). From naming and necessity. In D. Rosenthal (Ed.), *The nature of mind* (pp. 236–246). UK: Oxford University Press.

Kruger, J., & Dunning, D. (1999). Unskilled and unaware of it: How difficulties in recognizing one's own incompetence lead to inflated self-assessments. *J Pers Soc Psychol, 77*(6), 1121–1134.

Kruglanski, A. W. (1999). Motivation, cognition, and reality: Three memos for the next generation of research. *Psychological Inquiry, 10*(1), pp. 54–58.

Kuhnen, C. M., & Knutson, B. (2005). The neural basis of financial risk taking. *Neuron, 47*(5), 763–770.

LaBoeuf, R. A., & Shafir, E. B. (2005). Decision making. In K. J. Holyoak & R. G. Morrison (Eds.), *The Cambridge handbook of thinking and reasoning* (pp. 243–266). New York: Cambridge University Press.

LaFraniere, S. (2007, November 15). African crucible: Cast as witches, then cast out. *New York Times.*

Lahav, R. (1997). The conscious and the non-conscious: Philosophical implications of neuropsychology. In M. Carrier & P. K. Machamer (Eds.), *Mindscapes: Philosophy, science, and the mind.* Pittsburgh, PA: University of Pittsburgh Press.

Lai, C. S., Fisher, S. E., Hurst, J. A., Vargha-Khadem, F., & Monaco, A. P. (2001). A forkhead-domain gene is mutated in a severe speech and language disorder. *Nature, 413*(6855), 519–523.

Langford, D. J., Crager, S. E., Shehzad, Z., Smith, S. B., Sotocinal, S. G., Levenstadt, J. S., et al. (2006). Social modulation of pain as evidence for empathy in mice. *Science, 312*(5782), 1967–1970.

Langleben, D. D., Loughead, J. W., Bilker, W. B., Ruparel, K., Childress, A. R., Busch, S. I., et al. (2005). Telling truth from lie in individual subjects with fast event-related fMRI. *Hum Brain Mapp, 26*(4), 262–272.

Langleben, D. D., Schroeder, L., Maldjian, J. A., Gur, R. C., McDonald, S., Ragland, J. D., et al. (2002). Brain activity during simulated deception: An event-related functional magnetic resonance study. *Neuroimage, 15*(3), 727–732.

Larson, E. J., & Witham, L. (1998). Leading scientists still reject God. *Nature, 394*(6691), 313.

LeDoux, J. E. (2002). *Synaptic self: How our brains become who we are.* New York: Viking.

Lee, T. M., Liu, H. L., Chan, C. C., Ng, Y. B., Fox, P. T., & Gao, J. H. (2005). Neural correlates of feigned memory impairment. *Neuroimage, 28*(2), 305–313.

Leher, J. (2010, February 28). Depression's upside. *New York Times Magazine.*

Levine, J. (1983). Materialism and qualia: The explanatory gap. *Pacific Philosophical Quarterly, 64*, 354–361.

Levine, J. (1997). On leaving out what it's like. In N. Block, O. Flanagan, & G. Güzeldere (Eds.), *The nature of consciousness: Philosophical debates* (pp. 543–555). Cambridge, MA: MIT Press.

Levy, N. (2007). Rethinking neuroethics in the light of the extended mind thesis. *Am J Bioeth, 7*(9), 3–11.

Levy, N. (2007). *Neuroethics.* New York: Cambridge University Press.

Libet, B. (1999). Do we have free will? *Journal of Consciousness Studies, 6*(8–9), 47–57.

Libet, B. (2001). Consciousness, free action and the brain: Commentary on John Searle's article. *Journal of Consciousness Studies, 8*(8), 59–65.

Libet, B. (2003). Can conscious experience affect brain activity? *Journal of Consciousness Studies, 10*(12), 24–28.

Libet, B., Gleason, C. A., Wright, E. W., & Pearl, D. K. (1983). Time of conscious intention to act in relation to onset of cerebral activity (readiness-potential). The unconscious initiation of a freely voluntary act. *Brain, 106* (Pt. 3), 623–642.

Lieberman, M. D., Jarcho, J. M., Berman, S., Naliboff, B. D., Suyenobu, B. Y., Mandelkern, M., et al. (2004). The neural correlates of placebo effects: a disruption account. *Neuroimage, 22*(1), 447–455.

Litman, L., & Reber, A. S. (2005). Implicit cognition and thought. In K. J. Holyoak & R. G. Morrison (Eds.), *The Cambridge handbook of thinking and reasoning* (pp. 431–453). New York: Cambridge University Press.

Livingston, K. R. (2005). Religious practice, brain, and belief. *Journal of Cognition and Culture, 5*(1–2), 75–117.

Llinás, R. (2001). *I of the vortex: From neurons to self.* Cambridge, MA: MIT Press.

Llinás, R., Ribary, U., Contreras, D., & Pedroarena, C. (1998). The neuronal basis for consciousness. *Philos Trans R Soc Lond B Biol Sci, 353*(1377), 1841–1849.

Logothetis, N. K. (1999). Vision: A window on consciousness. *Sci Am, 281*(5), 69–75.

Logothetis, N. K. (2008). What we can do and what we cannot do with fMRI. *Nature, 453*(7197), 869–878.

Logothetis, N. K., Pauls, J., Augath, M., Trinath, T., & Oeltermann, A. (2001). Neurophysiological investigation of the basis of the fMRI signal. *Nature, 412*(6843), 150–157.

Logothetis, N. K., & Pfeuffer, J. (2004). On the nature of the BOLD fMRI contrast mechanism. *Magn Reson Imaging, 22*(10), 1517–1531.

Lou, H. C., Luber, B., Crupain, M., Keenan, J. P., Nowak, M., Kjaer, T. W., et al. (2004). Parietal cortex and representation of the mental self. *Proc Natl Acad Sci USA, 101*(17), 6827–6832.

Lou, H. C., Nowak, M., & Kjaer, T. W. (2005). The mental self. *Prog Brain Res, 150*, 197–204.

Lugo, L. D. (2008). *U.S. Religious Landscape Survey*, Pew Research Center.

Lutz, A., Brefczynski-Lewis, J., Johnstone, T., & Davidson, R. J. (2008). Regulation of the neural circuitry of emotion by compassion meditation: effects of meditative expertise. *PLoS ONE, 3*(3), e1897.

Lutz, A., Greischar, L. L., Rawlings, N. B., Ricard, M., & Davidson, R. J. (2004). Long-term meditators self-induce high-amplitude gamma synchrony during mental practice. *Proc Natl Acad Sci USA, 101*(46), 16369–16373.

Lutz, A., Slagter, H. A., Dunne, J. D., & Davidson, R. J. (2008). Attention regulation and monitoring in meditation. *Trends Cogn Sci, 12*(4), 163–169.

Lykken, D. T., & Tellegen, A. (1996). Happiness is a stochastic phenomenon. *Psychological Science, 7*(3), 186–189.

Mackie, J. L. (1977). *Ethics: Inventing right and wrong.* London: Penguin.

Macrae, C. N., Moran, J. M., Heatherton, T. F., Banfield, J. F., & Kelley, W. M. (2004). Medial prefrontal activity predicts memory for self. *Cereb Cortex, 14*(6), 647–654.

Maddox, J. (1981). A book for burning? *Nature, 293* (September 24), 245–246.

Maddox, J. (1995). The prevalent distrust of science. *Nature, 378*(6556), 435–437.

Maguire, E. A., Frith, C. D., & Morris, R. G. (1999). The functional neuroanatomy of comprehension and memory: The importance of prior knowledge. *Brain, 122* (Pt. 10), 1839–1850.

Mark, V. (1996). Conflicting communicative behavior in a split-brain patient: Support for dual consciousness. In S. Hameroff, A. W. Kaszniak, & A. C. Scott (Eds.), *Toward a science of consciousness: The first Tucson discussions and debates* (pp. 189–196). Cambridge, MA: MIT Press.

Marks, C. E. (1980). *Commissurotomy, consciousness, and the unity of mind.* Montgomery, VT: Bradford Books.

Marr, D. (1982). *Vision: A computational investigation into the human representation and processing of visual information.* San Francisco: W. H. Freeman.

Marx, K. ([1843] 1971). *Critique of Hegel's philosophy of right* (A. J. O'Malley, Trans.). Cambridge, UK: Cambridge University Press.

Mason, M. F., Norton, M. I., Van Horn, J. D., Wegner, D. M., Grafton, S. T., & Macrae, C. N. (2007). Wandering minds: The default network and stimulus-independent thought. *Science, 315*(5810), 393–395.

Masserman, J. H., Wechkin, S., & Terris, W. (1964). "Altruistic" behavior in rhesus monkeys. *Am J Psychiatry, 121*, 584–585.

Matsumoto, K., & Tanaka, K. (2004). The role of the medial prefrontal cortex in achieving goals. *Curr Opin Neurobiol, 14*(2), 178–185.

McCloskey, M. S., Phan, K. L., & Coccaro, E. F. (2005). Neuroimaging and personality disorders. *Curr Psychiatry Rep, 7*(1), 65–72.

McClure, S. M., Li, J., Tomlin, D., Cypert, K. S., Montague, L. M., & Montague, P. R. (2004). Neural correlates of behavioral preference for culturally familiar drinks. *Neuron, 44*(2), 379–387.

McCrone, J. (2003). Free will. *Lancet Neurol, 2*(1), 66.

McElreath, R., & Boyd, R. (2007). *Mathematical models of social evolution: A guide for the perplexed.* Chicago; London: University of Chicago Press.

McGinn, C. (1989). Can we solve the mind-body problem? *Mind, 98*, 349–366.

McGinn, C. (1999). *The mysterious flame: Conscious minds in a material world.* New York: Basic Books.

McGuire, P. K., Bench, C. J., Frith, C. D., Marks, I. M., Frackowiak, R. S., & Dolan, R. J. (1994). Functional anatomy of obsessive-compulsive phenomena. *Br J Psychiatry, 164*(4), 459–468.

McKiernan, K. A., Kaufman, J. N., Kucera-Thompson, J., & Binder, J. R. (2003). A parametric manipulation of factors affecting task-induced deactivation in functional neuroimaging. *J Cogn Neurosci, 15*(3), 394–408.

McNeil, B. J., Pauker, S. G., Sox, H. C., Jr., & Tversky, A. (1982). On the elicitation of preferences for alternative therapies. *N Engl J Med, 306*(21), 1259–1262.

Mekel-Bobrov, N., Gilbert, S. L., Evans, P. D., Vallender, E. J., Anderson, J. R., Hudson, R. R., et al. (2005). Ongoing adaptive evolution of ASPM, a brain size determinant in *Homo sapiens. Science, 309*(5741), 1720–1722.

Meriau, K., Wartenburger, I., Kazzer, P., Prehn, K., Lammers, C. H., van der Meer, E., et al. (2006). A neural network reflecting individual differences in cognitive processing of emotions during perceptual decision making. *Neuroimage, 33*(3), 1016–1027.

Merleau-Ponty, M. (1964). *The primacy of perception, and other essays on phenomenological psychology, the philosophy of art, history, and politics.* Evanston, IL: Northwestern University Press.

Mesoudi, A., Whiten, A., & Dunbar, R. (2006). A bias for social information in human cultural transmission. *Br J Psychol, 97*(Pt. 3), 405–423.

Mill, J. S. (1863). *Utilitarianism.* London: Parker, Son, and Bourn.

Miller, E. K., & Cohen, J. D. (2001). An integrative theory of prefrontal cortex function. *Annu Rev Neurosci, 24*, 167–202.

Miller, G. (2008). Investigating the psychopathic mind. *Science, 321* (5894), 1284–1286.

Miller, G. (2008). Neuroimaging. Growing pains for fMRI. *Science, 320*(5882), 1412–1414.

Miller, G. F. (2007). Sexual selection for moral virtues. *Q Rev Biol, 82*(2), 97–125.

Miller, K. R. (1999). *Finding Darwin's God: A scientist's search for common ground between God and evolution* (1st ed.). New York: Cliff Street Books.

Miller, W. I. (1993). *Humiliation: And other essays on honor, social discomfort, and violence.* Ithaca, NY: Cornell University Press.

Miller, W. I. (1997). *The anatomy of disgust.* Cambridge, MA: Harvard University Press.

Miller, W. I. (2003). *Faking it.* Cambridge, UK; New York: Cambridge University Press.

Miller, W. I. (2006). *Eye for an eye.* Cambridge, UK; New York: Cambridge University Press.

Mink, J. W. (1996). The basal ganglia: focused selection and inhibition of competing motor programs. *Prog Neurobiol, 50*(4), 381–425.

Mitchell, I. J., Heims, H., Neville, E. A., & Rickards, H. (2005). Huntington's disease patients show impaired perception of disgust in the gustatory and olfactory modalities. *J Neuropsychiatry Clin Neurosci, 17*(1), 119–121.

Mitchell, J. P., Dodson, C. S., & Schacter, D. L. (2005). fMRI evidence for the role of recollection in suppressing misattribution errors: The illusory truth effect. *J Cogn Neurosci, 17*(5), 800–810.

Mitchell, J. P., Macrae, C. N., & Banaji, M. R. (2006). Dissociable medial prefrontal contributions to judgments of similar and dissimilar others. *Neuron, 50*(4), 655–663.

Mlodinow, L. (2008). *The drunkard's walk: How randomness rules our lives.* New York: Pantheon.

Moll, J., & de Oliveira-Souza, R. (2007). Moral judgments, emotions and the utilitarian brain. *Trends Cogn Sci, 11*(8), 319–321.

Moll, J., de Oliveira-Souza, R., Garrido, G. J., Bramati, I. E., Caparelli-Daquer, E. M., Paiva, M. L., et al. (2007). The self as a moral agent: Linking the neural bases of social agency and moral sensitivity. *Soc Neurosci, 2*(3–4), 336–352.

Moll, J., de Oliveira-Souza, R., Moll, F. T., Ignacio, F. A., Bramati, I. E., Caparelli-Daquer, E. M., et al. (2005). The moral affiliations of disgust: A functional MRI study. *Cogn Behav Neurol, 18*(1), 68–78.

Moll, J., de Oliveira-Souza, R., & Zahn, R. (2008). The neural basis of moral cognition: sentiments, concepts, and values. *Ann NY Acad Sci, 1124,* 161–180.

Moll, J., Zahn, R., de Oliveira-Souza, R., Krueger, F., & Grafman, J. (2005). Opinion: The neural basis of human moral cognition. *Nat Rev Neurosci, 6*(10), 799–809.

Monchi, O., Petrides, M., Strafella, A. P., Worsley, K. J., & Doyon, J. (2006). Functional role of the basal ganglia in the planning and execution of actions. *Ann Neurol, 59*(2), 257–264.

Mooney, C. (2005). *The Republican war on science.* New York: Basic Books.

Mooney, C., & Kirshenbaum, S. (2009). *Unscientific America: How scientific illiteracy threatens our future.* New York: Basic Books.

Moore, G. E. ([1903] 2004). *Principia ethica.* Mineola, NY: Dover Publications.

Moran, J. M., Macrae, C. N., Heatherton, T. F., Wyland, C. L., & Kelley, W. M. (2006). Neuroanatomical evidence for distinct cognitive and affective components of self. *J Cogn Neurosci, 18*(9), 1586–1594.

Moreno, J. D. (2003). Neuroethics: An agenda for neuroscience and society. *Nat Rev Neurosci, 4*(2), 149–153.

Morse, D. (2009, March 31). Plea deal includes resurrection clause. *Washington Post,* B02.

Mortimer, M., & Toader, A. (2005). Blood feuds blight Albanian lives. September 23. Retrieved July 7, 2009, from http://news.bbc.co.uk/2/hi/europe/4273020.stm.

Muller, J. L., Ganssbauer, S., Sommer, M., Dohnel, K., Weber, T., Schmidt-Wilcke, T., et al. (2008). Gray matter changes in right superior temporal gyrus in criminal psychopaths. Evidence from voxel-based morphometry. *Psychiatry Res, 163*(3), 213–222.

Nagel, T. (1974). What is it like to be a bat? *Philosophical Review, 83*, 435–456.

Nagel, T. (1979). Brain bisection and the unity of consciousness. In *Mortal questions.* Cambridge, UK: Cambridge University Press, 147–164.

Nagel, T. (1979). *Mortal/Questions.* Cambridge, UK: Cambridge University Press.

Nagel, T. (1986). *The view from nowhere.* Oxford, UK: Oxford University Press.

Nagel, T. (1995). *Other minds.* Oxford, UK: Oxford University Press.

Nagel, T. (1997). *The last word.* Oxford, UK: Oxford University Press.

Nagel, T. (1998). Conceiving the impossible and the mind body problem. *Philosophy, 73*(285), 337–352.

Narayan, V. M., Narr, K. L., Kumari, V., Woods, R. P., Thompson, P. M., Toga, A. W., et al. (2007). Regional cortical thinning in subjects with violent antisocial personality disorder or schizophrenia. *Am J Psychiatry, 164*(9), 1418–1427.

National Academy of Sciences (U.S.). Working Group on Teaching Evolution. (1998). *Teaching about evolution and the nature of science.* Washington, DC: National Academies Press.

National Academy of Sciences (U.S.) & Institute of Medicine (U.S.) (2008). *Science, evolution, and creationism.* Washington, DC: National Academies Press.

Newberg, A., Alavi, A., Baime, M., Pourdehnad, M., Santanna, J., & d'Aquili, E. (2001). The measurement of regional cerebral blood flow during the complex cognitive task of meditation: A preliminary SPECT study. *Psychiatry Res, 106*(2), 113–122.

Newberg, A., Pourdehnad, M., Alavi, A., & d'Aquili, E. G. (2003). Cerebral blood flow during meditative prayer: Preliminary findings and methodological issues. *Percept Mot Skills, 97*(2), 625–630.

Newberg, A. B., Wintering, N. A., Morgan, D., & Waldman, M. R. (2006). The measurement of regional cerebral blood flow during glossolalia: A preliminary SPECT study. *Psychiatry Res, 148*(1), 67–71.

Ng, F. (2007). The interface between religion and psychosis. *Australas Psychiatry, 15*(1), 62–66.

Nørretranders, T. (1998). *The user illusion: Cutting consciousness down to size.* New York: Viking.

Norris, P., & Inglehart, R. (2004). *Sacred and secular: Religion and politics worldwide.* Cambridge, UK: Cambridge University Press.

Northoff, G., Heinzel, A., Bermpohl, F., Niese, R., Pfennig, A., Pascual-Leone, A., et al. (2004). Reciprocal modulation and attenuation in the prefrontal cortex: An fMRI study on emotional-cognitive interaction. *Hum Brain Mapp, 21*(3), 202–212.

Northoff, G., Heinzel, A., de Greck, M., Bermpohl, F., Dobrowolny, H., &

Panksepp, J. (2006). Self-referential processing in our brain—a meta-analysis of imaging studies on the self. *Neuroimage, 31*(1), 440–457.

Nowak, M. A., & Sigmund, K. (2005). Evolution of indirect reciprocity. *Nature, 437*(7063), 1291–1298.

Nozick, R. (1974). *Anarchy, state, and utopia.* New York: Basic Books.

Nunez, J. M., Casey, B. J., Egner, T., Hare, T., & Hirsch, J. (2005). Intentional false responding shares neural substrates with response conflict and cognitive control. *Neuroimage, 25*(1), 267–277.

O'Doherty, J., Critchley, H., Deichmann, R., & Dolan, R. J. (2003). Dissociating valence of outcome from behavioral control in human orbital and ventral prefrontal cortices. *J Neurosci, 23*(21), 7931–7939.

O'Doherty, J., Kringelbach, M. L., Rolls, E. T., Hornak, J., & Andrews, C. (2001). Abstract reward and punishment representations in the human orbitofrontal cortex. *Nat Neurosci, 4*(1), 95–102.

O'Doherty, J., Rolls, E. T., Francis, S., Bowtell, R., & McGlone, F. (2001). Representation of pleasant and aversive taste in the human brain. *J Neurophysiol, 85*(3), 1315–1321.

O'Doherty, J., Winston, J., Critchley, H., Perrett, D., Burt, D. M., & Dolan, R. J. (2003). Beauty in a smile: The role of medial orbitofrontal cortex in facial attractiveness. *Neuropsychologia, 41*(2), 147–155.

Oliver, A. M., & Steinberg, P. F. (2005). *The road to martyrs' square: A journey into the world of the suicide bomber.* New York: Oxford University Press.

Olsson, A., Ebert, J. P., Banaji, M. R., & Phelps, E. A. (2005). The role of social groups in the persistence of learned fear. *Science, 309*(5735), 785–787.

Osherson, D., Perani, D., Cappa, S., Schnur, T., Grassi, F., & Fazio, F. (1998). Distinct brain loci in deductive versus probabilistic reasoning. *Neuropsychologia, 36*(4), 369–376.

Parens, E., & Johnston, J. (2007). Does it make sense to speak of neuroethics? Three problems with keying ethics to hot new science and technology. *EMBO Rep, 8 Spec No*, S61–64.

Parfit, D. (1984). *Reasons and persons.* Oxford, UK: Clarendon Press.

Patterson, K., Nestor, P. J., & Rogers, T. T. (2007). Where do you know what you know? The representation of semantic knowledge in the human brain. *Nat Rev Neurosci, 8*(12), 976–987.

Patterson, N., Richter, D. J., Gnerre, S., Lander, E. S., & Reich, D. (2006). Genetic evidence for complex speciation of humans and chimpanzees. *Nature, 441*(7097), 1103–1108.

Patterson, N., Richter, D. J., Gnerre, S., Lander, E. S., & Reich, D. (2008). Patterson et al. reply. *Nature, 452*(7184), E4.

Paul, G. (2009). The chronic dependence of popular religiosity upon dysfunctional psychosociological conditions. *Evolutionary Psychology, 7*(3), 398–441.

Pauli, W., Enz, C. P., & Meyenn, K. von ([1955] 1994). *Writings on physics and philosophy.* Berlin; New York: Springer-Verlag.

Paulson, S. (2006). The believer. Retrieved July 24, 2009, from www.salon.com /books/int/2006/08/07/collins/index.html.

Paulus, M. P., Rogalsky, C., Simmons, A., Feinstein, J. S., & Stein, M. B. (2003). Increased activation in the right insula during risk-taking decision making is related to harm avoidance and neuroticism. *Neuroimage, 19*(4), 1439–1448.

Pavlidis, I., Eberhardt, N. L., & Levine, J. A. (2002). Seeing through the face of deception. *Nature, 415*(6867), 35.

Pedersen, C. A., Ascher, J. A., Monroe, Y. L., & Prange, A. J., Jr. (1982). Oxytocin induces maternal behavior in virgin female rats. *Science, 216*(4546), 648–650.

Pennisi, E. (1999). Are our primate cousins "conscious"? *Science, 284*(5423), 2073–2076.

Penrose, R. (1994). *Shadows of the mind.* Oxford, UK: Oxford University Press.

Perry, J. (2001). *Knowledge, possibility, and consciousness.* Cambridge, MA: MIT Press.

Persinger, M. A., & Fisher, S. D. (1990). Elevated, specific temporal lobe signs in a population engaged in psychic studies. *Percept Mot Skills, 71*(3 Pt. 1), 817–818.

Pessiglione, M., Schmidt, L., Draganski, B., Kalisch, R., Lau, H., Dolan, R. J., et al. (2007). How the brain translates money into force: A neuroimaging study of subliminal motivation. *Science, 316*(5826), 904–906.

Pierre, J. M. (2001). Faith or delusion? At the crossroads of religion and psychosis. *J Psychiatr Pract, 7*(3), 163–172.

Pinker, S. (1997). *How the mind works.* New York: Norton.

Pinker, S. (2002). *The blank slate: The modern denial of human nature.* New York: Viking.

Pinker, S. (2007, March 19). A history of violence. *The New Republic.*

Pinker, S. (2008). The stupidity of dignity. *The New Republic* (May 28).

Pinker, S. (2008, January 13). The moral instinct. *New York Times Magazine.*

Pinker, S., & Jackendoff, R. (2005). The faculty of language: What's special about it? *Cognition, 95*(2), 201–236.

Pizarro, D. A., & Bloom, P. (2003). The intelligence of the moral intuitions: comment on Haidt (2001). *Psychol Rev, 110*(1), 193–196; discussion 197–198.

Pizarro, D. A., & Uhlmann, E. L. (2008). The motivated use of moral principles. (Unpublished manuscript.)

Planck, M., & Murphy, J. V. (1932). *Where is science going*? New York: W. W. Norton.

Poldrack, R. A. (2006). Can cognitive processes be inferred from neuroimaging data? *Trends Cogn Sci, 10*(2), 59–63.

Polkinghorne, J. C. (2003). *Belief in God in an age of science.* New Haven, CT: Yale University Press.

Polkinghorne, J. C., & Beale, N. (2009). *Questions of truth: Fifty-one responses to questions about God, science, and belief* (1st ed.). Louisville, KY: Westminster John Knox Press.

Pollard Sacks, D. (2009). State actors beating children: A call for judicial relief. *U.C. Davis Law Review, 42,* 1165–1229.

Popper, K. R. (2002). *The open society and its enemies* (5th ed.). London; New York: Routledge.

Popper, K. R., & Eccles, J. C. ([1977] 1993). *The self and its brain.* London: Routledge.

Prabhakaran, V., Rypma, B., & Gabrieli, J. D. (2001). Neural substrates of mathematical reasoning: A functional magnetic resonance imaging study of neocortical activation during performance of the necessary arithmetic operations test. *Neuropsychology, 15*(1), 115–127.

Prado, J., Noveck, I. A., & Van Der Henst, J. B. (2009). Overlapping and distinct neural representations of numbers and verbal transitive series. *Cereb Cortex*, 20(3), 720–729.

Premack, D., & Woodruff, G. (1978). Chimpanzee problem-solving: A test for comprehension. *Science, 202*(4367), 532–535.

Previc, F. H. (2006). The role of the extrapersonal brain systems in religious activity. *Conscious Cogn, 15*(3), 500–539.

Prinz, J. (2001). Functionalism, dualism and consciousness. In W. Bechtel, P. Mandik, J. Mundale, & R. Stufflebeam (Eds.), *Philosophy and the neurosciences*. Oxford, UK: Blackwell, 278–294.

Pryse-Phillips, W. (2003). *The Oxford companion to clinical neurology.* Oxford, UK: Oxford University Press.

Puccetti, R. (1981). The case for mental duality: Evidence from split-brain data and other considerations. *Behavioral and Brain Sciences, (1981)*(4), 93–123.

Puccetti, R. (1993). Dennett on the split-brain. *Psycoloquy, 4*(52).

Putnam, H. (2007). The fact/value dichotomy and its critics. Paper presented at the UCD Ulysses Medal Lecture. Retrieved from www.youtube.com/watch?v=gTWKSb8ajXc&feature=player_embedded.

Pyysiäinen, I., & Hauser, M. (2010). The origins of religion: Evolved adaptation or by-product? *Trends Cogn Sci, 14*(3), 104–109.

Quiroga, R. Q., Reddy, L., Kreiman, G., Koch, C., & Fried, I. (2005). Invariant visual representation by single neurons in the human brain. *Nature, 435*(7045), 1102–1107.

Racine, E. (2007). Identifying challenges and conditions for the use of neuroscience in bioethics. *Am J Bioeth, 7*(1), 74–76; discussion W71–74.

Raichle, M. E., MacLeod, A. M., Snyder, A. Z., Powers, W. J., Gusnard, D. A., & Shulman, G. L. (2001). A default mode of brain function. *Proc Natl Acad Sci USA, 98*(2), 676–682.

Raine, A., & Yaling, Y. (2006). The neuroanatomical bases of psychopathy: A review of brain imaging findings. In C. J. Patrick (Ed.), *Handbook of psychopathy* (pp. 278–295). New York: Guilford Press.

Ramachandran, V. S. (1995). Anosognosia in parietal lobe syndrome. *Conscious Cogn, 4*(1), 22–51.

Ramachandran, V. S. (2007). The neurology of self-awareness, retrieved December 5, 2008, from www.edge.org/3rd_culture/ramachandran07/ramachandran07_index.html.

Ramachandran, V. S., & Blakeslee, S. (1998). *Phantoms in the brain.* New York: William Morrow and Company.

Ramachandran, V. S., & Hirstein, W. (1997). Three laws of qualia: What neurology tells us about the biological functions of consciousness. *Journal of Consciousness Studies, 4*(5/6), 429–457.

Range, F., Horn, L., Viranyi, Z., & Huber, L. (2009). The absence of reward induces inequity aversion in dogs. *Proc Natl Acad Sci USA, 106*(1), 340–345.

Raskin, R., & Terry, H. (1988). A principal-components analysis of the Narcissistic Personality Inventory and further evidence of its construct validity. *J Pers Soc Psychol, 54*(5), 890–902.

Rauch, S. L., Kim, H., Makris, N., Cosgrove, G. R., Cassem, E. H., Savage, C. R., et al. (2000). Volume reduction in the caudate nucleus following stereotactic placement of lesions in the anterior cingulate cortex in humans: A morphometric magnetic resonance imaging study. *J Neurosurg, 93*(6), 1019–1025.

Rauch, S. L., Makris, N., Cosgrove, G. R., Kim, H., Cassem, E. H., Price, B. H., et al. (2001). A magnetic resonance imaging study of regional cortical volumes following stereotactic anterior cingulotomy. *CNS Spectr, 6*(3), 214–222.

Rawls, J. ([1971] 1999). *A theory of justice* (Rev. ed.). Cambridge, MA.: Belknap Press of Harvard University Press.

Rawls, J., & Kelly, E. (2001). *Justice as fairness: A restatement.* Cambridge, MA: Harvard University Press.

Redelmeier, D. A., Katz, J., & Kahneman, D. (2003). Memories of colonoscopy: A randomized trial. *Pain, 104*(1–2), 187–194.

Resnik, D. B. (2007). Neuroethics, national security and secrecy. *Am J Bioeth, 7*(5), 14–15.

Richell, R. A., Mitchell, D. G., Newman, C., Leonard, A., Baron-Cohen, S., & Blair, R. J. (2003). Theory of mind and psychopathy: Can psychopathic individuals read the "language of the eyes"? *Neuropsychologia, 41*(5), 523–526.

Ridderinkhof, K. R., Ullsperger, M., Crone, E. A., & Nieuwenhuis, S. (2004). The role of the medial frontal cortex in cognitive control. *Science, 306*(5695), 443–447.

Rilling, J., Gutman, D., Zeh, T., Pagnoni, G., Berns, G., & Kilts, C. (2002). A neural basis for social cooperation. *Neuron, 35*(2), 395–405.

Rodriguez-Moreno, D., & Hirsch, J. (2009). The dynamics of deductive reasoning: An fMRI investigation. *Neuropsychologia, 47*(4), 949–961.

Rolls, E. T., Grabenhorst, F., & Parris, B. A. (2008). Warm pleasant feelings in the brain. *Neuroimage, 41*(4), 1504–1513.

Rosenblatt, A., Greenberg, J., Solomon, S., Pyszczynski, T., & Lyon, D. (1989). Evidence for terror management theory: I. The effects of mortality salience on reactions to those who violate or uphold cultural values. *J Pers Soc Psychol, 57*(4), 681–690.

Rosenhan, D. L. (1973). On being sane in insane places. *Science, 179*(70), 250–258.

Rosenthal, D. (1991). *The nature of mind.* Oxford, UK: Oxford University Press.

Roskies, A. (2002). Neuroethics for the new millennium. *Neuron, 35*(1), 21–23.

Roskies, A. (2006). Neuroscientific challenges to free will and responsibility. *Trends Cogn Sci, 10*(9), 419–423.

Royet, J. P., Plailly, J., Delon-Martin, C., Kareken, D. A., & Segebarth, C. (2003). fMRI of emotional responses to odors: Influence of hedonic valence and judgment, handedness, and gender. *Neuroimage, 20*(2), 713–728.

Rubin, A. J. (2009, August 12). How Baida wanted to die. *New York Times,* MM38.

Rule, R. R., Shimamura, A. P., & Knight, R. T. (2002). Orbitofrontal cortex and dynamic filtering of emotional stimuli. *Cogn Affect Behav Neurosci, 2*(3), 264–270.

Rumelhart, D. E. (1980). Schemata: The building blocks of cognition. In R. J. Spiro, B. C. Bruce, & W. F. Brewer (Eds.), *Theoretical issues in reading comprehension* (pp. 33–58). Hillsdale, NJ: Erlbaum.

Ryle, G. ([1949] 1984). *The concept of mind.* Chicago: University of Chicago Press.

Sagan, C. (1995). *The demon-haunted world: Science as a candle in the dark* (1st ed.). New York: Random House.

Salter, A. C. (2003). *Predators: Pedophiles, rapists, and other sex offenders: Who they are, how they operate, and how we can protect ourselves and our children.* New York: Basic Books.

Sarmiento, E. E., Sawyer, G. J., Milner, R., Deak, V., & Tattersall, I. (2007). *The last human: A guide to twenty-two species of extinct humans.* New Haven, CT: Yale University Press.

Sartre, J. P. ([1956] 1994). *Being and nothingness* (H. Barnes, Trans.). New York: Gramercy Books.

Saxe, R., & Kanwisher, N. (2003). People thinking about thinking people: The role of the temporo-parietal junction in "theory of mind." *Neuroimage, 19*(4), 1835–1842.

Schacter, D. L. (1987). Implicit expressions of memory in organic amnesia: learning of new facts and associations. *Hum Neurobiol, 6*(2), 107–118.

Schacter, D. L., & Scarry, E. (1999). *Memory, brain, and belief.* Cambridge, MA: Harvard University Press.

Schall, J. D., Stuphorn, V., & Brown, J. W. (2002). Monitoring and control of action by the frontal lobes. *Neuron, 36*(2), 309–322.

Schiff, N. D., Giacino, J. T., Kalmar, K., Victor, J. D., Baker, K., Gerber, M., et al. (2007). Behavioural improvements with thalamic stimulation after severe traumatic brain injury. *Nature, 448*(7153), 600–603.

Schiffer, F., Zaidel, E., Bogen, J., & Chasan-Taber, S. (1998). Different psychological status in the two hemispheres of two split-brain patients. *Neuropsychiatry Neuropsychol Behav Neurol, 11*(3), 151–156.

Schjoedt, U., Stodkilde-Jorgensen, H., Geertz, A. W., & Roepstorff, A. (2008). Rewarding prayers. *Neurosci Lett, 443*(3), 165–168.

Schjoedt, U., Stodkilde-Jorgensen, H., Geertz, A. W., & Roepstorff, A. (2009).

Highly religious participants recruit areas of social cognition in personal prayer. *Soc Cogn Affect Neurosci, 4*(2), 199–207.

Schmitt, J. J., Hartje, W., & Willmes, K. (1997). Hemispheric asymmetry in the recognition of emotional attitude conveyed by facial expression, prosody and propositional speech. *Cortex, 33*(1), 65–81.

Schneider, F., Bermpohl, F., Heinzel, A., Rotte, M., Walter, M., Tempelmann, C., et al. (2008). The resting brain and our self: Self-relatedness modulates resting state neural activity in cortical midline structures. *Neuroscience, 157*(1), 120–131.

Schnider, A. (2001). Spontaneous confabulation, reality monitoring, and the limbic system—a review. *Brain Res Brain Res Rev, 36*(2–3), 150–160.

Schreiber, C. A., & Kahneman, D. (2000). Determinants of the remembered utility of aversive sounds. *J Exp Psychol Gen, 129*(1), 27–42.

Schrödinger, E. (1964). *My view of the world* (C. Hastings, Trans.). Cambridge, UK: Cambridge University Press.

Schwartz, B. (2004). *The paradox of choice: Why more is less.* New York: Ecco.

Seabrook, J. (2008, November 10). Suffering souls. *New Yorker*, 64–73.

Searle, J. (1964). How to derive "ought" from "is". *Philosophical Review 73*(1), 43–58.

Searle, J. (2001). Free will as a problem in neurobiology. *Philosophy, 76*, 491–514.

Searle, J. R. (1992). *The rediscovery of the mind.* Cambridge, MA: MIT Press.

Searle, J. R. (1995). *The construction of social reality.* New York: The Free Press.

Searle, J. R. (1997). Consciousness and the philosophers. *New York Review of Books, XLIV*(4).

Searle, J. R. (1998). How to study consciousness scientifically. *Philos Trans R Soc Lond B Biol Sci, 353*(1377), 1935–1942.

Searle, J. R. (2000). Consciousness. *Annu Rev Neurosci, 23*, 557–578.

Searle, J. R. (2001). Further reply to Libet. *Journal of Consciousness Studies, 8*(8), 63–65.

Searle, J. R. (2007). Dualism revisited. *J Physiol Paris, 101*(4–6), 169–178.

Searle, J. R., Dennett, D. C., & Chalmers, D. J. (1997). *The mystery of consciousness* (1st ed.). New York: New York Review of Books.

Seeley, W. W., Carlin, D. A., Allman, J. M., Macedo, M. N., Bush, C., Miller, B. L., et al. (2006). Early frontotemporal dementia targets neurons unique to apes and humans. *Ann Neurol, 60*(6), 660–667.

Sergent, J., Ohta, S., & MacDonald, B. (1992). Functional neuroanatomy of face and object processing: A positron emission tomography study. *Brain, 115* Pt. 1, 15–36.

Seybold, K. S. (2007). Physiological mechanisms involved in religiosity/spirituality and health. *J Behav Med, 30*(4), 303–309.

Shadlen, M. N., & Kiani, R. (2007). Neurology: An awakening. *Nature, 448*(7153), 539–540.

Shadlen, M. N., & Movshon, J. A. (1999). Synchrony unbound: A critical evaluation of the temporal binding hypothesis. *Neuron, 24*(1), 67–77, 111–125.

Shadlen, M. N., & Newsome, W. T. (2001). Neural basis of a perceptual decision in the parietal cortex (area LIP) of the rhesus monkey. *J Neurophysiol, 86*(4), 1916–1936.

Shamay-Tsoory, S. G., Tibi-Elhanany, Y., & Aharon-Peretz, J. (2007). The green-eyed monster and malicious joy: The neuroanatomical bases of envy and gloating (schadenfreude). *Brain, 130*(Pt. 6), 1663–1678.

Sheldrake, R. (1981). *A new science of life: The hypothesis of formative causation.* London: Blond & Briggs.

Sheline, Y. I., Barch, D. M., Price, J. L., Rundle, M. M., Vaishnavi, S. N., Snyder, A. Z., et al. (2009). The default mode network and self-referential processes in depression. *Proc Natl Acad Sci USA, 106*(6), 1942–1947.

Shoebat, W. (2007). *Why we want to kill you: The jihadist mindset and how to defeat it.* [United States]: Top Executive Media.

Shweder, R. A. (2006, November 27). Atheists agonistes. *New York Times.*

Siebert, C. (2009, July 12). Watching whales watching us. *New York Times.*

Siefe, C. (2000). Cold numbers unmake the quantum mind. *Science, 287*(5454), 791.

Silk, J. B., Brosnan, S. F., Vonk, J., Henrich, J., Povinelli, D. J., Richardson, A. S., et al. (2005). Chimpanzees are indifferent to the welfare of unrelated group members. *Nature, 437*(7063), 1357–1359.

Silver, L. M. (2006). *Challenging nature: The clash of science and spirituality at the new frontiers of life.* New York: Ecco.

Simons, D. J., Chabris, C. F., Schnur, T., & Levin, D. T. (2002). Evidence for preserved representations in change blindness. *Conscious Cogn, 11*(1), 78–97.

Simonton, D. K. (1994). *Greatness: Who makes history and why.* New York: Guilford.

Singer, P. (2009). *The life you can save: Acting now to end world poverty.* New York: Random House.

Singer, T., Seymour, B., O'Doherty, J., Kaube, H., Dolan, R. J., & Frith, C. D. (2004). Empathy for pain involves the affective but not sensory components of pain. *Science, 303*(5661), 1157–1162.

Singer, W. (1999). Striving for coherence. *Nature, 397*(4 February), 391–393.

Singer, W. (1999). Neuronal synchrony: A versatile code for the definition of relations? *Neuron, 24*(1), 49–65, 111–125.

Sinnott-Armstrong, W. (2006). Consequentialism. *The Stanford encyclopedia of philosophy.* Retrieved from http://plato.stanford.edu/entries/consequentialism/.

Sirigu, A., Daprati, E., Ciancia, S., Giraux, P., Nighoghossian, N., Posada, A., et al. (2004). Altered awareness of voluntary action after damage to the parietal cortex. *Nat Neurosci, 7*(1), 80–84.

Sirotin, Y. B., & Das, A. (2009). Anticipatory haemodynamic signals in sensory cortex not predicted by local neuronal activity. *Nature, 457*(7228), 475–479.

Sloman, S. A., & Lagnado, D. A. (2005). The problem of Induction. In K. J. Holyoak & R. G. Morrison (Eds.), *The Cambridge handbook of thinking and reasoning* (pp. 95–116). New York: Cambridge University Press.

Slovic, P. (2007). "If I look at the mass I will never act": Psychic numbing and genocide. *Judgment and Decision Making, 2*(2), 79–95.

Smeltzer, M. D., Curtis, J. T., Aragona, B. J., & Wang, Z. (2006). Dopamine, oxytocin, and vasopressin receptor binding in the medial prefrontal cortex of monogamous and promiscuous voles. *Neurosci Lett, 394*(2), 146–151.

Smith, A., & Stewart, D. ([1759] 1853). *The theory of moral sentiments* (New ed.). London: H. G. Bohn.

Snowden, J. S., Austin, N. A., Sembi, S., Thompson, J. C., Craufurd, D., & Neary, D. (2008). Emotion recognition in Huntington's disease and frontotemporal dementia. *Neuropsychologia, 46*(11), 2638–2649.

Snyder, S. H. (2008). Seeking God in the brain—efforts to localize higher brain functions. *N Engl J Med, 358*(1), 6–7.

Sokal, A. (1996). Transgressing the boundaries: Toward a transformative hermeneutics of quantum gravity. *Social Text*(46/47), 217–252.

Sommer, M., Dohnel, K., Sodian, B., Meinhardt, J., Thoermer, C., & Hajak, G. (2007). Neural correlates of true and false belief reasoning. *Neuroimage, 35*(3), 1378–1384.

Soon, C. S., Brass, M., Heinze, H. J., & Haynes, J. D. (2008). Unconscious determinants of free decisions in the human brain. *Nat Neurosci, 11*(5), 543–545.

Sowell, E. R., Thompson, P. M., Holmes, C. J., Jernigan, T. L., & Toga, A. W. (1999). In vivo evidence for post-adolescent brain maturation in frontal and striatal regions. *Nat Neurosci, 2*(10), 859–861.

Spence, S. A., Farrow, T. F., Herford, A. E., Wilkinson, I. D., Zheng, Y., & Woodruff, P. W. (2001). Behavioural and functional anatomical correlates of deception in humans. *Neuroreport, 12*(13), 2849–2853.

Spence, S. A., Kaylor-Hughes, C., Farrow, T. F., & Wilkinson, I. D. (2008). Speaking of secrets and lies: The contribution of ventrolateral prefrontal cortex to vocal deception. *Neuroimage, 40*(3), 1411–1418.

Sperry, R. W. (1961). Cerebral organization and behavior: The split brain behaves in many respects like two separate brains, providing new research possibilities. *Science, 133*(3466), 1749–1757.

Sperry, R. W. (1968). Hemisphere deconnection and unity in conscious awareness. *Am Psychol, 23*(10), 723–733.

Sperry, R. W. (1976). Changing concepts of consciousness and free will. *Perspect Biol Med, 20*(1), 9–19.

Sperry, R. W. (1982). Some effects of disconnecting the cerebral hemispheres. Nobel Lecture, 8 December 1981. *Biosci Rep, 2*(5), 265–276.

Sperry, R. W., Zaidel, E., & Zaidel, D. (1979). Self recognition and social awareness in the deconnected minor hemisphere. *Neuropsychologia, 17*(2), 153–166.

Spinoza, B. S. F., Ed. (S. Shirley, Trans.). ([1677] 1982). *The ethics and selected letters*. Indianapolis, IN: Hackett Publishing.

Spitzer, M., Fischbacher, U., Herrnberger, B., Gron, G., & Fehr, E. (2007). The neural signature of social norm compliance. *Neuron, 56*(1), 185–196.

Sprengelmeyer, R., Schroeder, U., Young, A. W., & Epplen, J. T. (2006). Disgust in pre-clinical Huntington's disease: A longitudinal study. *Neuropsychologia, 44*(4), 518–533.

Squire, L. R., & McKee, R. (1992). Influence of prior events on cognitive judgments in amnesia. *J Exp Psychol Learn Mem Cogn, 18*(1), 106–115.

Stanovich, K. E., & West, R. F. (2000). Individual differences in reasoning: Implications for the rationality debate? *Behavioral and Brain Sciences, 23*, 645–726.

Stark, R. (2001). *One true God: Historical consequences of monotheism.* Princeton, NJ: Princeton University Press.

Steele, J. D., & Lawrie, S. M. (2004). Segregation of cognitive and emotional function in the prefrontal cortex: A stereotactic meta-analysis. *Neuroimage, 21*(3), 868–875.

Stenger, V. A. (2009). *The new atheism: Taking a stand for science and reason.* New York: Prometheus Books.

Stewart, P. (2008, May 29). Vatican says it will excommunicate women priests. Reuters.

Stoller, S. E., & Wolpe, P. R. (2007). Emerging neurotechnologies for lie detection and the Fifth Amendment. *American Journal of Law & Medicine, 33*, 359–375.

Stone, M. H. (2009). *The anatomy of evil.* Amherst, NY: Prometheus Books.

Strange, B. A., Henson, R. N., Friston, K. J., & Dolan, R. J. (2001). Anterior prefrontal cortex mediates rule learning in humans. *Cereb Cortex, 11*(11), 1040–1046.

Swick, D., & Turken, A. U. (2002). Dissociation between conflict detection and error monitoring in the human anterior cingulate cortex. *Proc Natl Acad Sci USA, 99*(25), 16354–16359.

Tabibnia, G., Satpute, A. B., & Lieberman, M. D. (2008). The sunny side of fairness: Preference for fairness activates reward circuitry (and disregarding unfairness activates self-control circuitry). *Psychol Sci, 19*(4), 339–347.

Takahashi, H., Kato, M., Matsuura, M., Mobbs, D., Suhara, T., & Okubo, Y. (2009). When your gain is my pain and your pain is my gain: Neural correlates of envy and schadenfreude. *Science, 323*(5916), 937–939.

Tarski, A. (1969). Truth and proof. *Sci Am., 220*(6), 63–77.

Tenenbaum, J. B., Kemp, C., & Shafto, P. (2007). Theory-based Bayesian models of inductive reasoning. In A. Feeney & E. Heit (Eds.), *Inductive reasoning: Experimental, developmental, and computational approaches* (pp. 167–204). Cambridge, UK: Cambridge University Press.

Teresi, D. (1990). The lone ranger of quantum mechanics. *New York Times.*

Thompson, J. J. (1976). Letting die, and the trolley problem. *The Monist, 59*(2), 204–217.

Tiihonen, J., Rossi, R., Laakso, M. P., Hodgins, S., Testa, C., Perez, J., et al. (2008). Brain anatomy of persistent violent offenders: More rather than less. *Psychiatry Res, 163*(3), 201–212.

Tom, S. M., Fox, C. R., Trepel, C., & Poldrack, R. A. (2007). The neural basis of loss aversion in decision-making under risk. *Science, 315*(5811), 515–518.

Tomasello, M. (2007, January 13). For human eyes only. *New York Times.*

Tomlin, D., Kayali, M. A., King-Casas, B., Anen, C., Camerer, C. F., Quartz, S. R., et al. (2006). Agent-specific responses in the cingulate cortex during economic exchanges. *Science, 312*(5776), 1047–1050.

Tononi, G., & Edelman, G. M. (1998). Consciousness and complexity. *Science, 282*(5395), 1846–1851.

Trinkaus, E. (2007). Human evolution: Neandertal gene speaks out. *Curr Biol, 17*(21), R917–919.

Trivers, R. (1971). The evolution of reciprocal altruism. *Quarterly Review of Biology, 46*(Mar.), 35–57.

Trivers, R. (2002). *Natural selection and social theory: Selected papers of Robert L. Trivers.* New York: Oxford University Press.

Turk, D. J., Heatherton, T. F., Kelley, W. M., Funnell, M. G., Gazzaniga, M. S., & Macrae, C. N. (2002). Mike or me? Self-recognition in a split-brain patient. *Nat Neurosci, 5*(9), 841–842.

Tversky, A., & Kahneman, D. (1974). Judgment under uncertainty: Heuristics and biases. *Science, 185*(4157), 1124–1131.

Ullsperger, M., & von Cramon, D. Y. (2003). Error monitoring using external feedback: Specific roles of the habenular complex, the reward system, and the cingulate motor area revealed by functional magnetic resonance imaging. *J Neurosci, 23*(10), 4308–4314.

Valdesolo, P., & DeSteno, D. (2006). Manipulations of emotional context shape moral judgment. *Psychol Sci, 17*(6), 476–477.

Van Biema, D. (2006, July 10). Reconciling God and science. *Time.*

van Leijenhorst, L., Crone, E. A., & Bunge, S. A. (2006). Neural correlates of developmental differences in risk estimation and feedback processing. *Neuropsychologia, 44*(11), 2158–2170.

van Veen, V., Holroyd, C. B., Cohen, J. D., Stenger, V. A., & Carter, C. S. (2004). Errors without conflict: Implications for performance monitoring theories of anterior cingulate cortex. *Brain Cogn, 56*(2), 267–276.

Viding, E., Jones, A. P., Frick, P. J., Moffitt, T. E., & Plomin, R. (2008). Heritability of antisocial behaviour at 9: Do callous-unemotional traits matter? *Dev Sci, 11*(1), 17–22.

Vocat, R., Pourtois, G., & Vuilleumier, P. (2008). Unavoidable errors: A spatiotemporal analysis of time-course and neural sources of evoked potentials associated with error processing in a speeded task. *Neuropsychologia, 46*(10), 2545–2555.

Vogel, G. (2004). Behavioral evolution. The evolution of the golden rule. *Science, 303*(5661), 1128–1131.

Vogeley, K., Bussfeld, P., Newen, A., Herrmann, S., Happé, F., Falkai, P., et al. (2001). Mind reading: Neural mechanisms of theory of mind and self-perspective. *Neuroimage, 14*(1 Pt. 1), 170–181.

Vogeley, K., May, M., Ritzl, A., Falkai, P., Zilles, K., & Fink, G. R. (2004). Neural correlates of first-person perspective as one constituent of human self-consciousness. *J Cogn Neurosci, 16*(5), 817–827.

Voight, B. F., Kudaravalli, S., Wen, X., & Pritchard, J. K. (2006). A map of recent positive selection in the human genome. *PLoS Biol, 4*(3), e72.

Wade, N. (2006). *Before the dawn: Recovering the lost history of our ancestors.* New York: Penguin.

Wade, N. (2010, March 1). Human culture, an evolutionary force. *New York Times.*

Wager, T. D., & Nichols, T. E. (2003). Optimization of experimental design in fMRI: A general framework using a genetic algorithm. *Neuroimage, 18*(2), 293–309.

Wager, T. D., Rilling, J. K., Smith, E. E., Sokolik, A., Casey, K. L., Davidson, R. J., et al. (2004). Placebo-induced changes in fMRI in the anticipation and experience of pain. *Science, 303*(5661), 1162–1167.

Wain, O., & Spinella, M. (2007). Executive functions in morality, religion, and paranormal beliefs. *Int J Neurosci, 117*(1), 135–146.

Wakin, D. J., & McKinley Jr., J. C. (2010, May 2). Abuse case offers a view of the Vatican's politics. *New York Times.*

Waldmann, M. R., & Dieterich, J. H. (2007). Throwing a bomb on a person versus throwing a person on a bomb: Intervention myopia in moral intuitions. *Psychol Sci, 18*(3), 247–253.

Waldmann, M. R., Hagmayer, Y., & Blaisdell, A. P. (2006). Beyond the information given: Causal models in learning and reasoning. *Current Directions in Psychological Science, 15*(6), 307–311.

Waters, E. (2010, January 8). The Americanization of mental illness. *New York Times Magazine.*

Watson, G. (1982). *Free will.* Oxford, UK; New York: Oxford University Press.

Weber, M. ([1922] 1993). *The sociology of religion.* Boston: Beacon Press.

Wegner, D. M. (2002). *The illusion of conscious will.* Cambridge, MA: MIT Press.

Wegner, D. M. (2004). Precis of the illusion of conscious will. *Behav Brain Sci, 27*(5), 649–659; discussion 659–692.

Weinberg, S. (2001). *Facing up: Science and its cultural adversaries.* Cambridge, MA: Harvard University Press.

Westbury, C., & Dennett, D. C. (1999). Mining the past to construct the future: Memory and belief as forms of knowledge. In D. L. Schacter & E. Scarry (Eds.), *Memory, brain, and belief* (pp. 11–32). Cambridge, MA: Harvard University Press.

Westen, D., Blagov, P. S., Harenski, K., Kilts, C., & Hamann, S. (2006). Neural bases of motivated reasoning: An fMRI study of emotional constraints on partisan political judgment in the 2004 U.S. presidential election. *J Cogn Neurosci, 18*(11), 1947–1958.

Wicker, B., Keysers, C., Plailly, J., Royet, J. P., Gallese, V., & Rizzolatti, G. (2003). Both of us disgusted in my insula: The common neural basis of seeing and feeling disgust. *Neuron, 40*(3), 655–664.

Wicker, B., Ruby, P., Royet, J. P., & Fonlupt, P. (2003). A relation between rest and the self in the brain? *Brain Res Rev, 43*(2), 224–230.

Wigner, E. (1960). The unreasonable effectiveness of mathematics in the natural sciences. *Communications in Pure and Applied Mathematics, 13*(1).

Williams, B. A. O. (1985). *Ethics and the limits of philosophy.* Cambridge, MA: Harvard University Press.

Wilson, D. S. (2002). *Darwin's cathedral: Evolution, religion, and the nature of society.* Chicago: University of Chicago Press.

Wilson, D. S., & Wilson, E. O. (2007). Rethinking the theoretical foundation of sociobiology. *Q Rev Biol, 82*(4), 327–348.

Wilson, E. O. (1998). *Consilience: The unity of knowledge* (1st ed.). New York: Knopf.

Wilson, E. O. (2005). Kin selection as the key to altruism: Its rise and fall. *Social Research, 72*(1), 159–166.

Wilson, E. O., & Holldobler, B. (2005). Eusociality: Origin and consequences. *Proc Natl Acad Sci USA, 102*(38), 13367–13371.

Wittgenstein, L. (1969). *Philosophical grammar* (A. Kenny, Trans.). Berkeley, CA: University of California Press.

Woolrich, M. W., Ripley, B. D., Brady, M., & Smith, S. M. (2001). Temporal autocorrelation in univariate linear modeling of fMRI data. *Neuroimage, 14*(6), 1370–1386.

Wright, N. T. (2003). *The resurrection of the Son of God.* London: SPCK.

Wright, N. T. (2008). *Surprised by hope: Rethinking heaven, the resurrection, and the mission of the church* (1st ed.). New York: HarperOne.

Yang, T., & Shadlen, M. N. (2007). Probabilistic reasoning by neurons. *Nature, 447*(7148), 1075–1080.

Yang, Y., Glenn, A. L., & Raine, A. (2008). Brain abnormalities in antisocial individuals: Implications for the law. *Behav Sci Law, 26*(1), 65–83.

Yang, Y., Raine, A., Colletti, P., Toga, A. W., & Narr, K. L. (2009). Abnormal temporal and prefrontal cortical gray matter thinning in psychopaths. *Mol Psychiatry, 14*(6), 561–562.

Ye'or, B. (2005). *Eurabia: The Euro-Arab Axis.* Madison, NJ: Fairleigh Dickinson University Press.

Yong, E. (2008). The evolutionary story of the "language gene." *New Scientist* (2669) Aug. 13, pp. 38–41.

Young, L. J., Lim, M. M., Gingrich, B., & Insel, T. R. (2001). Cellular mechanisms of social attachment. *Horm Behav, 40*(2), 133–138.

Young, L. J., & Wang, Z. (2004). The neurobiology of pair bonding. *Nat Neurosci, 7*(10), 1048–1054.

Yu, A. J., & Dayan, P. (2005). Uncertainty, neuromodulation, and attention. *Neuron, 46*(4), 681–692.

Zaidel, E., Iacoboni, M., Zaidel, D., & Bogen, J. E. (2003). The callosal syndromes. In *Clinical Neuropsychology* (pp. 347–403). Oxford, UK: Oxford University Press.

Zaidel, E., Zaidel, D. W., & Bogen, J. (undated). The split brain. Retrieved from www.its.caltech.edu/~jbogen/text/ref130.htm.

Zak, P. J., Kurzban, R., & Matzner, W. T. (2005). Oxytocin is associated with human trustworthiness. *Horm Behav, 48*(5), 522–527.

Zak, P. J., Stanton, A. A., & Ahmadi, S. (2007). Oxytocin increases generosity in humans. *PLoS ONE, 2*(11), e1128.

Zhang, J. X., Leung, H. C., & Johnson, M. K. (2003). Frontal activations associated with accessing and evaluating information in working memory: An fMRI study. *Neuroimage, 20*(3), 1531–1539.

Zhu, Y., Zhang, L., Fan, J., & Han, S. (2007). Neural basis of cultural influence on self-representation. *Neuroimage, 34*(3), 1310–1316.

Zuckerman, P. (2008). *Society without God.* New York: New York University Press.

INDEX

The letter *n* after a page number means "note"; the number following an *n* is the note's number; a double *nn* precedes a range of note numbers.

ABOUT THE AUTHOR

Sam Harris is the author of the *New York Times* bestsellers *The End of Faith* and *Letter to a Christian Nation. The End of Faith* won the 2005 PEN Award for Nonfiction. His writing has been published in over fifteen languages. He and his work have been discussed in *Newsweek, TIME, The New York Times, Scientific American, Nature, Rolling Stone*, and many other publications. His writing has appeared in *Newsweek, The New York Times*, the *Los Angeles Times, The Times* (London), the *Boston Globe, The Atlantic, Annals of Neurology*, and elsewhere. Dr. Harris is cofounder and CEO of Project Reason, a nonprofit foundation devoted to spreading scientific knowledge and secular values in society. He received a degree in philosophy from Stanford University and a PhD in neuroscience from UCLA. His website is www.samharris.org.